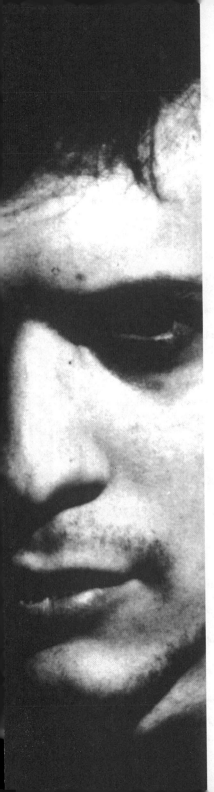

OBJECT LESSON

A ROMANCE, A METAPHYSICAL
MYSTERY, A STUNNING TOUR DE FORCE

"Orlando's skill in orchestrating
an elaborate plot is astonishing –
and even more impressive
is his narrative sleight-of-hand."

Miami Herald

JORDAN ORLANDO

SIMON &
SCHUSTER

GRANTA

CRIME

46

Editor: Bill Buford
Deputy Editor: Ursula Doyle
Managing Editor: Claire Wrathall
Editorial Assistant and Picture Researcher: Cressida Leyshon
Contributing Editor: Robert McSweeney

Managing Director: Catherine Eccles
Financial Controller: Geoffrey Gordon
Marketing and Advertising: Sally Lewis
Circulation Manager: Lesley Palmer
Subscriptions: Ruscha Fields

Picture Editor: Alice Rose George
Executive Editor: Pete de Bolla
US Publisher: Anne Kinard, Granta, 250 West 57th Street, Suite 1316, New York, NY 10107.

Editorial and Subscription Correspondence: Granta, 2–3 Hanover Yard, Noel Road, Islington, London N1 8BE. Telephone: (071) 704 9776. Fax: (071) 704 0474. Subscriptions: (071) 704 0470.
A one-year subscription (four issues) is £21.95 in Britain, £29.95 for the rest of Europe and £36.95 for the rest of the world.
All manuscripts are welcome but must be accompanied by a stamped, self-addressed envelope or they cannot be returned.

Granta is printed in the United States of America. The paper used in this publication meets the minimum requirements of American National Standard for Information Sciences—Permanence of Paper for Printed Library Materials, ANSI Z39.48-1984 ∞

Granta is published by Granta Publications Ltd and distributed by Penguin Books Ltd, Harmondsworth, Middlesex, England; Viking Penguin, a division of Penguin Books USA Inc, 375 Hudson Street, New York, NY 10014, USA; Penguin Books Australia Ltd, Ringwood, Victoria, Australia; Penguin Books Canada Ltd, 10 Alcorn Avenue, Toronto, Ontario, Canada M4V 3B2; Penguin Books (NZ) Ltd, 182–190 Wairau Road, Auckland 10, New Zealand. This selection copyright © 1994 by Granta Publications Ltd.

Cover by Senate. Cover photograph: Los Angeles Times Collection, UCLA Department of Special Collections.

Granta 46, Winter 1994
ISBN 0140 140 662

ROYAL COURT THEATRE

071 730 1745

INTO 1994

MAIN HOUSE
6 JAN UNTIL 5 FEB
The Abbey Theatre production of

THE *cavalcaders* by Billy Roche

FEBRUARY / MARCH

THE *kitchen* by Arnold Wesker

APRIL
Co-production with the Wrestling School

hated nightfall by Howard Baker

THEATRE UPSTAIRS
12 - 29 JANUARY

penetrator by Anthony Neilson

FEB / MARCH
In association with the Royal National Theatre Studio

THE *madness of esme and shaz*
by Sarah Daniels

FROM 19 MARCH
Presented by the Royal Court Young People's Theatre

pocahontas by Steve Shill/Stephen Warbeck

APRIL

my night with reg by Kevin Elyot

DUKE OF YORK'S THEATRE
BOOKING UNTIL MARCH

oleanna by David Mamet

PHONE NOW NO BOOKING FEE
FIRST CALL
071-836 2428
24HR CREDIT CARD SERVICE

Contents

Fresh Talent from Penguin

Bridie and Finn
Harry Cauley

A wonderful, funny, evocation of life in an east coast American university town, with a cast of acutely observed characters and misfits.

The Movie House
Steven Knight

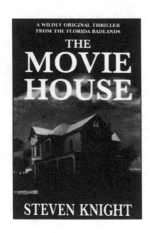

A hired screenwriter makes the gradual, horrible discovery that the plot of his new film is becoming reality. Dark and humorous, this is the very best in *thriller-noir*.

Dissociated States
Leonard Simon

A doctor and his wife are unwittingly treating the same patient - a psychokiller with a gruesome history and a habit for killing every doctor who's ever treated him.

All £4.99

GRANTA

JAMES ELLROY
DICK CONTINO'S BLUES

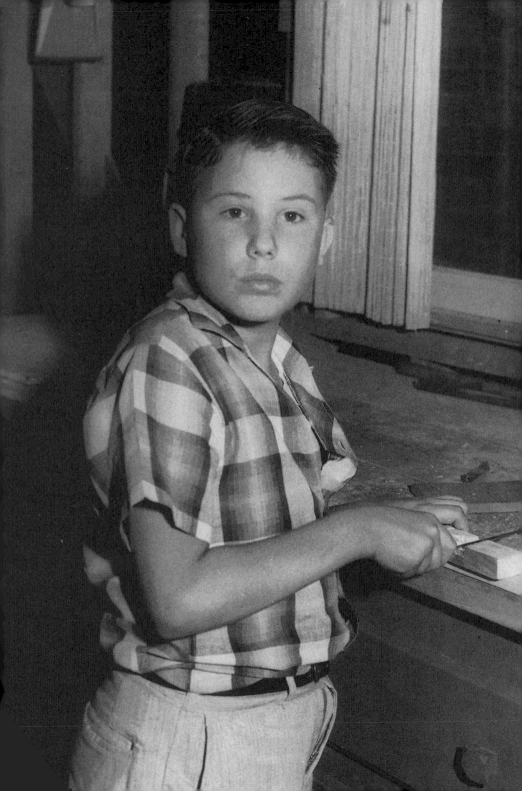

June 22, 1958. Dig, hepcats: it's me, five minutes after the fuzz told me my mother had been murdered.

My parents divorced in '54. The old man liked women; Mom grooved booze and men. Married life—not really their gig. They both exuded an intense sex vibe. She was a voluptuous redhead. He had a schvanze a yard long. I grew up weird.

I spend weekdays with my mother, weekends with my father. Friday, June 20, and Saturday, June 21—standard divorced father-disenfranchised son business. The old man and I had a blast: two double features, numerous cheeseburgers, boxing on TV.

Sunday, June 22. My father takes me back to El Monte—this dogdick town fifteen miles east of LA proper that the old lady had up and moved us to earlier in the year. He puts me in a cab and waits for a bus back to LA.

The cab drops me at my pad. The front yard is swarming with cops. I sense immediately that my mother is dead. An *LA Times* camera jockey poses me at a neighbor's workbench and flashbulb pops the moment for posterity.

The cops reconstructed the murder. My mother went out drinking the previous night. She was seen leaving the Desert Inn bar with a blond woman and a swarthy man about forty. Her body was found the following morning: dumped into some bushes on an access road adjoining Arroyo High School in El Monte. She had been strangled. She was nude, wrapped in an overcoat, one of her stockings loosely knotted around her neck. She scratched the shit out of the man who killed her. The killing was never solved.

I went to live with my father. I stayed up late watching crime movies on TV. I peeped in windows. I watched cars go by and wondered if the driver was a killer. I got scared for no reason and panicked if my father came home late.

I saw a man named Dick Contino belt the accordion on TV. Somebody called him a draft dodger. My initial Contino memory: just that obscure and contained.

Thirty-odd years passed. I picked up a video copy of *Daddy-O*—featuring Dick Contino. It was filmed in early '58. My mother and I were bopping towards our destinies.

I located Dick Contino. We became friends.

11

I was bombing.

Atom bombing: sweaty hands, shakes pending. My back-up combo sounded off-sync—I knew it was *me*, jumping ahead of the beat. BIG ROOM FEAR grabbed my nuts; headlines screamed:

CONTINO TANKS LACKLUSTER CROWD AT CRESCENDO!

CONTINO LAYS PRE-EASTER EGG AT SUNSET STRIP OPENING!

'Bumble Boogie' to 'Cirribirin'—a straight-for-the-jugular accordion segue. I put my whole body into a bellows shake; my brain misfired a message to my fingers. My fingers obeyed—I slammed out the 'Tico-Tico' finale. Contagious misfires: my combo came in with a bridge theme from 'Rhapsody in Blue'.

I just stood there.

House lights snapped on. I saw Leigh and Chrissy Staples, Nancy Ankrum, Kay Van Obst. My wife, my friends—plus a shitload of first nighters oozing shock.

'Rhapsody in Blue' fizzled out behind me. BIG ROOM FEAR clutched my balls and SQUEEZED.

I tried patter. 'Ladies and gentlemen, that was "Dissonance Jump", a new experimental twelve-tone piece.'

My friends yukked. A geek in a Legionnaire cunt cap yelled, 'Draft Dodger!'

Instant silence—big room loud. I froze on Joe Patriot: booze-flushed, Legion cap, Legion armband. My justification riff stood ready: I went to Korea, got honorably discharged, got pardoned by Harry S. Truman.

No, try this: 'Fuck you. Fuck your mother. Fuck your dog.'

The Legionnaire froze. I froze. Leigh froze behind a smile that kissed off two grand a week, two weeks minimum.

The whole room froze.

Cocktail debris pelted me: olives, ice, whisky sour fruit. My accordion dripped maraschino cherries—I slid it off and set it down behind some footlights.

My brain misfired a message to my fists: kick Joe Patriot's ass.

I vaulted the stage and charged him. He tossed his drink in my face; pure grain spirits stung my eyes and blinded me. I blinked, sputtered and swung haymakers. Three missed; one connected—the

---

Opposite: Dick Contino.

impact made me wah-wah quiver. My vision cleared—I thought I'd see Mr America dripping teeth.

I was wrong.

Joe Legion—gone. In his place, cut cheekbone-deep by my rock-encrusted guinea wedding ring: Cisco Andrade, the world's number one lightweight contender.

Sheriff's bulls swarmed in and fanned out. Backstopping them: Deputy Dot Rothstein, two hundred plus pounds of bull dyke with the hots for my friend Chris Staples.

Andrade said, 'You dumb son-of-a-bitch.'

I just stood there.

My eyes dripped gin; my left hand throbbed. The Crescendo main room went phantasmagoric.

There's Leigh: juking the cops with 'Dick Contino, Red Scare Victim' rebop. There's the Legionnaire, glomming my sax man's autograph. Dot Rothstein's sniffing the air—my drummer just ducked backstage with a reefer. Chrissy's giving Big Dot a wide berth—they worked a lezbo entrapment gig once—Dot's had a torch sizzling ever since.

Shouts. Fingers pointed my way. Mickey Cohen with his bulldog Mickey Cohen Jr—snout deep in a bowl of cocktail nuts. Mickey Sr, nightclub Jesus—slipping the boss deputy a cash wad.

Andrade squeezed my ratched-up hand—I popped tears. 'You play your accordion at my little boy's birthday party. He likes clowns, so you dress up like Chucko the Clown. You do that and we're even.'

I nodded. Andrade let my hand go and dabbed at his cut. Mickey Cohen cruised by and spieled payback. 'My niece is having a birthday party. You think you could play it? You think you could dress up like Davy Crockett with one of those coonskin caps?'

I nodded. The fuzz filed out—a deputy flipped me the bird and muttered, 'Draft Dodger.'

Mickey Cohen Jr sniffed my crotch. I tried to pet him—the cocksucker snapped at me.

Leigh and Chris met me at Googie's. Nancy Ankrum and Kay Van Obst joined us—we packed a big booth full.

Photo: Bob Willoughby/Redferns

Leigh pulled out her scratch pad. 'Steve Katz was furious. He made the bookkeeper pro-rate your pay down to one half of one show for one night.'

My hand throbbed—I grabbed the ice out of Chrissy's water glass. 'Fifty scoots?'

'Forty and change. They counted it down to the penny.'

Demons hovered: Leigh's obstetrician, the Yeakel Olds repo man. I said, 'They don't repossess babies.'

'No, but they do repossess three-month delinquent Starfire 88s. Dick, did you *have* to get the Continental Kit, "Kustom King" interior, and that hideous accordion hood ornament?'

Chrissy: 'It was an Italian rivalry thing. Buddy Greco's got a car like that, so Dick had to have one.'

Kay: 'My husband has an 88. He said the "Kustom King" interior is so soft that he almost fell asleep once on the San Bernardino Freeway.'

Nancy: 'Chester Boudreau, one of my *favorite* sex killers of all time, preferred Oldsmobiles. He said Oldsmobiles had a bulk that children found comforting, so it was easy to lure kids into them.'

Right on cue: my three-girl chorus. Chrissy sang with Buddy Greco and sold Dexedrine; Nancy played trombone in Spade Cooley's all-woman band and pen-palled with half the pervs in San Quentin. Kay: National President of the Dick Contino Fan Club. We go back to my Army Beef: Kay's husband Pete bossed the Fed team that popped me for desertion.

Our food arrived. Nancy talked up the 'West Hollywood Whipcord'—some fiend who'd strangled two lovebird duos parked off the Strip. Chris boo-hooed my Crescendo fracas and bemoaned the end of Buddy's Mocambo stand two weeks hence. Leigh let me read her eyes:

Your friends co-sign your bullshit, but I won't.

Your display of manly pique cost us four grand.

You fight the COWARD taint with your fists, you just make it worse.

Radioactive eyes—I evaded them via small talk. 'Chrissy, did you catch Dot Rothstein checking you out?'

Chris choked down a hunk of Reuben Sandwich. 'Yes, and it's been *five years* since the Barbara Graham gig.'

'Barbara Graham,' tweaked Nan the Ghoul. I elaborated: 'Chrissy was doing nine months in the Women's Jail downtown when Barbara Graham was there.'

Nancy, breathless: '*And?*'

'And she just happened to be in the cell next to hers.'

'*And?*'

Chris jumped in. 'Quit talking about me like I'm not here.'

Nancy: '*And?*'

'And I was doing nine months for passing forged Dilaudid prescriptions. Dot was the matron on my tier, and she was smitten by me, which I consider a testimonial to her good taste. Barbara Graham and those partners of hers, Santo and Perkins, had just been arrested for the Mabel Monohan killing. Barbara kept protesting that she was innocent, and the D.A.'s Office was afraid that a jury might believe her. Dot heard a rumor that Barbara went lez whenever she did jail time. Dot got the brainstorm to have me cozy up to Barbara in exchange for a sentence reduction. I agreed, but stipulated no Sapphic contact. The D.A.'s Office cut a deal with me, but I couldn't get Barbara to admit anything *vis-à*-goddamn-*vis* the night of March 9th, 1953. We exchanged mildly flirtatious napkin notes, which Dot sold to *Hush-Hush* magazine, and they published with my name deleted. I got my sentence reduction and Barbara got the gas chamber, and Dot Rothstein's got herself convinced that I'm a lezzie. She still sends me Christmas cards. Have *you* ever gotten a lipstick-smeared Christmas card from a two-hundred-pound diesel dyke?'

The whole booth howled. Kay squealed with her mouth full—some club soda spritzed out and hit Leigh. A flashbulb popped—I spotted Danny Getchell and a *Hush-Hush* camera jockey.

Getchell spritzed headlines. '"Accordion Ace Activates Lethal Left Hook at Crescendo Fistfest." "Draft Dodger Taunt Torches Torrid Temper Tantrum." "Quo Vadis, Dick Contino?—Comeback Crumbles in Niteclub Crack-Up."'

Nancy walked back to the pay phones. I said, 'Danny, this is publicity I don't need.'

'Dick, I disagree. Look at what that marijuana contretemps did for Bob Mitchum. I think this portrays you as a good-looking, hot-headed gavonne who's probably—excuse me, ladies—got a schvanze that's a yard long.'

I laughed. Danny said, 'If I'm lyin', I'm flyin'. Seriously, Dick, and again, excuse me, ladies, but this makes you look like you've got a yard of hard pipe and you're not afraid to show it.'

I laughed. Leigh sent up a silent prayer: save my husband from this scandal-rag provocateur.

Nancy shot me a whisper. 'I just talked to Ella Mae Cooley. Spade's been beating her up again . . . and . . . Dick . . . you're the only one who can calm him down.'

I drove out to Spade Cooley's ranch. Rain slashed my windshield; I tuned in Hunter Hancock's all-request show. The gang at Googie's got a call through: Dick Contino's 'Yours' hit the airwaves.

The rain got worse; the chrome accordion on my hood cut down visibility. I accelerated and synched bio-thoughts to music.

Late '47, Fresno: I glommed a spot on Horace Heidt's radio program. Amateur night stuff—studio audience/applause meter—I figured I'd play 'Lady of Spain', lose to some local babe Heidt was banging and go on to college.

I won.

Bobby-soxers swarmed me backstage.

I turned eighteen the next month. I kept winning—every Sunday night—weeks running. I beat singers, comics, a Negro trombonist and a blind vibraphone virtuoso. I shook, twisted, stomped, gyrated, flailed, thrashed, genuflected, wiggled, strutted and banged my squeeze-box like a dervish orbiting on Benzedrine, maryjane and glue. I pelvis-popped and pounded pianissimos; I cascaded cadenzas and humped harmonic hurricanes until the hogs hollered for Hell—straight through to Horace Heidt's grand finals. I became a national celebrity, toured the country as Heidt's headliner, and went solo BIG.

I played BIG ROOMS. I cut records. I broke hearts. Screen tests, fan clubs, magazine spreads. Critics marvelled at how I hipsterized the accordion—I said all I did was make schmaltz look sexy. They said where'd you learn to *move* like that?—I lied and said I didn't know.

The truth was:

I've always been afraid.

I've always conjured terror out of thin air.

Music and movement are incantations that help keep it formless.

1949, 1950—flying high on fame and callow good fortune. Early '51: FORM arrives via draft notice.

FORM: day sweats, night sweats, suffocation fears. Fear of mutilation, blindness, cancer, vivisection by rival accordionists. Twenty-four-hour heebie-jeebies; nightclub audiences packing shrouds. Music inside my head: jackhammers, sirens, Mixmasters stripping gears.

I went to the Mayo Clinic; three headshrinkers stamped me unfit for Army service. My draft board wanted a fourth opinion and sent me to their on-call shrink. He contradicted the Mayo guys—my 1-A classification stood firm.

I was drafted and sent to Fort Ord. FORM: the Reception Station barracks compressed in on me. My heart raced and sent

James Ellroy

live-wire jolts down my arms. My feet went numb; my legs
fluttered and dripped sweat. I bolted and caught a bus to Frisco.

AWOL, Federal fugitive—my desertion made front-page news.

I trained down to LA and holed up at my parents' house.
Reporters knocked—my dad sent them away. TV crews kept a
vigil outside. I talked to a lawyer, worked up a load of showbiz
panache and turned myself in.

My lawyer tried to cut a deal—the US Attorney wasn't buying.
I took a daily flailing from the Hearst rags: ACCORDION PRIMA
DONNA SUFFERS STAGE FRIGHT AT FORT ORD OPENING. 'Coward',
'Traitor', 'Yellow Belly', 'Chicken-Hearted Heart-Throb'. 'Coward,'
'Coward,' 'Coward.'

My BIG ROOM bookings were cancelled.

I was bound over for trial in San Francisco.

Fear:

Bird chirps made me flinch. Rooms closed in coffin-tight the
second I entered them.

I went to trial. My lawyer proffered Mayo depositions; I
detailed my fear on the witness-stand. The press kept resentment
fires stoked: I had it all, but wouldn't serve my country. My
response went ignored: so take away my fucking accordion.

The judge found me guilty and sentenced me: six months in
the Federal pen at McNeil Island, Washington.

I did the time. I put on a sadistic face to deter butt-fuckers.
Accordion slinging gave me big muscles—I hulked and popped
my biceps. Mickey Cohen, in for income tax evasion, befriended
me. My daily routine: yard trusty work, squeeze-box impromptus.
Ingratiating showman/psycho con—a schizophrenic performance
that got me through my sentence unmolested.

Released—January, '52. Slinking/creeping/crawling anxiety:
what happens next?

Winter '52—one big publicity watch. Big CONTINO OUT OF JAIL
coverage—most of it portrayed me as a coward case-hardened by
prison.

Photo: Wide World Photos

Opposite: Dick Contino leaves San Francisco Federal Court
accompanied by Deputy US Marshal Herbert Cole and Army
Psychiatrist Dr Percy Poliak, July 1951.

Residual fear: would I now be drafted?

Winter '52—no gigs, BIG ROOM or otherwise. My draft notice arrived—this time I played the game.

Basic training, communications school, Korea. Fear back-burner-boogied; I served in a Seoul-based outfit and rose from private to staff sergeant. Acceptance/taunts/shoving matches. Resentment oozing off guys who envied what they thought I'd come home to.

I came home to tapped-out momentum and DRAFT DODGER in Red-bait neon. I received an unsolicited presidential pardon—my COWARD taint rendered it toilet paper. I became a vanishing act: BIG ROOM stints replaced by lounge gigs; national TV shots down-graded into local stuff. Fear and I played peek-a-boo—it always seemed to grab my balls and twist just when it felt like something inside me could banish all the bullshit forever.

I hit Victorville. LA radio had faded out—I'd been listening to shitkicker ditties. Apt: I pulled up to the Cooley ranchhouse soundtracked by Spade's own, 'Shame, Shame on You'.

The porch reeked: marijuana and sourmash fumes. TV glow lit up windows bluish-gray.

The door stood ajar. I pressed the buzzer—hillbilly chimes went off. Dark inside—the TV screen made shadows bounce. George Putnam spritzed late local news: ' . . . the fiend the Los Angeles County Sheriff has dubbed the "West Hollywood Whipcord" claimed his third and fourth victims last night. The bodies of Thomas "Spike" Knode, 39, an out-of-work movie stuntman, and his fiancée Carol Matusow, 19, a stenographer, were discovered locked in the trunk of Knode's car, parked on Hilldale Drive a scant block north of the Sunset Strip. Both were strangled with a sash cord and bludgeoned post-mortem with a bumperjack found in the back seat. The couple had just come from the Mocambo nightclub, where they had watched entertainer Buddy Greco perform. Authorities report that they have no clues as to the slayer's identity, and—'

Opposite: Mickey Cohen (far right) is released from McNeil Island Penitentiary, October 1955.

A ratchet noise—metal on metal. That unmistakable drawl: 'From the size of your shadow, I'd say it's Dick Contino.'

'It's me.'

Ratch/ratch—trigger noise—Spade loved to get zorched and play with guns.

'I should tell Nancy 'bout that "Whipcord" sumbitch. She just might find herself a new pen pal.'

'She already knows about him.'

'Well . . . I'm not surprised. And this old dog, well . . . he knows how to put things together. My Ella Mae got a call from Nancy, and two hours later Mr Accordion himself shows up. Heard you tanked at the Crescendo, boy. Ain't that always the way it is when proving yourself runs contrary to your own best interests?'

A lamp snapped on. Dig it: Spade Cooley in a cowboy hat and sequin-studded chaps—packing two holstered six-guns.

I said, 'Like you and Ella Mae. You beg her for details on her old shack jobs, then you beat her up when she plays along.'

Fluttering flags replaced George Putnam—KTTV signing off for the night. The national anthem kicked in—I doused the volume. Spade slumped low in his chair and drew down on me. 'You mean I shouldn't have asked her if those John Ireland and Steve Cochran rumors were true?'

'You're dying to torture yourself, so tell me.'

Spade twirled his guns, popped the cylinders and spun them. Two revolvers, ten empty slots, one bullet per piece.

'So tell me, Spade.'

'The rumors were true, boy. Would I be sittin' here in this condition if those dudes were any less than double-digit bulls?'

I laughed.

I roared.

I howled.

Spade put both guns to his head and pulled the triggers.

Two loud clicks—empty chambers.

I stopped laughing.

Spade did it again.

Click/click—empty chambers.

I grabbed for the guns. Spade shot ME twice—empty chambers.

I backed into the TV. A leg brushed the volume dial—'The Star Spangled Banner' went very loud, then very soft.

Spade said, 'You could have died hearing your country's theme song, which might have gotten you the posthumous approval of all them patriotic groups that don't like you so much. And you also could have died not knowing that John Ireland had to tape that beast of his to his leg when he wore swimming trunks.'

A toilet flushed upstairs. Ella Mae yelled, 'Donnell Clyde Cooley, quit talking to yourself or God knows who, and come to bed!'

Spade aimed both guns at her voice and pulled the triggers.

Two empty chambers.

Four down per piece, two to go—50/50 odds next time. Spade said, 'Dick, let's get blotto. Get me a fresh bottle from the kitchen.'

I walked to the bathroom and checked the medicine cabinet. Yellow Jackets on a shelf—I emptied two into a glass and flushed the rest. Kitchen recon—a Wild Turkey quart atop the ice box.

I dumped it down the sink—all but three fingers' worth.

Loose .38 shells on a shelf—I tossed them out the window.

Spade's maryjane stash—right where it always was in the sugar bowl.

I poured it down the sink and chased it with Drano.

Spade yelled, 'I am determined to shoot somebody or something tonight!'

I swirled up a cocktail: bourbon, Nembutal, buttermilk to kill the barbiturate taste. Spade yelled, 'Go out to your car and get your accordion, and I'll put it out of its misery!'

On the breakfast table: a TV remote-control gizmo.

I grabbed it.

Back to Spade. On cue: he put down one gun and grabbed his drink. One six-shooter on the floor—I toed it under his chair.

Spade twirled gun number two.

I stood *behind* the chair. Spade said, 'I wonder if John used masking tape or friction tape.'

Blip, blip—I pushed remote-control buttons. Test pattern, test pattern, Rock Hudson and Jane Wyman in some hankie epic.

I nudged Spade. 'I heard Rock Hudson's hung like a horse. I

Above: Spade Cooley and his wife, Ella Mae.

Photo: Associated Press

heard he put the make on Ella Mae back when she played clarinet on your old *Hoffman Hayride Show.*'

Spade said, 'Ixnay—Rock's a fruit. I heard he plays skin flute with some quiff on the *Lawrence Welk Show.*'

Shit—no bite. Blip, blip, Caryl Chessman fomenting from his death row cell. 'Now there's your double-digit dude, Spade. That cat is legendary in criminal annals—Nancy Ankrum told me so herself.'

'Nix. Shitbird criminals like that are always underhung. I read it in *Argosy* magazine.'

Blip, blip, blip—beaucoup test patterns. Blip, blip, blip—test drive the new '58 Chevy, Ford, Rambler, et fucking al. Blip— Senator John F. Kennedy talking to reporters.

Spade pre-empted me. 'Hung like a cashew. Gene Tierney told me he screws from hunger. Hung like a cricket, and he expects a standing ovation for a two-minute throw.'

Shit—running out of channels. Blip—an American Legion chaplain with 2:00 a.m. prayers.

'And as always, we ask for the strength to oppose our Communist adversary at home and abroad. We ask—'

Spade said, 'This is for Dick Contino,' raised his gun and fired. The TV screen imploded—wood splintered, tubes popped, glass shattered.

Spade passed out on the floor rag-doll limp.

TV dust formed a little mushroom cloud.

I carried Spade upstairs and laid him down in bed next to Ella Mae. Cozy: inside seconds they were snoring in unison. I remembered Fresno, Christmas '47—I was young, she was lonely, Spade was in Texas.

Keep it hush-hush, dear heart—for both our sakes.

I walked out to my car. February 12th, 1958—what an all-time fucker of a night.

2

Bad sleep left me fried—hungover from my rescue run.

The baby woke me up. I'd been dreaming: I was on trial for Crimes Against Music. The judge said the accordion was obsolete; a studio audience applauded. Dig my jury: Mickey Cohen's dog, Jesus Christ, Cisco Andrade.

Leigh had coffee and aspirin ready. Ditto the a.m. *Mirror*, folded to the entertainment page.

BRAWL DEEP-SIXES CONTINO OPENING. NIGHTCLUB BOSS CALLS ACCORDION KING 'DAMAGED GOODS'.

The phone rang—I grabbed it. 'Who's this?'

'Howard Wormser, your agent, who just lost ten per cent of your Crescendo money *and* ten per cent of your sixty-day stand at the Flamingo Lounge. Vegas called, Dick. They get the LA papers early, and they don't like to sit on bad news.'

A *Mirror* sub-head: 'Draft Dodger Catcalls Plague Fading Star.' 'I was busy last night, or I would have seen this coming.'

'Seeing things coming is not your strong suit. You *should*

27

have accepted Sam Giancana's invitation to be on call for Chicago Mob gigs, and if you did you'd be playing big rooms today. You *should* have testified before that grand jury and named some Commies. You *should*—'

'I don't know any Commies.'

'No, but you *could* have gotten a few names from the phone book to make yourself look good.'

'Get me some movie work, Howard. Get me a gig where I can sing a few songs and get the girl.'

Howard sighed. 'There is a certain wisdom to that, since young snatch *is* your strong suit. I'll look into it. In the meantime, play a few bar mitzvahs or something and stay out of trouble.'

'Can you get me a few bar mitzvahs?'

'That was just a figure of speech. Dick, be calm. I'll call when I've got you 90 per cent of something.'

Click—one abrupt hang-up faded into noise outside—brake squeals, gear crunch. I checked the window—fuck—a tow-truck had my car bumper-locked.

I ran out. A man in a Teamster T-shirt held his hands up. 'Mr Contino, this wasn't my idea. I'm just a poor out-of-work union man with a family. Bob Yeakel said to tell you enough is enough, he read the papers this morning and saw the writing on the wall.'

The bumper winch ratched my trunk open. Record albums flew out—I grabbed an *Accordion in Paris*.

'What's your name?'

'Uh . . . Bud Brown.'

I pulled the pen off his clipboard and scrawled on the album cover. 'To Bud Brown, out-of-work union man, from Dick Contino, out-of-work entertainer. Dear Bud: why are you fucking with my beautiful Starfire 88, when I'm just a working stiff like you? I know that the evil McClellan Committee is harassing your heroic leader Jimmy Hoffa, in much the same way I was harassed during the Korean War, and thus you and I share a bond that you are trespassing on in your current scab status. Please do not fuck with my beautiful Starfire 88—I need it to look for work.'

The tow-truck driver applauded. Bud Brown fisheyed me—my McClellan schtick hit him weird.

'Mr Contino, like I said, I'm sorry.'

I pointed to the albums.

'I'll donate those to your Teamster Local. I'll autograph them. You can sell them yourself and keep the money. All I'm asking is that you let me drive this car out of here and hide it somewhere.'

Raps on the kitchen window—Leigh holding baby Merri up. Brown said, 'Mr Contino, that's fighting dirty.'

Worth the fight: my baby-blue/white-wall-tired/fox-tail-antennaed sweetie. Sunlight on the accordion hood hanger—I almost swooned.

'Have you guys got kids with birthdays coming up? I'll perform for free, I'll dress up like a—'

The tow-truck radio crackled; the driver listened and rogered the call. 'That was Mr Yeakel. He says Mr Contino should meet him at the showroom pronto, that maybe they can work out a deal on his delinquent.'

'And you know I've got my own TV show, *Rocket to Stardom*. My brothers and I do our own commercials and give amateur Angeleno talent a chance to reach for the moon and haul down a few stars. We put on a show here at the lot every Sunday, and KCOP broadcasts it. We dish out free hot dogs and soda pop, sell some cars and let the talent perform. We usually get a bunch of hot dog scroungers hanging around—I call them the "Yeakel Yokels". They applaud for the acts, and whoever gets the most applause wins. I've got a meter rigged up—sort of like that thingamajig you had on the Heidt show.'

Bob Yeakel: tall, blond, pitchman shrill. His desk: covered with memo slips held down by chrome hubcaps.

'Let me guess. You want me to celebrity MC one of your shows, in exchange for which I get to keep my car free and clear.'

Yeakel yuk-yuk-yukked. 'No, Dick, more along the lines of you produce *and* celebrity MC at least *two* shows, *and* perform at the Oldsmobile Dealers of America Convention, *and* spend some afternoons here at the lot auditioning acts and bullshitting with the customers. In the meantime, you get to keep your car, and we stop the clock on your delinquent interest payments, but not on the base sum itself. Then, if *Rocket to Stardom*'s ratings zoom, I

29

might just let you have that car free and clear.'

'Is that *all* I have to do?'

Yuk-yuk-yuk. 'No. You also have to pitch all your potential contestants on the '58 Oldsmobile line. And no jigaboos or beatniks, Dick. I run a clean family show.'

'I'll do it if you throw in two hundred a week.'

'A hundred and fifty, but off-the-books with no withholding.'

I stuck my hand out.

Work: The Oldsmobile Dealers Convention at the downtown Statler. Dig it: five hundred car hucksters and a busload of hookers chaperoned by a VD doctor. Bob Yeakel opened for me—schtick featuring 'Peaches, The Drag Queen With An Overbite.' Chris Staples sang, 'You Belong To Me' and 'Baby, Baby, All The Time'—Yeakel ogled her and cracked jokes about her 'tail fins'. I killed the booze-fried crowd with a forty-minute set and closed with the *Rocket to Stardom* theme song.

Work:

Birthday parties—Cisco Andrade's son, Mickey Cohen's niece. The Cisco gig was East LA SRO—Mex fighters and their families wowed by Dick Contino as 'Chucko the Birthday Clown'. Degrading?—yeah—but the guests shot me close to a C-note in tips. The Cohen job was more swank: a catered affair at Mickey's pad. Check the guest list: Lana Turner and Johnny Stompanato, Mike Romanoff, Moe Dalitz, Meyer Lansky, Julius La Rosa and the Reverend Wesley Swift—who explained that Jesus Christ was an Aryan, not a Jew, and that *Mein Kampf* was the lost book of the Bible. No gratuities, but Johnny Stomp kicked loose two dozen cases of Gerber's Baby Food—he bankrolled a fur van hijack, and his guys hit the wrong truck.

Work—long days at the Yeakel Olds lot.

I called the girls in to help me: Leigh, Chrissy, Nancy Ankrum, Kay Van Obst. Word spread quick: Mr Accordion and female coterie LIVE at Oldsmobile showroom!

We bullshitted with browsers and referred hard prospects to salesmen; we spritzed the '58 Olds line-up non-stop. We grilled burgers on a hibachi and fed the mechanics and Bud Brown and his repo crew.

Nancy, Kay and Leigh screened *Rocket to Stardom* applicants—I wanted to weed out the more egregious geeks before I began formal auditions. Bob Yeakel drooled whenever Chris Staples slinked by—I convinced him to put her on the payroll as my assistant. Grateful Chrissy gave Bob a thank-you gift: her *Nugget* magazine fold-out preserved via laminated wall plaque.

My Yeakel run nine days in: a righteous fucking blast.

Nine days sans 'Draft Dodger' jive—some kind of Contino world record.

We held auditions in a tent behind the lube rack; Bud Brown stood watchdog to keep obvious lunatics out. The girls had compiled a list: forty-odd individuals and acts to be winnowed down to six spots per show.

Our first finalist: an old geezer who sang grand opera. I asked him to belt a few bars of *Pagliacci*; he said that he possessed the world's largest penis. He whipped it out before I could comment—it was of average length and girth. Chrissy applauded anyway—she said it reminded her of her ex-husband's.

Bud hustled the old guy out. Pops was gone—but he'd set a certain tone.

Check this sampling:

Two roller-skating bull terriers—shark-like dogs with plastic fins attached to their backs. Their master was a Lloyd Bridges lookalike—the whole thing was a goof on the TV show *Sea Hunt*.

Nix.

An off-key woman accordionist who tried to slip me her phone number with Leigh right there.

Nix.

A comic with patter on Ike's golf game—epic Snoresville.

Nix.

A guy who performed silk scarf tricks. Deft and boring: he cinched sashes into hangman's knots.

Nix.

Over two dozen male and female vocalists: flat, screechy, shrill, hoarse—dud Presley and Patti Page would-bes.

A junkie tenor sax, who nodded out halfway through a flubbed-note 'Body and Soul'. Bud Brown dumped him in a demo car; the fucker woke up convulsing and kicked the windshield out.

Chrissy summoned an ambulance; the medics hustled the hophead off.

I confronted Nancy. She said, 'You should have seen the ones that *didn't* make the cut. I wish the West Hollywood Whipcord had a viable talent—it would be fun to put him on the show.'

I braced Bud Brown. 'Bud, the show's forty-eight hours off, and we've got nobody.'

'This happens sometimes. When it does, Bob calls Pizza De-Luxe.'

'What—'

'Ask Bob.'

I walked into Yeakel's office. Bob was eyeballing his wall plaque: Miss Nugget, June '54.

'What's Pizza De-Luxe?'

'Are your auditions going *that* bad?'

'I'm thinking of calling those roller-skating dogs back. Bob, what's Pizza De-Luxe?'

'Pizza De-Luxe is a prostitution racket. An ex-Jack Dragna goon who owns a greasy spoon called the Pizza Pad runs it. He delivers pizza twenty-four hours a day legit, and if you want a girl or a dicey boy on the side, a male or female prostitute will make the delivery. All of the hookers are singers or dancers or Hollywood riff-raff like that, you know, selling some skin to make ends meet until they get their so-called "big break". So . . . if I get strapped for decent contestants I call Pizza De-Luxe. I get some good pizza, some good "amateur" talent, and my top-selling salesman of the month gets laid.'

I checked the window. A transvestite dance team practiced steps by the grease rack—Bud Brown and a cop type shooed them off. I said, 'Bob, call Pizza De-Luxe.'

Yeakel blew his wall plaque kisses. 'I think Chrissy should win this next show.'

'Chrissy's a professional. She's singing back-up for Buddy Greco at the Mocambo right now.'

'I know that, but I want to do her a solid. And I'll let you in on a secret: my applause meter's rigged.'

'Yeah?'

'Yeah. It's a car battery hooked up to an oscilloscope screen.

I've got a foot pedal I tap to goose the needle. I'm sure Chris would like to win—it's a C-note and a free down payment on a snappy new Oldsmobile.'

I laughed. 'With debilitating *monthly* payments?'

'Normally, yes. But with Chrissy I'm sure we could work something else out.'

'I'll tell her. I'm sure she'll play along, at least as far as the "free" down payment.'

Bob's phone rang—he picked up, listened, hung up. I scoped the window—Bud Brown and the fuzz type saw me and turned away, nervous.

Bob said, 'I might have a way for you to buy out of your second *Rocket to Stardom* commitment.'

'I'm listening.'

'I've got to think it over first. Dick, I'm going to call Pizza De-Luxe right now. Will you . . . '

'Talk to Chrissy and tell her she just won an amateur talent contest rigged by this car kingpin who wants to stroke her "tail fins"?'

'Right. And ask for what she wants on her pizza.'

Chris was outside the sales shack, smoking. I spilled quick. 'Bob's bringing in some quasi-pro talent for Sunday's show. He wants you to sing a couple of songs. You're guaranteed to win, and he's got mild expectations.'

'If he keeps them mild, he won't be disappointed.'

Smoke rings drifted up—a sure sign that Chrissy was distracted.

'Something on your mind?'

'No, just my standard boogie man.'

'I know what you mean, but if you tell me you'll probably feel better.'

Chris flicked her cigarette at a Cutlass demo. 'I'm thirty-two, and I'll always earn a living as an entertainer, but I'll never have a hit record. I like men too much to settle down and have a family, and I like myself too much to sell my tush to clowns like Bob Yeakel.'

'And?'

'And nothing. Except that a car followed me after my Mocambo gig last night. I think it's Dot Rothstein. I think she got re-hipped on me after she saw me at your show at the Crescendo.'

'Was she at the Mocambo last night?'

'Yes. And it's in LA *County* jurisdiction, and she's an LA County Deputy Sheriff, which means . . . shit, I don't know. Dick, will you and Leigh come to Buddy's show tonight? Dot knows you're friends with Mickey Cohen, and it might discourage her from making any moves.'

'We'll be there.'

Chris hugged me. 'You know what I envy about your career?'

'What?'

'That at least you're *notorious*. At least that draft dodger thing gives you something to . . . I don't know, at least *overcome*.'

A lightbulb went POP!—but I didn't know what it meant.

3

The Mocambo JUMPED.

Buddy Greco was belting 'Around the World'—working it scat-man style. Buddy not only sells you the song—he drives it to your house and installs it. Chrissy and another girl sang counterpoint—nightclub eyeball magnets.

Leigh and I perched at the bar. She was pissed: I'd told her Bob Yeakel gave me an out on *Rocket to Stardom* number two—work repo back-up for Bud Brown and another finance clown named Sid Elwell. Bob had a shitload of Darktown delinquents—I was to divert the owners while Bud and Sid grabbed their sleds.

I accepted Bob's offer—the repo runs were scheduled for tomorrow. Leigh's response: it's another courage test. You don't know how to pass on things like that.

She was right. Chrissy's lightbulb POP! flickered: 'At least the draft dodger thing gives you something to *overcome*.'

Buddy snapped lyrics—'I traveled on when love was gone, to

keep a big fat swingin' rendezvous'—the crowd snapped fingers along with him. Danny Getchell hopped ringside tables—snouting for *Hush-Hush* 'Sinuendo'. Check Dot Rothstein by the stage: measuring Chrissy for a bunk at the Dyke Island Motel.

Leigh nudged me. 'I'm hungry.'

I leaned close. 'We'll go to Dino's Lodge. It won't be long—Buddy usually closes with this number.'

'No more will I go all around the world, 'cause I have found my world in you—*ooblay-oooh-oooh-baa-baa-doww!*'

Big-time applause—jealousy ditzed me. Dot sidled up to the bar and dug through her purse. Check it out: K-Y Jelly, .38 snubnose.

She threw me a sneer. Check her outfit: Lockheed jumpsuit, tire-tread sandals. Chrissy signalled from the stage door—the parking lot, five minutes.

Dot chug-a-lugged a Scotch; the bartender refused payment. I stood up and stretched—Dot bumped me passing by. 'Your wife's cute, Dick. Take good care of her or someone else will.'

Leigh stuck a leg out to trip her; Dot sidestepped and flipped me the finger. The barman said, 'She's supposed to be here on a stakeout for the West Hollywood Whipcord, but all she does is drool for the chorus girls.'

'Beautiful women can get away with anything.'

The barman roared. I doubled his tip and followed Leigh out to the parking lot.

Chrissy was waiting by the car. Dot Rothstein stood close by—bugging loiterers for IDs. She kept one eyeball on Chris: strictly X-ray, strictly a scorcher.

I unlocked the sled and piled the girls in. Ignition, gas, zoom—Dot's farewell kiss fogged my back windshield.

Heavy traffic on the Strip—we slowed to a crawl. Chris said, 'I'm hungry.'

I said, 'We'll hit Dino's Lodge.'

'Not there, please.'

'Why?'

'Because Buddy's taking a group from the club there, and I'm betting Dot will crash the party. Really, Dick, anyplace but Dino's.'

Leigh said, 'Canter's is open late.'

I hung a sharp right. Headlights swept my Kustom King interior—the car behind us swung right abruptly.

South on Sweetzer, east on Fountain. Dildo Dot had me running edgy—I checked my back mirror.

That car was still behind us.

South on Fairfax, east on Willoughby—that car stuck close. A sports job—white or light gray—I couldn't make out the driver.

Odds on: Deputy Dot Rothstein.

South on Gardner, east on Melrose—those headlights goose goose goosed us. Leigh said, 'Dick, what are you doing?'

'We're being followed.'

'What? Who? What are you—'

I swung into a driveway sans signal; my tires plowed some poor fucker's lawn. The sports car kept going; I backed out and chased it.

It zooooomed ahead; I flicked on my brights and blipped its tail. No fixed license plate—just a temp sticker stuck to the trunk. Close, closer—a glimpse of the last four digits: 1116.

The car ran a red on 3rd Street. Horns squealed; oncoming traffic held me back. Taillights flickered eastbound: going, going, gone.

Leigh said, 'I've got no more appetite.'

Chris said, 'Can I sleep at your place tonight?'

4

Repo adventures.

Cleotis De Armand ran a crap game behind Swanky Frank's liquor store on 89th and Central, flaunting his delinquent 98 right there on the sidewalk. Bud Brown and Sid Elwell came in with cereal box badges and shook him down while I fed Seconal-laced T-Bird to the winos guarding the car. BIG fear: this was combustible LA Darktown, cop impersonation beefs probable if the ubiquitous LAPD swooped by. They didn't—and *I* was the one who drove the sapphire-blue jig rig to safety while the guard contingent snored. Beginner's luck: I found a bag of maryjane in the glove compartment. We toked a few reefers en route to our next job: boost a '57 Starfire off Big Dog Lipscomb, the southside's #1 streetcorner pimp.

The vehicle: parked by a shoeshine stand at 103 and Avalon. Customized: candy-apple red paint, mink interior, rhinestone-studded mud flaps, radio aerials topped with plastic streamers. Bud said, 'Let's strip the upholstery and make our wives fur stoles'—Sid and I were thinking the same thing.

The team deployed.

I unpacked my accordion and slammed 'Lady of Spain' right there. Sid and Bud walked point on Big Dog Lipscomb: across the street browbeating whores. Someone yelled, 'Hey, that's Dick Contino'—Watts riff-raff engulfed me.

I was pushed off the sidewalk—straight into Big Dog's coon coach. An aerial snapped; my back hit the hood; I played prostrate and didn't miss a note.

Look, Mom: no fear.

Foot scrapes, yells—dim intrusions on my reefer reverie. Hands yanked me off the hood—I went eyeball to eyeball with Big Dog Lipscomb.

He swung on me—I blocked the shot with my accordion. Contact: his fist, my keyboard. Sickening cracks: his bones, my bread-and-butter baby.

Big Dog yelped and clutched his hand; some punk kicked him in the balls and picked his pocket. Car keys in the gutter—Bud Brown right there. Flipped, tossed, sprawled—in fur and chauffeur driven: Sid with white knuckles on a mink steering wheel.

Look, Mom: no fear.

We rendezvoused at Teamster Local 1819—Bud brought the back-up sled. My accordion needed a face-lift—I was too weed-wafted to sweat it.

Sid borrowed tools and stripped the mink upholstery; I signed autographs for goldbricking Teamsters. That lightbulb POP! flickered anew: 'Draft dodger thing . . . gives you something

Opposite: police officers break up a fight in South Central Los Angeles.

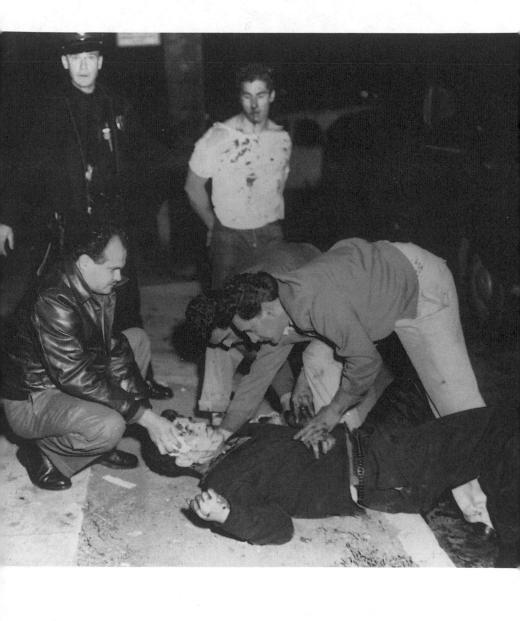

to overcome.' That car chase crowded my brain: temp license 1116; Dot Rothstein after Chrissy or something else?

Bud shmoozed up the local prez—more information pump than friendly talk. A Teamster begged me to play 'Bumble Boogie'—I told him my accordion died. I posed for pix instead—the prez slipped me a Local 'Friendship Card'.

'You never can tell, Dick. You might need a real job someday.'

Too true—a wet towel on my hot fearless day.

Noon—I took Sid and Bud to the Pacific Dining Car. We settled in behind T-bones and hash browns—small talk came easy for a while.

Sid put the skids to it. 'Dick . . . ask you something?'

'Sure.'

'You know . . . your Army rap?'

'What about it?'

'You know . . . you don't impress me as a frightened type of guy.'

Bud piped in: 'As Big Dog Lipscomb will attest to. It's just that . . . you know.'

I said, 'Say it. It feels like I'm close to something.'

Sid said it. 'You know . . . it's like this. Someone says "Dick Contino", and the first thing you think of is "Coward" or maybe "Draft Dodger". It's like a reflex, when you should be thinking "Accordion Player" or "Singer" or "Good repo back-up".'

I said, 'Finish the thought.'

Bud: 'What Sid's saying is how do you get around that? Bob Yeakel says it's a life sentence, but isn't there something you can *do*?'

Closer now—lightbulb hot—so HOT I pushed it away. 'I don't know.'

Sid said, 'You can always do something, if you've got nothing to lose.'

I changed the subject. 'A car was tailing me last night. I think it might be this lezbo cop who's hipped on Chrissy.'

Bud whooped. 'Put her on *Rocket to Stardom*. Let her sing

Opposite: Dick Contino in Korea, 1952.

"Once I had a Secret Love".'

'I'm not 100 per cent sure it's her, but I got the last four digits of the license plate.'

'So it was just a temporary sticker? Permanent plates only have three letters and three digits.'

'Right, 1116. I thought Bob could call the DMV and get a make for me.'

Bud checked his watch, antsy. 'Not without all nine digits. But ask Bob anyway, *after* the show tomorrow. It's a Pizza De-Luxe gig, and he always bangs his favorite "contestant" *after* the show. Mention it to him then, and maybe he'll call some clerk he knows and tell him to look up all the 1116s.'

A waitress crowded up menu first. 'Are you Dick Contino? My daddy doesn't like you 'cause he's a veteran, but my mom thinks you're *real* cute. Could I have your autograph?'

Ladies and Gentlemen, this is Dick Contino welcoming you to *Rocket to Stardom*—where tomorrow's stellar performers reach for the moon and haul down a few stars! Where all of you in our television audience and here at Yeakel Oldsmobile can seal your fate in a Rocket 88!'

Canned applause/hoots/yells/whistles—a rocket launch straight for the toilet.

Somebody spiked the punch—our live audience got bombed pre-showtime.

Sid Elwell ID'd the crowd: mostly juiceheads AWOL from the County dry-out farm.

Act #1: a Pizza De-Luxe male hooker. Topical patter de-luxe: Eisenhower meets Sinatra at the 'Rat Pack Summit'. Ring-a-fucking-ding: Ike, Frank and Dino swap stale one-liners. The crowd booed; the applause meter went on the fritz and leaked steam.

Act #2: a Pizza De-Luxe prostie/songbird. Tight capris, tight sweater—mauling 'Blue Moon' made her bounce in two directions. A pachuco by the stage kept a refrain up: 'Baby, are they real?' Bud Brown sucker-punched him silent off-camera; the sound man said his musings came through un-squelched.

Act #3: 'Ramon and Johnny'—two muscle queen acrobats.

Dips, flips, cupped-hand tosses—nice, if you dig shit like that.

Whistles, applause. Bob Yeakel said the guys worked shakedowns: extorting married fags with sodomy pix.

Some spurned lover-out-of-nowhere yelled, 'Ramon, you bitch!'

Ramon blew the audience a pouty kiss.

Johnny spun in mid-toss; Ramon neglected to catch him. Johnny hit the stage flat on his back.

The crowd went nuts; the applause meter belched smoke. Kay Van Obst drove Johnny to Central Receiving.

#4, #5: Pizza De-Luxe torch singers. Slit-legged gowns, cleavage, goosebumps—both sang Bob Yeakel-lyriced ditties set to hit records. 'The Man I Love' became 'The Car I Love'; 'Fly Me to the Moon' got raped thusly: 'Fly me to the stars, in my souped-up 88; it's got that V-8 power now, and its traction holds straight! In other words, OLDS IS KING!!!'

Cleavage out-tractioned lyrics—the drunks cheered. Sid Elwell hustled a new car battery/applause meter on stage for Chris Staples's bit and final bows.

Chrissy:

Running on fear—that car chase spooked her. I told her I'd have Bob Yeakel tap some DMV slave to trace the license—my backstage pitch shot her some last-minute poise.

Chrissy:

Scorching 'Someone to Watch Over Me' like the Gershwins ALMOST wrote it for her—going hushed so her voice wouldn't crack—the secret of mediocre songsters worldwide.

Chrissy:

Shaking it to 'You Make Me Feel So Young'; putting the make out implicit: *she'd* call *you* at three in the morning.

Chrissy:

Wolf-whistles and scattered claps first time out. Better luck at final bow time: Bob Yeakel hooked the applause rig up to an amplifier.

Chrissy won.

The crowd was too drunk to know it got bamboozled.

Bob congratulated Chris and stroked her tail-fins on-camera— Chris swatted his hand.

Ramon moaned for Johnny.

The sales crew snarfed Pizza De-Luxe pizza.

Leigh called to say she'd caught the show on TV. 'Dick, you were better off as Chucko the Clown.'

I grabbed Chrissy. 'Tell Bud and Sid to meet us at Mike Lyman's. You gave me an idea the other day.'

Bud and Sid made Lyman's first. I slipped the headwaiter a five spot; he slipped us a secluded back booth.

We huddled in, ordered drinks and shot the shit. Topics covered: *Rocket to Stardom* as epic goof; would my repo work spring me from my second producing gig? Bud said he spieled the car chase to Bob Yeakel; Bob said he'd try to DMV-trace the temp license. Sid reprised the Big Dog repo—I used it to steer talk down to biz.

'I've been stuck with this "Coward" tag for years, and I'm tired of it. My career's going nowhere, but at least I've got a name, and Chrissy doesn't even have that. I've got an idea for a publicity stunt. It would probably take at least two extra men to pull off, but I think we could do it.'

Bud said, 'Do *what?*'

Chris said, 'I've got a hunch I know where this is going.'

I whispered. 'Two hoods kidnap Chrissy and I at gunpoint. The hoods are psycho types who've got this crazy notion that we're big stars who can bring in ransom money. They contact Howard Wormser—he's the agent who gets both of us work—and demand some large amount. Howard doesn't know the gig's a phony, and either calls the fuzz or doesn't call the fuzz. In either case, Chrissy and I heroically escape. We can't identify the kidnappers, because they wore masks. We fake evidence at the place where we were held hostage and tough it out when the cops question us. We're bruised up and fucked up from the ordeal. The kidnappers, of course, remain at large. Chrissy and I get a boatload of publicity and goose our careers. We pay off the fake kidnappers with a percentage of the good money we're now making.'

Three deadpans.

Three-way silence—I clocked it at one minute.

Sid coughed. 'This is certifiably nuts.'

Chris coughed and lit a cigarette. 'I like it. If it works, it works. If it doesn't, Dick and I go to jail. We've both been to jail, so we know we can survive. I say maybe this is the real *Rocket to Stardom*, and if it isn't, *c'est-la*-goddamn-*guerre*. I say better to try it than not. I say the entertainment business thrives on bullshit, so why not try to shovel some of our own?'

Bud strafed me: wary eyes, working on sad. 'It's dangerous. It's illegal, probably to the tune of a couple of years in jail. And you're what the cops would call a "known associate" of me and Sid. I could probably set you up with some guys more removed, so the cops couldn't link you to them. See, Dick, what I'm thinking is: if you're *determined* to do it, then maybe we could make some money by cutting down the chance you'll get caught. *If you're determined to do it, hell or high water.*'

Those eyes—why so *sad*?

'I'm determined.'

Bud pushed his drink aside. 'Then it has to look real. Let's go, there's a place you should see.'

We convoyed up to Griffith Park and went hiking. There it was: a shack tucked into a box canyon a mile north of the Observatory.

Hard to spot: scrub bushes blocked the canyon entrance off.

Tumbleweeds covered the roof—the shack couldn't be seen from the air.

The door was open. Stink wafted out: dead animals, dead something. Dig the interior: a mattress on the floor, blood-encrusted pelts stacked on a table.

Chris said, 'Scalps,' and covered her nose.

I looked closer—yeah—SCALPS.

Sid crossed himself. Bud said, 'I found this place a few years ago. I was on a hiking jaunt with a buddy and stumbled on to it. Those scalps spooked the living bejeezus out of me, and I checked with this cop pal of mine. He said back in '46 some crazy Indian escaped from Atascadero, killed six people and scalped them. The Indian was never captured, and if you look close, you'll see six scalps there.'

I looked close. Six scalps, all right—one replete with braids

45

and a plastic barette.

Chris and Sid lit cigarettes—the stink diminuendoed. I said, 'Bud, what are you saying?'

'That at least one of your kidnappers should be made up to look like an Indian. That this dump as the kidnapper's stash place would gain you some points for realism. That a psycho Indian who might be long dead makes a good fall guy.'

Chris said, 'If this works and my career takes off, I'll give you each ten per cent of my gross earnings for the next ten years. If it doesn't work, I'll cash in some stocks my dad left me and split the money between you, and I'll sleep with both of you at least once.'

Sid howled. Chris poked a scalp and said, 'Ick. Icky lizard.'

I said, 'Count me in, minus the bed stuff. If the gig doesn't fly or get results, I'll fork over the pink slip on my 88.'

Four-way handshakes. A bird squawked outside—I flinched wicked bad.

5

Scalps.

Indian fall guys.

Teamster goons.

Encore: Dick Contino, truculent guinea hood.

Who *didn't* tell his wife: I'm knee-deep in a hot kidnap caper.

Monday morning twinkled new-beginning-bright. I walked out for the paper—a fuzz type was lounging on my car. I'd seen him before: hobnobbing with Bud Brown at Yeakel Olds.

I eased over guinea hood cool. Fear: my legs evaporated.

He held up a badge. 'My name's DePugh. I'm an investigator for the McClellan Senate Rackets Committee. Bud Brown snitched you for Conspiracy to Kidnap, Conspiracy to Defraud and Conspiracy to Perpetrate a Public Hoax, and believe me, he did you a big favor. Hand me the contents of your outside jacket pockets.'

I complied. Felony bingo: repo run reefers. Bud Brown: lying rat motherfucker.

DePugh said, 'Add Possession of Marijuana to those charges, and put that shit back in your pockets before your neighbors see it.'

I complied. DePugh whipped out a sheet of paper. 'Dear Dick: I couldn't let you and Chrissy go through with it. You would have gotten caught in your lies and everybody would have gotten hurt, me and Sid included. I told Mr DePugh, who is a nice guy, so that he would stop you but not get you in trouble. Mr DePugh said there is a favor you could do for him, so my advice is to do it. I'm sorry I finked you off, but I did it for your own good. Your pal, Bud Brown.'

My legs returned—this wasn't a jail bounce. Shit clicked in late: Bud pressing the Teamster Prez for info: Bud hinky on the kidnap plan from jump street. 'Brown's an informant for the McClellan Committee.'

'That's correct. And I am a nice guy with a beautiful and impetuous nineteen-year-old daughter who may be heading for a fall that you can help avert.'

'*What?*'

DePugh smiled and clicked into focus: a cop from Moosefart, Minnesota, with a night-school law degree. 'Dick, you are one good-looking side of beef. My daughter Jane, God bless her, goes for guys like you—although I'm pretty sure she's still a virgin, and I want to keep her that way until she finds herself some nice pussy-whipped clown that I can control and marries him.'

'*What?*'

'Dick, you keep asking me that, so I will now tell you that one hand washes the other, a stitch in time saves nine, and if you scratch my back I'll scratch yours, i.e.: I'll let your fake kidnapping happen, and I'll even supply you with some muscle far superior to Bud and Sid—if you do me a favor.'

I checked the kitchen window—no Leigh—good. 'Tell me about it.'

DePugh tossed an arm around me. 'Jane's an undergrad at UCLA. She's flirting with pinko politics and attending some sort of quasi-Commie coffee klatch every Monday night. The klatch is an open thing, so anybody can show up, and with that bum Korean War deal of yours, you'd be a natural. See, Dick, I'm afraid the Feds have infiltrated the group. I'm afraid Janie's going to get her name on all kinds of lists and fuck her life up. I want you to infiltrate the group, woo Janie, but don't sleep with her, and make it look like she just joined the group to chase men, which Janie implied to her mother is true. You join the "Westwood People's Study Collective", put some moves on Jane DePugh and pull her out before she gets hurt. Got it?'

Holy Jesus Christ.

'And no reprisals against Bud and Sid. Really, Dick, Bud did you an all-time solid by bringing me into this scheme of yours. You'll see, I'll find you some good boys.'

I said, 'I like the scalp angle. I want to keep it.'

DePugh pulled out photos. The top one: a dead Indian on a morgue slab. Three bullet holes in his face; SIOUX CITY, S.D. CORONER'S OFFICE 9/18/51 stamped on back.

'Bud Brown and I are old pals from Sioux City. When I was on the Sheriff's there, Chief Joe Running Car here got drunk and scalped his wife. I picked him up, and he copped to those Griffith Park snuffs. Chief tried to escape, and I killed him. Bud and I are the only ones who know that he confessed to the LA killings, and the only ones who've got the shack pegged. Chief Joe here—he's your fall guy.'

Three bullet holes/one tight circle—DePugh took on a new panache. 'Show me the other picture.'

He held it up. 'Aah, my Janie.'

Nice: a redhead hot for some mischief. Sleek—Julie London minus 10,000 miles.

Leigh banged on the window and drew a question mark.

DePugh caught it. 'You'll think of something. Just don't fuck my daughter, or I'll kill you.'

6

Green eyes scorched me—I shaved a few miles off Jane De Pugh's odometer.

In session: the Westwood People's Study Collective.

The Boss Pinko droned on: the labor strike aesthetic, blah, blah. Some collective: me, a few beatniks, a Hollywood 'Producer' named Sol Slotnick—a wolf with fangs for sweet Janie.

My mind wandered. Sol and Jane made me walking in—Jane's horns grew right on cue. Now it was Commie biz as usual.

Blah, blah—the LAPD as management enforcers. A cheap one-room pad; shit-strewn cat boxes placed strategically. Bum furniture—my chair gouged my ass.

'It is well known that Chief William H. Parker has formed anti-labor goon squads at the request of wealthy contributors to LAPD fund drives.'

I called Chrissy and spilled on Dave DePugh's shakedown—she agreed not to tell Leigh about it. I told her the kidnap scheme was still on—with DePugh supplying some pro muscle. Scared Chris: a light-colored sports car tailed her briefly last night. I mentioned Yeakel's DMV contacts—a temp license trace might be possible.

'It is thus not untoward to state that police violence is violence aimed at subjugating the lower stratas of society.'

I flicked a cat turd off my chair. Jane crossed her legs my way—ooooooh, daddy!

A man walked in and sat down. Thirty-fiveish, hipster garb: sandals, Beethoven T-shirt. *I* made *him*: an FBI face in the crowd at my desertion trial.

He made *me*: a half-second quizzical look.

He didn't make *me* make *him*—I glued on a deadpan quicksville.

Fed sharks circling—Janie, watch your mouth.

The Head Red called for questions. Jane said, 'My dad's an investigator with the McClellan Committee. They're investigating corrupt labor unions, so I hope you're not going to tell us that all unions are squeaky clean.'

Sol Slotnick raised a hand. 'I ditto that sentiment. I made a picture once called *Picket Line!* I had some connections in the garment rack—I mean trade, and I had a kickback—I mean a reciprocal agreement going with the owner of a sweat sh—I mean factory, who let me film his peons—I mean workers, at work. Uh . . . uh . . . uh, I saw good on both sides of the picket line, which . . . uh . . . is why *Picket Line!* was the title of the movie.'

Sol looked at Jane. Jane looked at me. The Fed inched his

49

chair away from a cat box.

The beatniks walked out oozing boredom. The Commie Commissar harumphed.

Sol, eyes on Jane: 'I'm, uh, thinking of making a picture about that killer that's strangling those kids up on the Strip, you know, the West Hollywood Whipcord. I want to show him as a . . . uh . . . out-of-work union guy who got fucked—I mean loused up by corrupt management practices. And . . . uh . . . when the cops shoot him, he's gonna decry the corruption of the system while he spits blood and repents. It's gonna be like *Picket Line!* I'm gonna show good and bad on both sides of the fence. I might even go the whole hog and have a Negro cop! See, this schvartze gas station attendant I know has taken some acting classes. I think I could do good business with this picture and do some social good to boot. I think I'll call it *Sunset Strip Strangler!*'

Sol looked at Jane.

Jane looked at me.

The Fed looked at Sol.

The Boss Pinko said, 'Mr Contino, you're acquainted with the dark side of the police experience. Would you care to offer comments?'

'Yeah. I agree with everything Jane said.'

Jane threw me a swoon. Sol muttered, 'Goyische prick'—I barely caught it. Mr Commissar sighed. 'Sometimes I think I'm running a lonely hearts club. And on that note, let's call it a night. We'll have coffee at the usual place, and I'll do my best to upgrade the conversation.'

We hit Truman's Drive-In and commandeered a booth. Sol slid in next to Jane; I sandwiched her from the flip side.

The Fed and the Red sat buddy-buddy close. Jane pressed into me—her nylons went scree-scree.

I signalled a waitress—coffee all round.

The Fed said, 'My name's Mitch Rachlis.'

Introductions flew quick—the Commie tagged himself Mort

Photo: Hulton/Bettmann

Opposite: Jimmy Hoffa testifies before the Senate Labor Rackets Committee, chaired by John L. McClellan, August 1957.

Jastrow. I ditzed Rachlis: 'You look familiar, Mitch.'

Smart fucker: 'My wife's a fan of yours. We caught you at the El Rancho Vegas way back when, and a couple of times at the Flamingo Lounge. We always sit up close, so maybe that's why I look familiar.'

Smart fucker/good improvisor.

Sol moved on Jane. 'Have you ever considered a career in motion pictures?'

Jane scrunched my way. 'I'm keeping that option open. In fact, right now I've narrowed my career choices down to doctor, lawyer or movie star.'

'I could help you. If *Sunset Strip Strangler!* floats, you could play one of the victims. Can you sing?'

'I certainly can. In fact, that's my fourth career option: recording star.'

'Sweetie, that's wonderful. See, I could cast you as a nightclub songstress that attracts men like flies on sh—I mean like moths to the flame. The West Hollywood Whipcord gets a big boner—I mean a big thing going for you, and you get to perform a few numbers to showcase your singing skills.'

Mitch Rachlis butted in. 'What are you working on now, Mr Slotnick?'

'A picture called *Wetback!* It blows the lid off the treatment of migrant fruit pickers. It's gonna stir up a load of shit—I mean controversy, and establish me as a producer of socially conscious pictures that deliver a message but don't fuck with—I mean sacrifice a good story in the process. Sweetie, write your number down for me. I might need to call you soon for an audition.'

Jane complied—twice. One napkin slip went to Sol; one snaked into my pants pocket. Jane's hand/my thigh—oooh, daddy!

Mitch the Fed looked at Sol—stone puzzled. Mort the Red scoped the whole group—stone disgusted.

Janie pressed up to me. 'We should get together. I'd love to hear about your political struggle and what it's like to play the accordion.'

'Sure, I'd like that,' came out hoarse—our leg-to-leg action crossed the line.

The Fed said, 'See you all next week,' and hotfooted it. Jane lit a cigarette—Miss Teen Sophisticate, 1958. I checked the window—and spotted Rachlis outside by the pay phones.

Janie smiled—teen steam wilted my pompadour. I put a dollar on the table, mumbled good nights and split.

The parking lot spread out behind the phone bank. Rachlis stood in an open booth, his back to me. I eased by just inside earshot.

'. . . and of all people, Dick Contino was at the meeting.'

'. . . the whole thing wasn't exactly what you'd call subversive.'

'. . . no, I don't think Contino made me . . . yeah, right, I was there at his trial.'

'. . . yes, sir . . . yes, sir . . . Slotnick *is* the one we're interested in. Yes, that wetback movie does sound pro-Communist . . . yes, sir, I'll . . . '

I walked down Wilshire, relieved: Joe Fed wasn't after Jane—or me. Then guilt goosed me: this extortion gig felt like a blight on my marriage. Another phone bank by the bus stop—I called Chrissy.

Her service answered: 'Miss Staples will be spending the night at OL-23464.'

My number. Chris probably called Leigh and asked to sleep over—that car must have tailed her again.

Shit—no kidnap scheme/extortion scheme confidante.

A directory by the phone. I looked up Truman's, dialed the number and paged trouble.

Jane came on. 'Hello?'

'This is Dick. Would you like to have dinner tomorrow night?'

'Oh, yes! Yes, I would!'

Please God: get me out of this morass intact and protect me from myself and this Teenage Temptress.

7

The mail arrived early. I went through it on the sly—half expecting notes from the dangerous DePughs. Irrational: I only met them yesterday.

Leigh was still asleep; Chrissy sawed wood on the couch. She confirmed it last night: the light-colored sports car tailed her again. I insisted: you're our guest until this bullshit resolves. Her DePugh Dilemma advice: warn Sol Slotnick on the Feds and let Jane down easy. Buy her dinner, be her pal—but no wanka-wanka. PROTECT OUR RELATIONSHIP WITH DAD AND OUR BOSS KIDNAP CAPER.

Bills, *Accordion Quarterly* magazine. A letter to Miss Christine Staples, no return address on the envelope.

Waa! Waa!—baby Merri back in her bedroom.

Chrissy stirred and yawned. I said, 'There's a letter here for you.'

'That's odd, because nobody knows I've been staying here on and off.'

I tossed the envelope over; Chris opened it and pulled a sheet of paper out. Instant heebie-jeebies—she trembled like Jell-O with the DTs.

I grabbed it—one yellow legal pad page.

Swastika decals circling the borders—model airplane stuff. Glued-on newspaper letters: I WANT TO FUCK YOU TO DEATH.

My brain zipped:

Dot Rothstein? The tail car, temp license 1116—who? The tail car geek might have followed Chris here and glommed the address—but why send a letter here? The fiend might have seen Chris and I on *Rocket to Stardom*; he could have bagged my address from the phone book. Longshot: he could have resumed his tail after *I* chased *him* that first night Chrissy slept here.

Chris reached for her cigarettes; a half dozen match swipes got one lit. I said, 'I'll take this to the cops. We'll get you some proper protection.'

'No! We can't! It'll screw the kidnap thing up if we've got cops nosing around!'

'Sssh. Don't wake Leigh up. And don't mention the kidnap gig when she might hear you.'

Chris spoke *sotto voce*. 'Talk to Bob Yeakel about checking with his DMV people on the license again. Maybe we can get a name that way and turn it over to Dave DePugh. Then maybe he can lean on the guy to make him stop. I don't think this is Dot Rothstein, because I don't think she could squeeze into a sports car.'

'I'll talk to Bob. And you're right, this isn't Dot's style.'

Chris stubbed her cigarette out. Shaky hands—the ashtray jittered and spilled butts. 'And ask Bob to give us some time off. Remember, he said he'd cut you loose on your second show if you helped out with those repossessions.'

I nodded. Leigh walked in cinching her robe; Chris held her mash note up show-and-tell style. My stoic wife: 'Dick, go to your father's house and get his shotguns. I'll call Nancy and Kay and have them bring some ordnance over.'

My dad kicked loose two .12 gauge pumps. I called Bob Yeakel and batted 500: yes, Chris and I could have a few more days off; no, his DMV contact was out of town—there was no way he could initiate a license check. I buzzed Dave DePugh's office to pitch a kidnap skull session—the fucker was 'out in the field.'

The White Pages listed Sol Slotnick Productions: 7481 Santa Monica Boulevard. I drove out to West Hollywood and found it: a warehouse down the block from Barney's Beanery.

I shoved the door open; industrial smells wafted up. Sweatshop City: rows of garment racks, sewing machines and pressers. Signs in Spanish posted, easy to translate: FASTER WORK MEANS MORE MONEY; MR SOL IS YOUR FRIEND.

I yelled—nobody answered.

Cramped—I scissor-walked to the back. Three Border Patrol cars stood on blocks; a nightclub set stood on a platform: bar, tables, dancefloor.

Homey: sleeping bag, portable TV. Foodstuffs on the bar: crackers, Cheez Whiz, canned soup.

'Yeah, yeah, I live here. And now that you have witnessed this ignominy, state your business.'

Sol Slotnick, popping through bead curtains in a bathrobe.

'I also swiped this robe from the Fountainbleu Hotel in Miami Beach. Contino, what is this? First you steal Jane DePugh's heart, and now you come to torment me?'

Why mince words?

'I'm happily married, and I've got no interest in Jane. I was sent in to pull her out of that Commie group before she hurts herself. You should get out, too. There's an FBI plant in the group, and he's interested in *you.* The local FBI's got some bee in its bonnet that *Wetback!* is pro-Red.'

Sol grabbed a bar stool and steadied himself. Rainbow time: he want pale, then flushed bright red. Lunch time: he wolfed a stack of saltines and Cheez Whiz.

His color stabilized. A belch, a smile—this clown digested grief fast. 'I'll survive. I'll shift gears like when I lost my backing for *Tank Squadron!* and doctored the script into *Picket Line!* Besides, I just joined that fakoktah group to chase trim. I saw Jane on the street up by UCLA and followed her to my first meeting. You know, I think I want to marry her as well as drill her. I'm forty-nine years old, and I've had three heart attacks, but I think a young cooze like that could add another twenty years to my lifespan. I think this is one Jew she could seriously reJEWvinate. I could make her a star, then trade her in for some younger poon before she starts cheating on me with handsome young greaseballs like you. Contino, tell me, do you think she'd consent to a nude screen test?'

The spritz had me reeling. Sol built a cracker/Cheez Whiz skyscraper and snarfed it. Fishbelly white to red and back again—the spritz hit overdrive. 'You know, I'd love to use *you* in a movie—you and Janie, what a pair of filmic lovebirds you could be. Most of your publicity has been poison, but it's not like you're Fatty Arbuckle, banging starlets with Coke bottles. Dick, a wholesome young slice of low-fat cheese like Jane DePugh could ream me, steam me, dry-clean me and get me off this B-movie treadmill to Nowheresville that has had me exploiting aggrieved schvartzes and taco benders to glom the cash to make these lox epics that have given me three heart attacks and a spastic colon. Dick, I own this factory. I hired illegal aliens to sew cut-rate garments until the INS nailed me for harboring wetbacks, because I let them sleep here on the premises in exchange for a scant one-half of their pay deducted from their checks. The INS nailed me and fined me and shipped most of my slaves—I mean workers—back to Mexico, so I glommed some Border Patrol cars for bubkes at a police auction and decided to make *Wetback!* to atone for my exploitation sins and defer the cost of my fine. Now the Feds want to crucify me for my egalitarian tendencies, so I won't be able to shoot *Wetback!* I've got these Mex prelim boxers lined up to play illegals, but they're *really* illegals, so if I shoot the movie, the INS will round them up and put them on the night bus to Tijuana. Dick, all I want to do is make serious movies that explore social issues and turn a profit, and slip the schnitzel to Jane DePugh. Dick, I am at a loss for words. What do *you* recommend?'

My head whizzed. I ate a cracker to normalize my blood sugar. Sol Slotnick stared at me.

I said, 'I've got a date with Jane tonight, and I'll put in a good word for you. And I know an FBI man pretty well. I'll tell him that you're not making *Wetback!* and ask him to pass the word along.'

'*You're* friends with one of J. Edgar Hoover's minions?'

'Yeah, Special Agent Pete Van Obst. His wife's the President of my National Fan Club.'

'What's the current membership? We might make a picture together, and statistics like that impress financial backers.'

'The current membership is sixty-something.'

'So you add a few zeros and hope they don't check. Dick, be a gentleman with Jane tonight. Tell her I think she has movie-star potential. Tell her you've heard rumors that I'm hung like Roy Rogers' horse Trigger.'

Dismissal time—Sol looked exhausted. I grabbed a few crackers for the road.

Kay Van Obst brought three .45 autos—FBI issue, 'borrowed' from husband Pete. Nancy Ankrum brought a sawed-off loaded with rat poison-dipped buckshot—Caryl Chessman told her where to find one. Add my dad's .12 gauge pumps and call the pad 'Fort Contino'—LA's cut-rate Alamo.

Ammo boxes on the coffee-table.

Front and back window eyeball surveillance—four women in rotating shifts.

Four women packing kitchen knives in plastic scabbards—Kay hit a toy store on her way over.

Time to kill before my 'date'—I took a snooze.

Ink-smeared dreams:

COWARD REDEEMED; KIDNAPPERS STILL AT LARGE!

CONTINO FOILS FIENDS; SAVES BACK-UP SINGER FROM TORTURE AND RAPE!

LA FUZZ NIX PUBLICITY STUNT SPECULATION: 'THIS CAPER WAS REAL!'

Chris held down by salivating psychopaths.

Cops swarming the kidnap shack.

Chief William H. Parker holding up scalps.

CONTINO KIDNAP PLOT REVEALS BIZARRE LINKS TO UNSOLVED MURDERS!!!

REDSKIN RESERVATIONS RAIDED IN SEARCH FOR KIDNAPPERS!!!

APACHE CHIEF SAYS, 'HEAP BAD BUSINESS! ME SEND UP SMOKE SIGNALS TO TRAP SCALP KILLER!'

Chris woke me up. 'You should get ready. I told Leigh you were jamming with some studio guys, so take your accordion.'

A last headline flickered out:

CONTINO CONQUEST CONTINUES! KIDNAP TOPS LINDBERGH SNATCH IN POPULAR POLL!

I'm sure you must think that I'm just a naive young thing. You must think that any girl who hasn't narrowed her career choices down any better than doctor, lawyer, movie star or recording star must be rather silly.'

Jane picked the restaurant: a dago joint off Sunset and Normandie. The Hi-Hat Motel stood cattycorner—VACANCY in throbbing neon made me sweat.

I drank wine. Jane drank ginger ale under protest—feeding minors liquor was a contributing beef.

'I don't think you're silly. When I was nineteen I was a recording star, but I just fell into it. You should finish college and let things happen to you for a while.'

'You sound like my dad. Only he doesn't push the "let things happen" part, because he knows that I have the same appetites my mom had when I was her age. I look like my mom, I act like my mom and I talk like my mom. Only my mom married this rookie cop from Sioux Falls, South Dakota, who got her pregnant when she was eighteen, and I'm too smart for that.'

Scorch/scorch/twinkle—green eyes offset by Chianti bottle candlelight. 'Sol Slotnick might fit that "let things happen to you" bill. He likes you, and he's a legit movie producer who could get you work.'

Jane futzed with her bread plate. 'He's a lech and a fatty-patty. He followed me to my first Collective meeting, so he's one step up from a wienie wagger. My dad used to drive me around when he was a detective in Sioux Falls. He wanted to show me what I had to look forward to as far as men were concerned. He showed me all the pimps and panty sniffers and winos and wienie waggers and rag sniffers and gigolos that he dealt with, and believe me, Sol Slotnick fits right in. Besides, he has small hands, and my mom told me what *that* means.'

I sipped dago red. Jane said, 'You have *big* hands.'

VACANCY throbbed.

Questions throbbed: Who's gonna know? Who's gonna care? Who's gonna tell?

Easy—you/you/you—straight across.

'Jane, Sol's the kind of guy that makes dreams come true.'

'Sol Slotnick is a long-distance wrong number. My mom reads *Variety*, and she said *Picket Line!* was one of the big low-grossing losers of 1951. Sol Slotnick, ick.'

I dipped some bread in my wine glass and bit off a crust. Jane said, 'You're both earthy and sensitive. You're politically aware, but not didactic. You've been wronged by society, but you're not a martyr. My mom said that men with ambiguous qualities like that make the best lovers, because they keep you guessing, and that postpones the inevitable letdown of sex getting stale.'

'Your dad must be quite a guy.'

Jane giggled. 'You mean my dad's brother Phil. I figured that out because Uncle Phil used to come around a lot when my dad was out of town on extradition assignments, and I got sent to the movies all the time. *And*, I used to sneak peeks at my mom's diaphragm, which sure was out of its case a lot when Uncle Phil was around. And you know what? Uncle Phil's hands were *much* bigger than my dad's.'

I checked out my own mitts. Big—accordion practice gave them their girth.

A waiter hovered—I signalled him away. Jane laced fingers with me. 'Did you ask me out just to shill for Sol Slotnick?'

'Did you join the Westwood People's Study Collective just to chase men?'

'No fair. You answer first.'

I pulled my hands free. 'I was bored and shopping around for kicks, so I went to the meeting. You looked like kicks, but I've decided not to cheat on my wife.'

Hot potato—Jane winced. 'OK, so I joined the group for the same reason. And you can tell Sol Slotnick that I won't sleep with him until the twelfth of never, but I will audition and strip down to a bikini if you'll chaperone me.'

'I'll tell him, and I'll chaperone you. And I'll warn you now: you should quit going to those meetings, or your name will end up on some goddamn blacklist that could break your heart.'

Jane smiled. My heart swelled—just a little.

'There's a meeting tomorrow night that I *have* to go to, because Mort's going to discuss FBI malfeasance, and I want to get some lines to tease my dad with. Besides, that man with the Beethoven sweatshirt looks cute.'

'He's an FBI agent taking names.'

'Well, then at least my dad will approve of him. My dad's *so* right-wing. He thinks that slavery should be reinstated and that streets should be privately owned, so the owners can charge protective tariffs. My mom's a liberal, because she had a Brazilian lover once. He had really big hands, but he tried to pimp her out to cover some track bets he made, and my mom said "No, sir," and called a cop.'

'What did the cop do?'

'The cop was my dad. He got her pregnant.'

I called for the check. 'Come on, I'll drive you home.'

Jane snuggled close in the car. Chanel #5 tickled my nose—I cracked the window for relief. The McGuire Sisters on the radio—I let 'Sincerely' wash over me like Jane and I were for real.

It started drizzling. I hit the wipers and adjusted the rearview—a car was glued to my back bumper.

Spooky.

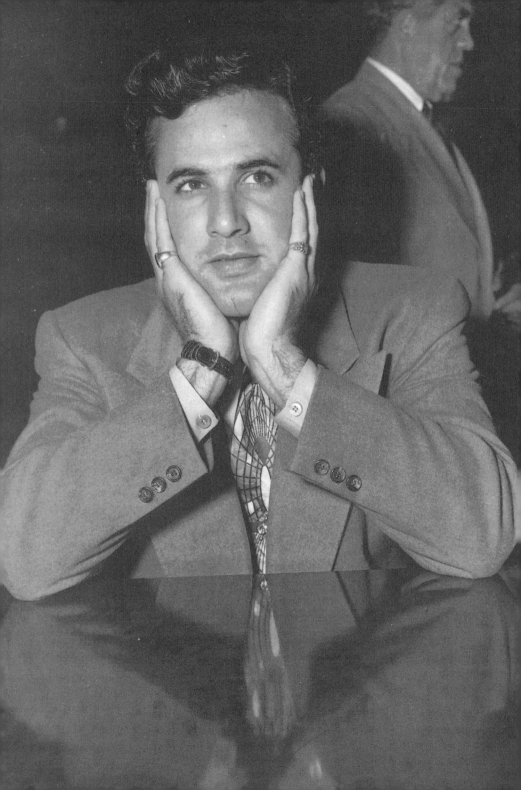

I punched the gas; the car behind us accelerated.

Jane slid off my shoulder and into my lap.

I hung a sharp left, sharp right, sharp left—that car bird-dogged collision close.

Jane burrowed into my lap.

I felt myself responding.

Left turn, right turn—the steering wheel brushed Jane's hair. Hands on my zipper—something told me to hit the brakes.

BAM!—two-car bumper-locked pile-up—in the middle of a pissant LA side street.

I quit responding. Jane said, 'Shit, I think I chipped a tooth.'

I got out. French kissing: my Continental Kit and a '56 De Soto grille.

???—no white sports job—???

I ran back.

The De Soto driver got out, weak-kneed. Streetlamp glow lit him up good: Danny Getchell, *Hush-Hush* magazine.

'Dick, don't hit me, I've got pictures!'

I charged him. A flashbulb popped and blinded me—Getchell bought some seconds.

'The waiter at the restaurant recognized you and called me!'

My sight came back blurry—I charged and sideswiped a tree.

'Dick, I've got pix of you and the redhead holding hands!'

Flashbulb pops—I picked myself up seeing stars.

'I've got a shot of you and the twist walking by the Hi-Hat Motel!'

I charged the voice—'Dick, you can buy out with money or trade out with a story! Don't you know some queers you can rat?'

I tripped on a hubcap and went sprawling. Jane yelled, 'My Dad's a policeman *and* a lawyer, you extortionist cocksucker!'

Flashbulb pop-pop-pop—my whole world went bright white.

'Dick, your zipper's down!'

I flailed on my knees and glimpsed trouser legs. Those legs went spastic—I caught a blurred shot of Jane shoving Getchell.

Gray flannel up close—I grabbed and yanked. Getchell hit the pavement; Jane smashed his camera on the curb.

'I dropped the film off, you dumb guinea shitbird!'

My hands/his neck—made for each other. *My* voice, surreal to *my* own ears: 'If you tell Leigh, I'll kill you. I've got no money, and the only story I've got is too good for you.'

Choking out raspy: 'You bluff. I call.'

I tightened my grip. Choking out bone dry: 'You bluff. I call.'

Door slams, background voices. Jane said, 'Dick, there's witnesses. My Dad says eyewitnesses get killers the death penalty.'

Getchell, bedrock bone dry: 'You bluff. I call.'

I let go. Getchell hunkered up and ass-scooted away. I pulled him back by the hair and whispered, 'I'm working out a fake kidnap thing with some pros. I won't give you the exclusive, but I'll give you first crack at my own account.'

Getchell choked out, 'Deal.'

Jane helped me up. Miss Teen Temptress was snaggle-toothed now.

8

Fort Contino, cabin-fevered up.

Leigh and Chris practiced knife throws: the 'I want to fuck you to death' note corkboard-mounted served as a target. Nancy Ankrum kept her snout stuck in the *Herald*: the West Hollywood Whipcord hit again. Kay Van Obst on maintenance duty: oiling pistols and shotguns.

The girls had spent the night—'Barracks Contino'. Bob Yeakel sent a food supply over: a half-dozen Pizza De-Luxe pizzas. A note accompanied them: 'Chrissy Dear, be of strong heart. My pal at the DMV goes back to work in a week, and I'll have him start checking temporary licenses then. Dinner soon? Romanoff's or Perino's?'

Leigh kept me under fisheye surveillance: I came home last night with ripped pants and a mangled car. My excuse: some punks tried to hijack my accordion. Leigh was skeptical. I kept smelling Jane's shampoo—maybe Alberto VO5, maybe Breck.

I got Kay alone. 'Can you call Pete and deliver sort of a cryptic message? I'll explain later.'

'Well . . . sure.'

'Tell him to talk to the agent assigned to the Westwood People's Study Collective. Tell him to tell the agent that I know for a fact that Sol Slotnick is not going to shoot the movie *Wetback!* Tell Pete that Slotnick is *not a Red*, he's just a movie clown trying to make money and get laid.'

Kay got it straight and grabbed the hall phone; I covered her so Leigh wouldn't hear. Whispers, whispers—a nudge in my back.

'Pete said he'll pass it along, and he said that you've got a certain credibility. He said that if the agent isn't at the meeting tonight, you'll know he bought your story.'

Good—some intrigue resolving my way. The doorbell rang—Nancy checked the peephole and opened up smiling.

Pizza De-Luxe with three piping hot pies. Sizzling cheese and anchovies—unmistakable. Ramon of 'Ramon and Johnny' trilled, '*Buon Appetite!*'

I got lost: lunch by myself, a cruise to the beach, dinner solo. I stewed, I fretted—shakedown Danny Getchell, my ratched-up car. Dave DePugh and Janie, Sol Slotnick, the kidnap—some four-or-five-or-six-horse parlay buzz-bombed my brain. Wires crossed, sputtered and finally made contact—I drove straight to the Westwood Collective and parked with an eye on the door.

7:58—Sol Slotnick walked in.

8:01 to 8:06—assorted beatniks walked in.

8:09—Jane DePugh walked in.

8:09 to 9:02—no Fed man in sight—Pete Van Obst probably put the fix in.

9:04—I stationed myself by that door.

Jane and Sol walked out first; I gathered them up in one big embrace. 'Not *Wetback!*, *Border Patrol!* You've got the cars, and you can hire some non-illegals to play illegals! The movie stars Janie and me, and we can start working on the script tonight! Sol, I pulled the Feds off your ass, so now we can work this deal free and clear!'

Jane said, 'I'll call my dad and tell him I'll be home late.'

Sol said, '*Border Patrol!* . . . Riiiiiight . . .'

I zoomed by Googie's and copped some Bennies off Gene the Queen, this transvestite that deals shit from the men's room. Va-va-voom!—I chased a handful with coffee and hit Sol's warehouse hummingbird buzzed.

Sol and Jane filled their fuel tanks: Maxwell House, double-X Benzedrine. Pencils, notebooks, the *Wetback!* script to work from, go—

We changed heroic fruit picker Pedro to Big Pete—a Border Patrolman/accordionist hot to fill a Communist band exporting wetbacks to a secret slave-labor camp in the Hollywood Hills. Big Pete is in love with torch singer Maggie Martell, formerly leftist earth mother Maria Martinez. Maggie is being pursued by evil scientist Dr Bob Kruschev, who's brainwashing the wetbacks and implanting slogan devices inside their heads. Big Pete/Maggie/Kruschev—a hot love triangle!!! Big Pete serenades illegals from the back of a truck; his accordion lures them into surrender and deportation! Kruschev sends his sloganeering robots into the bracero community, where they spout Commie rebop and corrupt a youth group that Big Pete has been indoctrinating into Americanism. The robots and corrupted youths advance on a Border Patrol station; Big Pete makes an impassioned anti-Red speech that instantly un-corrupts the young pachucos and inspires them to attack their corruptors. The robots are demolished; Dr Bob Kruschev makes a last-ditch effort to corrupt Maggie with a pinko love potion that makes all Commies and fellow travelers irresistible! Maggie unknowingly drinks the evil brew and puts the make on a roomful of visiting Soviet spies! Big Pete arrives on the scene, lures the spies outside with accordion music and guns them down! The movie ends with a citizenship swear-in: all the wetbacks that fought the Reds are issued green cards!

We finished the script at 6:00 a.m.—Benzedrine blasted, exultant. Jane called her dad to say she was a movie star—Sol just offered her five hundred scoots to play Maggie Martell.

I wondered how 'Dad' would react.

Jane cupped a whisper. 'Dick, Dad wants to talk to you.'

I grabbed an extension; Jane hung up. DePugh came on the line. 'I approve, Contino. But I want this Slotnick clown to up the

65

payoff to *six* hundred. Plus: no gratuitous cleavage during her nightclub scenes. Plus: no heavy make-out scenes with you. Plus: I say we tie the kidnapping in to the movie. I say we do it just as the movie starts shooting. I've got some Teamster guys to play the kidnappers, and I think you should audition them. Dick, this caper is tied to Janie's career now, so I want to do this right. We want a realistic abduction backed by eyewitness testimony. We want—'

Rabid dog stage-daddy—whoa!

'We want—'

I said, 'Dave, I'll call you,' and hung up. Sol was taking his Bennie-jacked pulse—at 209 when I walked over.

'Can you stand some more excitement?'

'Just barely. The way Jane rewrote that love scene is gonna get us Auschwitz'd by the Legion of Decency.'

I whispered. 'I'm getting kidnapped right before we start shooting. It's a put-up job with some pro muscle working back-up.'

Sol whispered. 'I like it, and you can count on me to keep mum. What about Jane as your co-victim? Add cheesecake to beefcake for a *real* publicity platter.'

'That spot's already filled.'

'Shit. Why are we whispering?'

'Because amphetamines induce paranoia.'

The warehouse door slid open; two pachucos struck lounging poses. Slit-bottom khakis, Sir Guy shirts—bantamweight punks on the stroll.

'Hey, Mr Sol. You got trabajo?'

'When we get our movie work? Hey, Mr Sol, what you got for us?'

Sol flipped. 'I'm doing a new picture! No trabajo! No work! Get your green cards and you can play robots in *Border Patrol!* Amscray! Get out of here, I'm having a heart attack!'

The punks split with middle finger farewells; Sol broke out the saltines, took his pulse and noshed simultaneously. My fair co-star: dozing in a Border Patrol car.

I walked outside for some air. *Heralds* in a curbside newsrack—NEW WHIPCORD SLAYINGS! on page one. Photos of the dead couple—the woman looked oddly like Chris Staples.

My Bennie jag was wearing down—I stifled a yawn. A carload of pachucos cruised by; one vato eyeballed me mean. I walked back in to give the script a last look.

Sol had a saltine Dagwood going: peanut butter, lox spread, sardines. Jane was scoping her chipped tooth in a compact. I said, 'Get your dad to set you up with a good dentist.'

'No. I've decided it will be my trademark. Dick, we were so close when that car hit us. We were so close that you couldn't have refused me.'

Sol sprayed cracker crumbs. 'What the fuck are you talking about?'

Noise: front door scrapes, a bottle breaking. Then KAAA-WHOOOOOOSH—fire eating sewing machines, garment racks, air.

Rushing at us, oxygen fed—

Sol grabbed his Cheez Whiz and ran. Jane's knees went; I picked her up and stumbled towards the back exit. Big-time heat behind us—I caught an over-the-shoulder glimpse of mannequins sizzling.

Sol hit the exit door—cool air, sunshine. Jane moaned in my arms and actually smiled. I risked a look back—flames torched the Border Patrol cars.

BOOM—an air clap hit me. Jane and I went topsy-turvy airborne.

A dim voice: ' . . . yeah, and we held it back from the press. Right . . . we had an eyeball witness on the last Whipcord snuffs. No, he only saw the killer's vehicle. No license numbers, but the guy got away in a '53 Buick Skylark, light in color. Yeah, needle in a haystack stuff . . . there's probably six thousand of the fuckers registered in California. Yeah, right, I'll call you—'

Bench slats raked my back. Not so dim: a phone slammed receiver to cradle. My eyes fluttered open behind a huge headache—a police squadroom came into focus.

A cop said, 'You're supposed to say "Where am I?"'

Lightish '53 Skylark/Whipcord vehicle/Chrissy.

I said, 'Did the eyewitness say the car had a *temporary* license?'

Quick on the uptake: 'No, the witness didn't specify, and temp licenses only account for 8 per cent of all registered vehicles, so I'd call it a longshot that's none of your business. *Now*, you're supposed to say, "How did I get here?" and "Where's the redhead that I was passed out with?"'

My head throbbed. My bones ached. My lungs belched up a smoke aftertaste. 'OK, I'll bite.'

Fat Joe Plainclothes smiled. 'You're at the West Hollywood Sheriff's Sub-Station. You may not recall it, but you refused medical help at the arson scene and signed autographs for the ambulance attendants. The driver asked you to play "Lady of Spain", and you passed out again walking to your car to get your accordion. Sol Slotnick is in a stable condition at the cardiac ward at Queen of Angels, and the redhead's father picked her up and drove her home. There's an APB out for the spics that tossed the Molotov, and Mr DePugh left you a note.'

I reached out woozy; the cop forked a memo slip over.

Dick—the bar at the Luau tonight at 8:00. There's some boys I want you to meet. P.S.—Slotnick got the script pages out, so we're still on schedule. P.P.S.—what happened to Janie's tooth?

Woozy—weak legs, hand tremors. The cop said, 'Your car's in the back lot with the keys under the mat. Go home.'

I woozy-legged it outside. Clear, smogless, so bright my eyes stung. Soot hung in the eastbound air—R.I.P., Sol Slotnick Productions.

Leigh was waiting on the Fort Contino porch. Armed: a .45 in her belt, a black-and-white glossy held up.

Jane DePugh and I—passed out entwined behind Sol Slotnick's sweatshop.

'Marty Bendish from the *Times* brought this by. He owes Bob Yeakel a favor, so it won't be printed. Now, will you explain your behavior for the past week or so?'

I did.

Chrissy, Bud Brown, scalps, redskin fall guys—publicity kidnap extraordinaire. Dave DePugh and horny daughter

extrication; the People's Collective/Sol Slotnick/*Border Patrol!*
The off-chance that the tail car man and Whipcord were one;
DePugh as the new kidnap mastermind.

Leigh said, 'When you get out of prison I'll be waiting.'

'That won't happen.'

'My mother said Italians were all suckers for big gestures,
which is why they wrote such great operas.'

'Yeah?'

'Don't act disingenuous and don't look so handsome, or I'll
try to talk you out of it. And don't let that chipped-toothed vixen
french kiss you during your love scenes, or I will fucking *kill* you
both.'

Anchovy pizza on Leigh's breath—I kissed her long and
hard anyway.

9

'This is my daughter's movie debut, so I want a good deal of
publicity surrounding it. You need men with no police records to
play the kidnappers, in case any eyewitnesses get called in to look
at mugshots, but they've got to be real hard boys who can act the
parts convincingly. Now, check these guys out. Are they not the
stuff criminal nightmares are made of?'

Introducing:

Fritz Shoftel—blond, crew-cut, fireplug-thick Teamster thug.
Wire-rimmed glasses, acne scars, six extra knuckles minimum per
hand. Pop/pop/pop—he stretched a few digits to show me they
worked. Loud—a man in the adjoining booth winced.

Pat Marichal—dark-skinned Paraguayan beanpole with a
stark resemblance to the morgue pic of Chief Joe Running Car. A
smiler—tiki table torch light made his too-bright dentures gleam.

I said, 'I'm impressed. But Slotnick's Border Patrol cars got
fried, so I'm not entirely sure there's going to *be* a movie.'

DePugh sipped his Mai-Tai. 'I have faith in Sol. Any man
that can eat cheese dip in the middle of a heart attack is
resourceful.'

Shoftel stretched his fingers. 'I studied acting under Stella

Adler. My kidnapper's motivation is that he's a rape-o. I'll maul the Staples babe a little bit for verisimilitude's sake, you know, give her a few hickeys.'

Marichal chewed the fruit out of his Zombie. Those teeth—fucking incandescent. 'I was a contract Indian at Universal until I got my Teamster card. My motivation's a hatred of the white man. I drop a load of redskin grievance shit on you and Chris while I get ready to scalp you. You grab my tomahawk and slice me, then make your getaway. When you bring the cops back to the shack, they'll see those scalps from those unsolved snuffs back in '46. See, Fritzie's the guy with the ransom-sex perv motives, and I'm the out-of-control guy that fucks this genius plan up.'

I said, 'Who do you hit up for the ransom?'

DePugh: 'Sol, and Charlie Morrison, the owner of the Mocambo. You see, Dick, I'm a cop, and I know what all cops know: that kidnappers are brainless scum who don't know shit from Shinola. You and Chris are not exactly big-name kidnap bait, and Morrison and Sol wouldn't lift a finger to save you. This crime has to *reek* of vicious incompetence, and Fritz and Pat are two guys who know how to play the part.'

Shoftel said, 'My parents abused me when I was a kid, so that's why I'm a rapist.'

Marichal said, 'The white-eyes stole my people's land and got me hooked on firewater. I need scalps to sate my blood lust and the ransom money to set up an Indian curio shop outside Bisbee, Arizona.'

DePugh tiki-torched a cigar. 'We do the snatch in broad daylight outside your house. Pat and Fritz will haul you and Chris out to a mud-smeared Chevy, then transfer you to another car and drive you to Griffith Park. Fritz will call Sol with the first ransom demand, and Sol will haul ass to the Hollywood Police Station. You said that Getchell guy gets first crack at the story, and you said he hangs out at the Hollywood Station chasing tips. OK, he'll be there and overhear Sol tell the cops about the ransom

Opposite: Dick Contino and Leigh Snowden celebrate their engagement, June 1956.

demand. These are solid embellishments, and we've got time to set things up right, because we can't move until Sol gets financing for the movie and it's ready to shoot.'

Fiends by torchlight: rape-o/scalper/stage-door dad/rogue accordionist. We shook hands all around—Shoftel's knuckles popped castanet-loud.

I went by Queen of Angels to see Sol. A clerk told me he'd checked out against doctor's advice. His forwarding address: Pink's Hot Dogs, Melrose and La Brea.

I doubled back west. Pink's was SRO—feed lines counter to curb. Sol hogged a pay phone and table at the rear—spritzing with one eye on a row of half-gnawed wienies.

Spritzing: 'I'm not wedded to *Border Patrol!* at the expense of your script, and I can get you Contino for an even grand!'

Spraying: sauerkraut strands, french-fry morsels.

His color rose and fell; his medic-alert bracelet jangled. 'Elmer, all right, your girlfriend can co-star. Yes, Elmer, I'll relinquish my producer's credit for a profit percentage! Listen, there's a publicity angle rigged to Contino's participation that I can't reveal the details of, but believe me, it's a doozie!'

Hot dog meat flew.

A pickle chunk hit a babe in a low-backed sweater; the mid-spine bulls-eye made her go, 'EEEK!'

Sol saw me and smothered the phone to his chest. '*Border Patrol!* is now *Daddy-O*.'

10

Genealogies:

Wetback! into *Border Patrol!* into *Daddy-O*. Pedro into Big Pete into Phil 'Daddy-O' Sandifer: truck driver/singer/romantic lead. Maria Martinez to Maggie Martell to Jana Ryan; Jane DePugh to Sandra Giles—pitch-girl for Mark C. Bloome Tires, semi-regular on Tom Duggan's TV gabfest.

Jane gave up her 'movie star' option and switched her major to pre-law—'So I can be more like my dad.' She sent me a farewell gift: her chipped tooth enshrined in a locket.

Dave DePugh continued to boss the kidnap plot—
'Hollywood publicist might be a shrewd career switch.'

Pat Marichal and Fritz Shoftel stayed on board—Sol Slotnick
promised them SAG cards if the scheme succeeded.

Ten days raced by.

Chris, Kay and Nancy continued to bunk at Fort Contino.

Bob Yeakel sent Pizza De-Luxe over with daily injections of
grease.

Chrissy seduced pizza boy Ramon.

Ramon renounced his homosexuality.

Ramon told Kay he had to pretend Chris was a man.

Yeakel double delivered: some DMV flunky was collating
license slips. Leigh was helping him out—she wanted the Chrissy
problem resolved and the Fort Contino red alert suspended.

No more FUCK YOU TO DEATH notes arrived.

No cars tailed Chris on her out-of-fort journeys. My
journeys ditto—no suspicious vehicles, period.

I spilled my insider lead to Nancy and Chris: the West
Hollywood Whipcord drove a light-colored '53 Skylark. Crime
Queen Nancy cut me off short: the Whipcord only snuffed
couples; single-o women and hate notes weren't his M.O.

'Sex killers never change their *modus operandi*. I've been
intimate with enough of them to know that's true.'

Sol Slotnick found a pad down the street from Pink's and
secured his *Daddy-O* financing via a high-interest loan from
Johnny Stompanato. Stomp said he'd use his pay-back cash to
market a new woman's tonic—a Spanish fly compound guaranteed
to induce instant and permanent nymphomania.

Chris and I joined Pat and Fritz for acting practice. Both
men were 'Motivation' obsessed. Fritz picked up a lightweight
case of paranoia—sometimes he imagined a primer-gray sports
car tailing him. Practice, dress rehearsals—waiting for a *Daddy-O*
GO date.

Schizo days.

I rehearsed with the Scalper and the Rapist; I rehearsed with
the *Daddy-O* director, Lou Place. David Moessinger's *Daddy-O*
script replaced *Border Patrol!*—it was tighter, but lacked political

punch. Sol rescued his nightclub set from sweatshop rubble—it would serve as both the 'Rainbow Gardens' and 'Sidney Chillis' Hi-Note'—major *Daddy-O* venues. The new screenplay called for me to sing—I learned 'Rock Candy Baby,' 'Angel Act' and 'Wait'll I Get You Home' pronto. My *Daddy-O* co-stars—Sandra Giles, Bruno VeSota, Ron McNeil, Jack McClure, Sonia Torgesen—were swell, but Scalp Man and Rape Man claimed my soul.

We'd hike up into the Griffith Park hills and bullshit. Pat Marichal brought firewater—he was working the 'Method' on his Chief Joe Running Car persona. A few shots, a few yuks. Then the inevitable segue to the topic of courage.

My best take: you never knew when it was real or just moonshine to impress other people.

Pat's best take: *you* know when you're scared, but do what you're scared of anyway—nobody else can ever know.

Fritzie's best take: give the world what it respects to get you what you want, and keep close watch on your balls when nobody's looking.

Time schizzing by—this fine LA winter fading out breezy.

Sol called and hit the brakes: *Daddy-O* was set to go four days hence.

The word flashed:

Mastermind/Scalper/Rapist to Victims—48 hours until kidnap morning.

11

Tick tick tick tick tick tick tick tick tick.

Leigh left for the DMV early.

Nancy and Kay left with her—baby Merri ditto.

Tick tick tick tick tick.

Chris and I watched the door.

Tick tick tick—my pulse worked triple-digit overtime. Chrissy's neck veins pop-pop-popped—every cigarette drag made them throb.

8:00 p.m. even—the doorbell.

'Hello? Is anyone home? My car's broken down and I need

to call the Auto Club.'

Good neighbor Dick opens up.

Two men in stocking masks sap him prone. He's grabbed and hauled outside, good neighbor Chris likewise—she gets off her muffled scream right on cue.

Manhandled across the street—Stanislavsky Method tough. Weird: no mud-smeared Chevy in view.

More weird:

I made Pat Marichal through his mask. Nix on the other man—he was half a foot taller than Fritz Shoftel.

Slammed into a copper-colored sports coupé. Skewed glimpses: 'Skylark' in longhand chrome, a spanking new metal license plate. My shoulder rubbed the door—paint smeared—a primer-gray spot showed through.

The car MOVED—Chris and I backseat-tangled—Pat driving.

The other man held a cocked roscoe on us.

Down into Hollywood, speed-limit cautious. Pat spoke out of character. 'This is Duane. Fritz had an appendicitis and sent him in as a sub. He says he's solid.'

Blip: Fritz said *he'd* been tailed by a primer-gray car.

Blip: Skylark/fresh paint/new permanent license.

Blip: tails on Chrissy.

Blip: light-colored and primer-gray = similar.

Chris shook from plain tension—she didn't waft hink. The other man spoke in character. 'Baby, you look so goooooooooood. Baby, it's gonna be so goooooooooooood.'

Talking stretched his mask. I recognized him: the scarf trick geek from the *Rocket to Stardom* try-outs.

Silk sashes—fashioned into hangman's knots.

Blip: THE WHIPCORD.

Fountain and Virgil looming—the car switch—our only chance.

Chris, improvising nice: 'You're a filthy degenerate shitbird.'

Whipcord/sash man: 'Baby, I want to fuck you to death.'

Neon bright hink—Chris flashed me this big HOLY SHIT!

On cue—Pat pulled into the deserted Richfield Station.

Off cue—I kicked the Whipcord's seat and slammed him against the dashboard.

Go—

Whipcord—stunned. Pat, stunned—this wasn't in the script. A '51 Ford by some gas pumps—the transfer/getaway car.

Very very fast:

I kicked the seat again.

Chris tumbled out the passenger door. I got one leg out—and kicked Whipcord with the other.

Chrissy stumbled and fell.

Whipcord shot Pat in the face—brains spattered the windshield.

I tripped and fell out of the car. Whipcord kicked me—I rolled into a ball and dervish-spun towards Chris. Shots zinged the pavement—asphalt exploded shrapnel-like.

Chrissy got to her feet.

Whipcord grabbed her.

I stood up, charged, and tripped over a pump hose. Whipcord pistol-whipped Chris into the Ford and peeled out eastbound.

'I Want To Fuck You To—'

DEATH.

I pulled Pat out of the car and wiped his brains off the windshield with my sport coat. Keys in the ignition—*I* peeled eastbound.

25, 40, 60, 70—double the speed limit. Blood streaks on my windshield—I hit the wipers and thinned it red to pink. No sight of the Ford; sirens behind me.

Sticky hands—I wiped them on the seat to grip the wheel better. Sirens in front of me, sirens wailing from both sides, ear-splitter loud.

Black-and-white police cars—a four-point press descending. Bullhorn roar—garbled—something like, 'Buick Skylark pull over!'

I obeyed—very very slow.

I got out of the car and raised my brain-crusted hands.

Cop cars fishtailed up and boxed me in. Somebody yelled, 'That's Contino, not the Whipcord!' Harness bull stampede—

Opposite: Hollywood and Vine.

gun-wielding fuzz surrounded me.

A plainclothesman got up in my face. 'Your wife called us from the DMV. She got a make on that 1116 temp license and traced it to the Skylark, which just got a paint job and some permanent plates. She told us how the car was tailing your friend the Staples woman, and Sheriff's Homicide just got a second eyewitness who tagged this as the West Hollywood Whipcord's very own—'

I cut in. 'I'll explain all this later, but right now you've got to be looking for a light-blue '51 Ford. The Whipcord's got Chris Staples, and he's heading east with her in that car.'

The cop shrieked orders; black-and-whites shrieked eastbound rapidamente. My brain shrieked—

Spill on the kidnap caper?—no, don't implicate Chrissy. Dead certain—the Whipcord killed Fritzie—don't reveal that either. Would Whipcord take Chris to the Griffith Park shack?— NO—he wouldn't go near it.

'Fuck You To Death' implied slow torture implied Chris with a chance to survive.

The plainclothesman said, 'The Whipcord's got an apartment near here. Follow me in the Skylark, maybe you'll see something that will help us.'

I saw:
Plastic dolls sash-cord-strangled, dripping nail-polish blood.

Stuffed dolls ripped open, spilling kapok.

Polaroids of bumper-jack-bludgeoned lovers.

Thousands of silk scarves tossed helter-skelter.

Chris Staples publicity pix, semen-crusted.

Chrissy's *Nugget* fold-out defaced with swastikas.

Barbie and Ken dolls going 69. Crudely glued-on photograph faces: Chris Staples, Dick Contino.

A photo-faced pincushion voodoo doll: Dick Contino with a hatpin stuck in his crotch.

It hit me:

He thinks Chris and I are lovers. He wants to kill us both. This fixation will make him indecisive—he'll keep Chrissy alive for a while.

The plainclothesman said, 'His name's Duane Frank Yarnell, and I don't think he takes too kindly to you and Miss Staples.'

Those dolls—Jesus fuck. 'Can I go now? Can I take the Skylark and drop it off later?'

'Yeah, you can. I yanked the APB on it, but the Sheriff's have a want on it, so you'll have to get it back by tonight. And I want to see you downtown at LAPD Homicide tonight, no later than 6:00. There's a dead man with a stocking on his face and a bullet in his head that you have to explain, and I'm just dying to hear your story.'

I said, 'Just find Chris and save her.'

He said, 'We will make every effort. Are you sure there's nothing you can tell us *now* that will help us?'

I lied: 'No.'

Tears in my eyes, a blood-smeared windshield—luck got me to Fritz Shoftel's pad intact. I laid some jive and a tensky on his landlady—she unlocked his apartment and bugged out.

The living-room and kitchen—nothing amiss. The bedroom—

Fritzie hung from a ceiling beam—cinched up by at least fifty neckties. Eviscerated: entrails oozing from deep torso rips. Viscera piles on the floor—shaped into a swastika.

I ran for the bathroom and hurled just short of the door. Towels atop a hamper—I soaked one in cold water, swabbed my face and got up the juice for a search.

The bedroom, first glance:

A bookshelf crammed with acting texts. Knife wounds on Fritzie's arms—figure Whipcord tortured him for kidnap info. A dresser and closet—be thorough, now.

Work clothes. Teamster T-shirts. A photo of Fritz and Jimmy Hoffa—someone drew devil's horns on the big man. Rubbers, women's undies—Fritz admitted he was a longtime panty sniffer. Rolls of dimes, *Playboy* magazines, a Playboy rabbit keychain. A group picture: Fritzie's World War Two outfit. More panties, more rubbers, more *Playboy*s, an LA Parks and Recreation Field Guide dog-eared to a Griffith Park page.

I examined it. The kidnap shack location was X-marked; pencil press indentation lines grew out of it. I found a magnifying glass and traced them to their terminus: a cave area a half mile southwest of the shack.

I re-checked the map. Tilt—dirt roads marked off— Observatory to cave turf access.

Somebody charted escape routes and other hide-outs on tracing paper. They weren't part of the initial kidnap plan—I would have known. Double tilt: Whipcord gets us to the shack and kills Marichal *there*. It's just a short hop to the caves—where he can kill Contino and Staples at leisure.

Leisure=Time=go NOW, don't buzz the fuzz.

I hauled up to Griffith Park. Danny Getchell lurked by the Greek Theatre, backstopped by some movie camera schmuck. Oblivious shitbird—he didn't know the whole scheme had gone blooey.

I ditched the Skylark in the Observatory lot. Access roads would take me straight to the caves—but I couldn't risk car noise that close to Whipcord. Sprint time—I ran straight up to the kidnap shack.

Empty—scalps on the table, biz as usual. I followed tracing paper lines southwest; adrenaline jacked my heart up to my pompadour.

There—a clearing offset by cave-dotted hills. Tire marks on the road; a '51 Ford covered with camouflage shrubs.

Four cave openings.

I crept up and re-conned, ears cocked for horror. One, two—silent. Three—squelched screams and insane ramblings.

'I have worshipped the Great Fire God for lo these years, and I have heeded the teachings of His only son, Adolf Hitler. He has asked me for silk scarf sacrifices, and I have given them to Him. Now the Great Fire God wishes me to take a wife, and first consecrate her with the markings of His son.'

I crept in. Pitch dark, twisty, damp—I hugged the cave wall. Motor hum, then light—Whipcord had an arc lamp set up.

Shadows, shapes half-visible. Shadow bounces, full light on pale skin: Chrissy's back, marked with a red swastika.

Trickling blood—not a gouge—still TIME.

I tiptoed outside to the Ford. Adrenaline: one good yank ripped the back seat out clean. I found a siphon tube in the trunk, popped the gas cap and sucked.

Lip traction caught—I soaked the seat cushion with ethyl. Springs and a baseboard to grip—I hoisted the hundred pounds of vinyl and foam up easy.

Unwieldy—but I got a match lit. WHOOOOOOOOOSH—the Fire God stormed the cave.

Smoke, screams up ahead. Flames snaking sideways—my arm hair sizzled. Godawful heat, shots—I felt foam rip close to my heart.

Chris screamed.

Whipcord screamed gobbledygook. Bullets smashed my shield of fire and exploded.

Heat, smoke, wind sucking flames *away* from me.

Whipcord kept firing—two guns—very close range. The top of the seat cushion blew off—I held on to red-hot springs and kept coming.

A blue halo behind Whipcord: clear sky.

I piled into him.

His hair caught fire.

I kept pushing towards the blue.

Whipcord ran backwards, screaming.

I chased him.

He hit thin air—I hurled the cushion at him.

Flaming pinwheels off a hundred-foot cliff.

I grabbed Chris, ran her out to the Ford, tucked her low in the passenger seat. Fire God fast: down dirt roads, through the lot, Vermont south. Roadblocks by the Greek Theatre; Danny Getchell, camera ready. Cops yelled, 'Stop!'—I got the notion this Fire God Buggy could fly. I worked the clutch/gas/shifter just right—the fucker went airborne. Shots behind me, residual shouts—magically audible. I heard 'CONTINO,' but no one yelled, 'COWARD.'

That was thirty-five years ago. History in ellipses: the cops covered all of it up.

I skated on kidnap plot charges—a police bullet meant for the Ford killed an old lady. Shoftel, Marichal and the Whipcord—stonewalled.

Chris Staples healed up nicely—and avoids low-cut gowns

that expose her faint scarring. She married a right-wing nut who digs swastikas—they're big in Born-Again Christian TV fraud.

Sol Slotnick has survived nineteen heart attacks on an all-junk-food diet.

Spade Cooley beat Ella Mae to death in 1961.

Jane DePugh had an affair with President John F. Kennedy.

Dave DePugh is a major JFK snuff suspect.

Leigh died of cancer in '82. Our three kids are grown up now.

Daddy-O bombed critically and nosedived at the box office. My career never regained its early momentum. Lounge gigs, dago banquets—I earn a decent living playing music I love.

'Draft Dodger', 'Coward'—every once in a while I still hear it. It's only mildly annoying.

LAPD goons muscled Danny Getchell for his flying car footage.

He dumped it on the *Daddy-O* cinematographer. It was spliced into the movie—not too convincingly.

People who've seen the raw film stock deem my driving feat miraculous. The word has spread in a limited fashion: one day in 1958 I touched God or something equally powerful. I believe it—but only to an ambiguous point. The truth is that at any given moment anything is possible.

Every word of this memoir is true.

Opposite: Dick Contino and James Ellroy, 1993.

GRANTA

HUGH COLLINS
HARD MAN

I'm five and a half years old, attending the Saint Roche primary school in Glasgow. The teacher, Miss O'Donnell, has asked us each to stand, walk to the front of the class and tell the others what our fathers do.

My da's a railway worker, says one and sits down.

My da makes ships, says another.

My da's a postman. He delivers the mail.

It is my turn and, with considerable pride, I walk to the front of the class. My da, I say, is the famous Wullie Collins. He's the Robin Hood of Scotland. He takes from the rich and gives money to the poor. My da's a bank robber.

The class erupts into screaming, shrieking laughter, and I'm taken by surprise. I can feel my face reddening. Miss O'Donnell is also surprised. And panicking. She puts an immediate halt to the exercise and marches me out of class to phone my granny.

Granny arrives. She is concerned.

He's not a bank robber, Hughie. You mustn't say that. You mustn't ever say that.

But where did I get the idea from?

Didn't I get it from Ginger McBride? Ever since Granny Collins told me to write my da at Peterhead Prison, we've had regular visits from those who have been in with him and now been released. They come to tell me and my granny stories—how Wullie has the run of the prison; how all the screws are scared of him; how he won't speak to them, even to give them the time of day; how he's still the boss. They always come with something—a little gift for Wullie Collins's only son. Tony Smith, the skinny man with a nose hooked like a claw hammer, brings me a small jewellery box. He is younger than my da, but one of his best mates (Skinny's brother, Granny tells me one night in a solemn voice, after Skinny has just left us, will be hanged in the new year). Gypsy Winning is another. Gypsy is tall—six foot two, he says—and towers over my granny and me. He's another one of my da's best mates. When he comes, he brings me a toy gun. And then there is Ginger McBride.

I'm sure in fact that it was Ginger McBride who said that my

Opposite: Hugh Collins, aged twelve.

da is the Robin Hood of Scotland, a bank robber who helps the poor. The last time he was here Ginger McBride brought me a knife. The knife is very heavy and has a tartan handle and a long, narrow blade like a dagger. It is my first knife.

My first memory is not of my da—I know him only by the pictures my granny shows me: it's of my ma on a cold, blustery night. I cannot be more than two years old and am wrapped in a blanket and held in her arms. We're walking fast, looking into deserted buildings. I remember the gaslights and the shadowy emptiness of the streets. My mother is frightened. She's been unable to find the address that she is looking for and knows that she needs to find a place for us to sleep. She is crying and her face is wet from tears. We spend the night in a room in an empty tenement. I sleep on the floorboards, my mother huddled next to me, clutching her knees.

The next morning we cross the city to Granny Collins's house, near the Royston Road. Granny Collins has such a large family—there's Alex, Jack, Shug, Charlie and Cathie—and now there will be me as well. I'm to live with Granny Collins. I don't remember my mother going. I look for her and she's gone.

I will have two mothers. My 'ma': my real mother, whom I will rarely see again. And my 'maw': my granny. At school, I start to invent parents; I seem to have so many. I take them from comic strips and make them into heroes.

I learn later that my mother's parents were against her marrying my father. Wullie Collins was a troublemaker and always in fights: he was notorious, even then. And my mother's father—a Clyde shipyard worker and lecturer for the Socialist party, a conscientious objector during the war who then spent the rest of his life fighting the label of coward—wasn't going to have Wullie Collins in the house. He was a bad sort. My mother's father refused to take her back, even for the night, even with a child in her arms. She'd just have to sleep out in the cold.

That's the night my father is sent to prison. My granny has to explain what a prison is and why my father has been sent to one. Later I will learn about the Glasgow knife fights and the razor slashings and the judge—one Lord Charmont—who was determined to make an example of my father: as a deterrent to the other slashers. Until then, no sentence for a slashing had been longer than two years. Usually no one did time at all. But knife slashings had become a Glasgow epidemic, and my father, having slashed the manager of the Locarno, a dancehall in the city centre, was given ten years. The dancehall manager got nine stitches. Ten years for nine stitches. That's thirteen months and ten days for each stitch. It doesn't seem right. Everyone tells me it isn't right; every visitor who comes with stories and gifts says it isn't right. Later still, in prison myself for a slashing, I will hunt out the newspaper clippings and trace my father's fame. I will tape them on to the wall and stare at them. His name and picture were in all the papers. There was even a 'bin the knives' campaign on television—led by Frankie Vaughan—and every bampot in the city came out to make a show of dropping off their sticks and broken bottles and used razor-blades.

It didn't seem right. It still doesn't. A judge, for his own private purposes, took Wullie Collins away from me, deprived a child of his father.

I don't know this man, the father I've never lived with, but my loyalty to him is powerful and undeniable. Where do they come from, feelings like these: so strong and yet based on so little? The man, after all, is just an idea, a thought, existing before I have any experience of being his son, and yet I want to look after and defend him. I want to protect him from injustice. And I want to be looked after by him. I want him to teach me—things, everything: how to be like him. I want to be a son he is proud of. When, later, my real mother remarries while my father is still in prison, I explode with rage at the terrible unfairness of it all. I long for my parents to be together. How can she take up with another man, when her real man, her husband, my father, is in prison, suffering from a publicity-stunt jail sentence? I will never forgive her, and years later, still inflamed by the treachery, will call her a whore (and then hate myself afterwards for saying it).

Another picture. I am eight years old, asleep, in the same cot with Alex. I think of Alex as my brother, but, even then, I know he's not. He's my granny's son, and, although only eighteen months older than me, is really my uncle. Granny is shaking Alex by the shoulders. She is fully dressed, and crying.

Wake up, Alex, she is saying. Wake up. Yer faither's just died.

For days, everyone is crying. I cry, too, although I'm not sure why. I don't think I understand what has occurred, but I'm infected by the sadness.

I remember that several days later the children—me, Alex and Cathie—find ourselves alone in a room with Granpa. He is in a coffin. We poke his face, and the skin is cold and tough like a football. Someone finds some lipstick. What would Granpa look like with red lips? Alex is giggling as I rub great gobs of the stuff across Granpa's face. He's like Coco the Clown, I say, and everyone laughs uncontrollably.

It's when we arrive at the funeral that I see my da. He's been let out of prison to attend his father's funeral. I've seen him only once before, but it was behind a plate glass window: he was dressed in blue and had black curly hair and a big smile. He is different now. He doesn't acknowledge me, his only son. He doesn't acknowledge anyone. He is there to witness the burying of his father. Wullie Collins is dressed in black—a long and immaculate black overcoat, a black suit, shiny black shoes, a black tie and steel handcuffs. He is surrounded by four screws and stands by the grave, silent. Everyone around him—the family, the friends—are weeping. My father is still. His face, covered with scars, doesn't reveal a thing. I study the face and will remember it forever: it is hard, like a stone. Wullie, the hard man, people say. Yes, my da, the hard man.

(He will attend another funeral with a prison escort, my granny's, in 1968. By then, he will have completed his ten-year sentence, but will be in prison on another conviction—assault of some kind. But this time, so am I. I am only seventeen and have been sentenced to Borstal for a knifing. This time, I'm the one surrounded by screws and held in steel handcuffs: I'm the hard one, who doesn't speak and is too dangerous to be allowed near anyone else. I'm kept far from the grave. I see my father on the other side. He has been accompanied by a single copper. His hands are free. He is telling someone a joke and laughing. And then I am taken away.)

(And then, twenty years later—at the age of thirty-seven—on my first weekend's leave from a life sentence, I will return to that grave to grieve properly and pay homage to this small, heavy woman who was stronger than so many men I've known and who was more of a parent than my real parents. I found her grave some time after midnight and broke down into hysterical crying and couldn't leave. I spent the night with her, sleeping atop her, and then, in the morning, returned to prison.)

In 1977, I was given a life sentence for murdering a man by stabbing him in the heart and sent to Perth Prison in Scotland. In the first months of my imprisonment, I stabbed three prison officers, was tried for attempted murder, pleaded guilty, and was given an additional seven-year sentence. I was put in solitary confinement, where I remained for a year. In 1978, I was transferred to the Special Unit at Barlinnie Prison, in Glasgow. The transfer, I remember being told, was meant to create in me a feeling of hope: faced with an eternity in prison, a living death sentence, I would now find, people said, a reason to live.

I had no reason to live, although I knew all about the Special Unit, and was, I admit, pleased to have been sent there. The Unit had come into existence following the abolition of the death sentence; prison officers had found they were unable to cope with this new generation of lifers: what is to stop a murderer from murdering again? What does he get—another life sentence? Cages and disciplinary regimes and long bouts of solitary confinement weren't working, and the idea was advanced by the officers themselves to create a new environment—one characterized by trust and a limited sense of freedom.

In the Special Unit, the cells are not locked; there is a public telephone; visitors are welcome; there is a kitchen where prisoners prepare their own meals (with real plates *and* knives and forks), a weight-room where they can exercise, a studio where they can draw and paint, a computer where they can write. Prisoners are not automatically punished for bad behaviour, but encouraged by specially trained staff to talk through their problems. That, in any case, was the theory. It was not always the practice, but there was no denying that the Special Unit was different. Only five prisoners were accepted at any one time; there were fifteen officers to take care of them.

The Unit opened in 1974 and, in Scotland at least, has never been long out of the news. Journalists seem incapable of accepting that a murderer can be rehabilitated or placed in something other than a locked cell with a bucket for slopping out. And since 1974, there has been a steady run of stories about drugs and drink and sex. In 1978, just before I was admitted, there was a suicide, Larry Winters, who died from a barbiturate overdose. The suicide, in the eyes of many, was conclusive evidence of both the availability of drugs and, more damningly, the experiment's failure: as much as society might like to see its murderers killed off, the idea was not that the murderers should do it themselves.

The Unit's most famous member was Jimmy Boyle. While there, he was the subject of a television documentary and wrote a book, *A Sense of Freedom*, about his experiences as 'one of Scotland's most dangerous men.' Jimmy Boyle now lives in Edinburgh, drives a Rolls-Royce, and is a highly successful wine merchant, specializing in vintage champagnes. But in 1978, when I first arrived at the Unit, Jimmy was its undeniable leader.

I was, I now understand, extremely confused when I was admitted into this odd, L-shaped section of Barlinnie Prison, a space suddenly so large, especially for me, emerging from solitary confinement, that I spent days wandering along its walls, trying to understand its layout. Several times I got lost. I thought, though, that my disorientation was probably normal, because, otherwise, I didn't believe there was anything wrong with me. But there did seem to be something wrong with the people around me. They weren't behaving like prisoners. For a start, they were all friendly with the screws, joking and laughing and talking, as if they were normal people. It made me uncomfortable; more than uncomfortable, it made me sick: I was stuck in a place surrounded by sanctimonious bastards looking for parole—or maybe this was the pay-off for the treats and favours that they all got in the Unit. It was ugly, and I didn't like it. Then I noticed that even Jimmy Boyle was friendly with the screws. Boyle's reputation preceded him: he had attacked prison officers in Inverness and had been involved in the rioting there. He knew that he was never to fraternize with the enemy.

On the second day, Jimmy invited me into his cell. He knew my father—he was about halfway between my father's age and mine.

You're fucked up, he said. You don't think you are, but you're completely fucked up. So was I when I arrived here. It took me six months to recover.

And he was right: I was fucked up. A few days later, a visitor brought me some drugs, and by the afternoon I had 'snowballed'—a concoction of cocaine and heroin, a subdued high, but one intense enough to allow my feelings to erupt. I threatened to attack the prison staff unless I was transferred immediately. What was I asking for really? I know what I was expecting: punishment or solitary or a beating or even the very transfer I demanded. What I got instead was the 'hot seat', a meeting where I was questioned by all of them—officers *and* prisoners. The meeting's resolution was not to mete out punishment, but to develop ways of supporting me through my difficulties.

What the fuck was going on?

I woke the next morning and, before breakfast, drank a bottle of whisky. I don't drink whisky and had never had a whole bottle before. I was full of anger and feelings of rebellion and defiance. I walked round to Jimmy Boyle's cell and had a go at him, until the other prisoners had to restrain me. Again, I expected to be punished; perhaps I wanted to be punished, if only to reinforce my sense of self and place. Instead another meeting was convened, and I was put back into the 'hot seat'. This time, though, I wasn't going to be interrogated; I was spewing with rage—at everyone about everything: the prisoners for being such obsequious arse-lickers, the staff for being so intrusive and nosey, the endless visitors who came parading through the Unit as if we were all animals in the zoo, and these stupid meetings that we had every day, sometimes twice a day, sometimes more.

I was bundled up—I had expected this—and put in a cell: but, again, not to be punished, as I had thought I would be. No: I was put in a cell so I could sober up in peace.

I didn't understand.

The next morning, Jimmy asked to see me again.

93

You have to understand, he said, how really fucked up you are. You don't believe me, but you need to write out all these different emotions. There are too many of them. They're all jumbled together. Get them on paper. Try to find out who you are and what has made you this way.

But how do I do that?

Who is Hugh Collins?

Caucasian male, born of William Collins and Betty Norrie Collins on 17 June 1951.

Height?

Five feet, ten inches.

Weight?

Eleven stone.

Build?

Muscular.

Hair?

Grey-brown.

Eyes?

Grey.

Vision?

A slight astigmatism. Corrective lens required for reading and watching television.

Tattoos or distinguishing characteristics?

A tattoo the length and width of my back, consisting of a network of concentric circles and different coloured stars.

Other distinguishing characteristics?

Scars. From the bottom up. One in the shape of a *W* on my calf: from a gang fight with the Tongs when I was fifteen. Twelve stitches.

What else?

Two scars on my back. The first is about an inch to the left of my spine. After I was arrested for murder, and while awaiting trial, I tried to escape. My plan was to become so 'ill' I'd be removed to the Royal Infirmary, where a friend had stashed clothing and a weapon in a closet. The trick was to get there. Another friend had been arrested with me. I had a piece of a mirror, which I broke into long slivers, wrapping the end of one with a blanket to make a crude dagger. I got my friend to ram it into my back, but, in his enthusiasm, he pushed it both too far in and too close to the spine. I lost consciousness before I had a chance to make my getaway.

And the second?

On the right, higher up. Another gang fight with the Tongs. I was eighteen. I was stabbed with a bayonet.

Other scars?

One on my hand, from the day that Wee Joe, a school friend, pinned my hand to a table with a carving knife. A scar on my upper arm, the right one, from Saughton Prison, when I tried to break up a fight.

The head?

About five on my scalp, mainly from the police. One is from a steel bar—from when I was beaten up in prison by William Mooney, the man I later killed. Also, a scar behind the right ear, which Wee Joe had tried to lop off in 1971.

And the face?

Principally the seven-inch scar along the jaw line. It's my badge, my calling card. Nobody fails to notice it: shop detectives single me out, children ask me if it still hurts, civilized people at dinner parties stare at it when they think I'm not looking. In prison, a psychiatrist suggested that I have plastic surgery—that, unless removed, the scar, like the scars on my father's face, would mean that people always responded to me as a violent man. An operation was arranged, but on the day I changed my mind: the scar is me, and to remove it would be to deny what I am.

How did it happen?

I was surprised by a butcher's cleaver. I believe the intention had been to kill me and that the jugular in my throat had been the target. They missed.

They?

My school friends.

There were four of us, all from the Royston Road. We met between the ages of five and ten at Saint Roche's: Catholic boys from a rough Catholic school. But by the time we were ten, none of us remained: we'd all been expelled. (In my case, it was after head-butting the headmaster when he tried to lash my hands because he found the length of my hair unacceptable—'Do you wear girl's clothing when you get home as well?' he asked. I broke his nose, knocked him unconscious and then ran away, never to return.)

There was the Bear, who even at five years old was large for his age. Since I can remember, the Bear was in fights, at first with the other boys at our school, usually held at the 'coop', the area behind the football parks. A day didn't pass when the Bear hadn't thumped someone (it was why I first sought his friendship: to protect me from him). Soon the Bear was thumping the boys from the next school. And then it was boys from the other side of Glasgow. The Bear had a knack for finding trouble and putting himself at the front of it—for 'steaming in'. In fact, it was the Bear who taught me how to head-butt, my first experiment being the headmaster's unhappy nose. As the Bear got older, he got bigger. He developed curious, brooding moods and a taciturn manner and had unpredictable fits of rage. He also developed an impeccable sense of dress, with a gangster's flair for long coats: it's where he concealed his weapons.

There was Joe Mulligan. Wee Joe, we called him. While he wasn't all that short—he probably came to about five-foot-seven—he had a terribly wee frame, and a relentless capacity for violence to make up for it. Wee Joe looked like some kind of animal, a weasel or ferret, a ferocious rodent-like thing that you'd never want to feed with your hands for fear that he'd sink his teeth in and never let go. He had an animal's head—slightly snout-like, as if he could sniff things out that normal humans might miss—with slitty eyes and thin, pointy, jagged teeth. Wee Joe had a small man's dexterity with an open razor, and whenever things became a little violent, he would become hysterical and start slashing. Wee Joe and I also had our difficulties. It was Wee Joe who surprised me when I stopped at the Yellow Bird café on Buchanan Street to pick up some fish and chips by chopping the side of my head with a butcher's cleaver. I can still recall the crunching sound as it slammed into my back teeth. And then, as I spun round, he sliced across the gums above my front teeth with a razor-blade. It was his 'comeback': the two scars that run in tandem from the top of his forehead, through his eyelid and down his cheek, came from me.

I met Albert Faulds the year I was expelled. He was Irish, with jet-black hair that he kept cropped close and short to accommodate fighting: to ensure that no one had anything to grab. Albert rarely spoke—it was his way—and was always superbly fit. He had just got out of an approved school, and the two of us used to spend afternoons in the upstairs cafeteria in Woolworth's, pretending to our parents—or, in my case, to my granny—that we were in class. At one point, we got proper jobs working in a garment factory; but, having spotted some fabric that I was convinced was mohair, and having clocked the fire escapes and alarms (out of habit, if nothing else), I couldn't resist returning late on the Saturday night and making off with great rolls of our rare cloth (which we then sold on to friends and punters to make suits; but our rare cloth turned out to be synthetic—it was intended to line suits, not to make them—and as it stretched and sagged and came apart, more and more unhappy customers came looking for us).

Our employment, however, was an aberration (it turned out to be the only job I held). And after one week, Albert and I were back at the cafeteria in Woolworth's. Soon, the Bear was joining us, and then Wee Joe, and before we knew it, we had the makings of a gang. We called it the Shamrock and would eventually have about fifty members. We were fourteen years old. We'd all been in fights and had a brief history of trouble of one kind or another with the authorities. We'd all done a bit of shoplifting or some burglaries—going through the floorboards of derelict tenements, say, so as to break through the ceilings of the places below. But the point was this: we hadn't done that much. We weren't criminals. Nor were we all that violent—yet. We were just boys in search of an adventure, looking for our part in the black-and-white gangster movie that was playing inside our heads. One moment we were hanging out; the next we had a gang.

That was 1965. My father was finally out of prison. Everywhere you heard the Beatles. I'd grown my hair long. I had money in one pocket and a lump of hashish in the other. On Saturdays, I'd be at the Celtic match. And I'd become a good fighter—I knew this because people were already afraid of me. I had a wildness about me and I loved it.

And I loved being in a gang. I don't know what I was getting from it, but it had something I wanted. I lived for the gang. We all did. I was seeing girls and going to clubs, but my heart was down on the South Side, fighting with open razors, the adrenalin crack. And, from the ages of fourteen to twenty-two, from 1965 to 1973, when I was released from Perth Prison, that was my life. It's a Glasgow story that has been told and retold; its history is carved into my body; it's the *W* across my calf; the crusty lump that has formed along my back; the knot still bulging, arthritic now, that rests atop my hand. But it was, more than anything else, the period that made me.

Now, when I think back to that time, I see it in two parts. In the first, I'm fifteen years old—out of school, on the loose, on my own. That ends when I'm seventeen and sentenced, for the second time, to Borstal (where I'll be when my granny dies).

In the second, I'm in custody: always (or so it seems). I'm in Borstal or the Young Offenders' Prison at Barlinnie. Most of the offences are absurd—silly mistakes made by an arrogant guy who doesn't know better. One evening I go out to rob a bank—me, aged eighteen, on my own, standing outside the Royal Bank of Scotland with a brick in my hand, at two in the morning, until chased away by an old woman in the flat above, who suddenly throws open her window—startling the hell out of me—and tells me to bugger off before I get arrested. So what do I do? I walk down the street until I come across a display of red apples looking so delicious that, with the brick still in my hand, I feel compelled to break the window and grab one. *Three months.* In another instance, I, along with Wee Joe and Albert, have been asked to testify about a gang fight (the one where I got bayonetted in the back). The case is heard on the very day that I'm released from the Young Offenders' Prison, and I'm confused and disoriented. I should have realized what I needed to do on learning that Wee Joe has absconded to England. I have no excuse when, later, Albert appears, having purchased a bottle of lemonade which he insists I break over his head. I do, knocking him out, and when he regains consciousness, he thanks me profusely. He then goes to the Royal Infirmary, declares that he has concussion and is unable to testify. I, however, do testify: and (determined not to grass on anyone, including the guy who stabbed me in the back) I am caught out committing perjury. *Eighteen months.* In all, between 1968 and 1973, I am sent to prison five times, for sentences totalling four years. Is that where my real education took place?

I ask myself that, I have to, it's the assumption: prison is where hard men get educated. But I also ask because I now see how I am changed by my time inside, and how the person who now emerges is different from the child who was sent to Borstal. He's a man now, quick and violent, a slasher, with few scruples or regrets. This is the third part, my final chapter. It begins in 1973. I'm twenty-three and am returning to Glasgow from Perth Prison. But this is not the Glasgow I left. There are still gangs—there will always be gangs—but there is something else: drugs. And a lot of money.

Today, the drug scene is different: more sophisticated, more dangerous. Today if there's trouble, you get shot: no argument. But this was 1973. There were only about twenty people dealing in all of Glasgow, and many were still the hippy-types, middle-class, with long hair, attracted to the city centre for the glamour of its violence or its atmosphere of danger. In a few years, these dealers would have gone: if not dead, then they'd be back at a university or in a job somewhere.

The drugs had been here before, but the money hadn't. You could find acid, but you'd never pay for it. Now it was being sold—fifty pence a tab, a pound, sometimes five pounds. There was hash, as there always had been. And there was also morphine and heroin, and everyone was using needles. There were downers, diconal, mandrax: and money, everywhere.

It's easy to picture: arrogant, young Glasgow hard man arrives home to find naïve hippy-types, unused to fighting of any kind—not to mention knives, bayonets, open razors and guns—making lots of money. What does arrogant, young Glasgow hard man do?

My day began by visiting my six regular dealers in preparation for the evening. (Before I was finally put away, I had stabbed most of them. Three are now dead.) I'd then return to the flat or else meet up with a friend and have a drink. Around six o'clock, I'd start my rounds. On a normal evening, I might have had, say, fifty tabs of LSD, two or three ounces of hashish and some tablets; occasionally I had heroin. A gram fetched eight pounds.

Everything took place in the pubs in the city centre, and eventually the pubs themselves became part of my routine. Most were owned by the big breweries who were always afraid of losing their licences if too much violence occurred on their premises. Therefore, with the help of some friends, I made a point of introducing too much violence and then demanding protection money. It was a time when—with a little imagination and a great deal of fearlessness—anything was possible. The drug squads were just starting out, but they weren't working undercover yet. They'd arrive in suits, looking conspicuously like policemen, with the result that, in the drug-friendly pubs, someone usually flicked the lights off and on to warn of a possible bust. What, therefore, would the arrogant, young Glasgow hard man do? He'd put on a suit—expensive, hand-made, silk—and, with one or two mates, go out for the evening pretending to be the drug squad: he'd enter a pub; its lights would be flicked off and on by the accomplice already in place; and drugs, in little pouches and sachets, would be dropped on the floor as their owners fled through the first available door; arrogant, young Glasgow hard man then had the opportunity to increase his stockholding by a brief, highly efficient sweeping operation.

What had I become? I cite an incident as an illustration. I could cite any number of others.

A publican approached me and asked if, for a hundred quid, I would slash someone who was giving him trouble. I performed my service and was duly paid. The following week I returned for another hundred quid. The publican was surprised to see me and refused to pay. I returned the following week. This time, I demanded two hundred quid—one hundred for this week, and one hundred for the week before. Again, the publican refused to pay, but I could tell that he was frightened. And with good reason.

My success in this new Glasgow rested on my reputation for being capable of limitless violence. I was both menace and protector, and I couldn't be one effectively without being the other. When the publican refused to make another payment, he knew that, eventually, he would have trouble: from me. He then made another mistake. Just as he had hired me to slash a man who had been a problem, so now he asked his bouncer to slash me—for an extra hundred quid. The news, when I learned it from a friend, filled me with an icy rage.

The bouncer did not have to look for me. That evening I presented myself at the pub. He was at the door.

'Are you looking for me?' I asked. I stepped right up to him, with my face inches from his. I had an open razor in the palm of my hand.

'Why, Collie,' he said, surprised, but very, very friendly. 'How the fuck are you?'

I then reached up behind him, grabbed him by the hair, jerked his head back and slashed him—straight along the jaw line, the blood spurting suddenly on to my face and hair and shirt, a steady stream. He buckled, knowing he had been slashed, and I pulled back harder on his hair.

'Naw, mate,' he said, 'I'm not looking for you. There's been some mistake.'

'You're right there's been a mistake,' I said. 'Tell your fuckin' gaffer that he owes me money.' And then I slashed him across the other jaw.

I had known, from the moment I heard the news that morning, what I was going to have to do that evening. The entire operation was carried out mechanically; no reflection, no regrets. It was business. (But then, later that night, I went home, smoked a joint, relaxed, and, as I was sitting on my own, listening to some music, I saw his face, the skin stretched back from the way I was holding his hair, and him looking confused and frightened. It was the eyes: suddenly so vulnerable in a man otherwise so hard. And I hated myself, grew sick and vomited.)

It is a feature of this kind of memoir—a villain's autobiography, a murderer remembering—to dress up the nasty bits. I've read books of this kind in which the murderer disappears entirely, and you're left with this nice guy telling lots of nice, colourful stories. What was all the fuss about, you want to ask? I don't want to prettify what was ugly. I don't want to persuade anyone that I was innocent, when I wasn't. From 1973 to 1977, my life was as I describe it here. I was at war—with everyone, even the members of the Shamrock. Albert, Wee Joe, the Bear: during this time, I slashed them all. And many, many others. I never went anywhere without being armed—tooled up—and would never tool myself up unless I was prepared to use my weapons. I knew what it was like to savage someone with a blade; I had felt the thrill of it, the intensity of the experience. I knew what it was to take someone's life. I was a very powerful man, and I was powerful because I was dangerous, and I was dangerous because I was prepared to be, and everyone knew I was fully capable of being so very, very violent. I had become my father.

Or perhaps I had become nothing more than what I thought my father was.

For the first time in my life, I was seeing him regularly. History and chance had conspired to keep both of us out of prison. He was living nearby, a ten-minute bus-ride away. But I didn't like what I saw.

I was at some awful club—everyone in platform shoes and three-piece suits—when I was tapped on the shoulder: there was an old man at the door asking after me.

An old man? I didn't know any old men. I went to the door and discovered my father, covered in blood. He'd been done over and had come to me for help. His face had been slashed and he was without his dentures. His hair was long and unkempt, and his clothes smelt of drink and urine.

My father: the old man.

I took him home in a taxi. I cleaned him up and discovered who'd slashed him. Once he was in bed, I went out and stabbed the guy who did it. I returned home and assured my father that the guy would no longer be a problem.

Which he wasn't. But the next week, late, there was a knock on the door. It was my father: the puckered face without its dentures, the hair, the blood, the soiled clothes, the smells. And so the routine: I brought him inside, cleaned him up, asked him who did it, put him to bed, then went out and did the guy. And so it continued. And every time it happened, I duly went out into the night and chibbed the person (except one, a black guy, whose flat I broke into—perfectly prepared to stab him as well—when I came upon an old-fashioned iron; I used that instead; I learned later that, having cracked his skull, I had put him into Intensive Care).

I started to suspect that my father was allowing himself to get into trouble—or at least wasn't too bothered when he found himself in a bit of bother—knowing that his son would sort it out for him. I started to suspect that he was revelling in my reputation as Glasgow's violent hard man—as if he was living off me in some way: or, more frightening, living through me.

And then one night, I couldn't take any more. And I beat him up. He was there in the flat with his girlfriend, a prostitute he picked up every night at the end of her run—the tartan mini-skirt, the white plastic boots, the battered, swollen face. He was pissed again, knocking over the furniture, spraying beer on the carpet, repeating, in his drunken slur, that I was his boy, his fuckin' boy.

And I hit him: I smacked him across the forehead with the butt of my sawn-off shotgun, then aimed it at him. Both barrels were loaded, and I went as far as pulling back the hammers. I was within a muscle's twitch of blowing my father away.

He lay there in the recess of the flat, his flies undone, his genitals hanging out, his hard, scarred face in a spasm of fear.

And for the first time, I saw him for what he was. My father was not a hard man. The hard man was a lie. Robin Hood? He was a drunk, poncing money from a burnt-out prostitute half his age. He was not someone I wanted to be. What I wanted to be had been a lie. It didn't exist.

But just look at what the lie had created.

I knew William Mooney, the man I murdered. I didn't like him, but I didn't like a lot of people. In any case, it's not the reason I murdered him. There was no reason to murder him.

Mooney was a big man, about my age, and weighed about fourteen or fifteen stone: stocky, but fit. I'd heard of him—he was from a gang called the Peg—but I didn't meet him until 1968. We were both at the Young Offenders' Prison at Barlinnie:

he was on his way out just as I was settling in to serve an eighteen-month sentence. I had my father's firm principles, not to talk to, or in any way be friendly with, the screws, and so Mooney's manner was bound to irritate me. He was a screws' pet, making them tea, doing them little favours. The day before he was due to be liberated, we had an argument. I don't remember what it was about. I suspect I resented that he was about to walk free—that he'd probably got parole because he got on so well with the screws—whereas I was on my way to serving my full sentence, down to the last possible minute. I offered him a 'square go', but he wasn't having any of it: after all, he'd be having a pint with his friends by this same time the next day. I then went to the screws and asked if Mooney and I could have a square go. They almost always obliged, leaving the two of you in a room alone, intervening only if the fighting got out of hand. But the screws told me to fuck off. I drifted back into the television room and then went to bed.

At Barlinnie, the cells are opened at six-fifteen on the dot, but the next morning they were opened at six. I had been asleep and just opened my eyes to see Mooney rushing through my cell door, coming at me with a steel bar. He hammered my nose with it, then pulled a blanket over me, picked up the steel washing basin nearby and slammed it repeatedly on my head. He went on to pound my joints, one after the other: one shoulder, then the other, the elbows, the spine, the pelvis, the knees. Then he left, closing the door behind him. I couldn't follow even if I'd been able to; I was locked in. In fact, I could hardly walk.

Mooney was freed fifteen minutes later.

I didn't see him again until the day I killed him. I had run into Wee Joe, who asked me if I could score some dope for Johnny Gemmell. Johnny Gemmell had been the husband of the woman I was living with, but Johnny and I remained good friends. Johnny was in prison, and Wee Joe would be seeing him the next day. By this time, there was no trust between me and Wee Joe, but I liked Johnny and wanted to help, so I told Wee Joe that I would meet him later at a pub called the Lunar Seven—around seven o'clock.

With Wee Joe was Mooney (Mooney, I learned later, was

seeing Wee Joe's sister, and all three of them—Wee Joe, the Bear and Mooney—had an informal gang of sorts). I hadn't come upon Mooney in nearly ten years, and, while I hadn't forgotten the beating, I was happy to let it pass. I was pleased to see him.

Wee Joe went off, and I joined Mooney for a drink. Mooney was already half-pissed and in a boisterous mood. Two women were with them and he was showing off a bit. He wanted to do things: shoplifting or thieving. He asked if I'd help him slash a guy—that there was money in it and that, in any case, the guy was a mug. I agreed, mainly to keep Mooney happy, although I thought that he'd been watching too many gangster movies. He kept jabbering away. He had a round, innocent face, with a turned-up nose and a permanent half-smile while he talked. As the pub closed, he suggested that all of us head off to one of the women's flats.

And so we set off, running into a nephew of mine along the way. He was with his mates, a gang called the Pickpockets, and Mooney decided to have a go at him. The Pickpockets was one of Glasgow's most organized gangs. It had about a dozen members, all young, between the ages of twelve and sixteen, and dedicated to making money. They avoided violence; they were thieves, especially adept at stealing jewellery. They travelled regularly—the previous week, they'd been in Switzerland—and always had cash. They could also be remarkably generous: if you stepped in front of a copper during a chase, they'd make a point of rewarding you later—as much as three hundred quid. But they didn't respond to bullying, and Mooney was bullying them: he wanted money.

I think I would have objected to the bullying in any case. That the one being bullied was my fourteen-year-old nephew—who couldn't fight sleep, let alone a fifteen-stone, body-building maniac in a half-drunken state—meant I was bound to get involved. And so it happened: Mooney pulled out a bread knife, threatening my nephew; I told him to leave it out, and he turned on me instead. 'I'll give it to you again,' he said.

It appeared that Mooney, too, hadn't forgotten the beating. In the circumstances, it wasn't going to take much to provoke me; this was certainly enough. And I told him so: I told Mooney to meet me at the Lunar Seven that evening; then, I, too, would be tooled up and we could go for a walk. By now, I was extremely angry, and my nephew—who, a moment before, I was protecting—now stepped between us to calm things down.

As the day wore on, I became angrier still. A friend, Felix, sought me out and told me not to go the pub that night: that it wasn't going to be a fair go after all, that everyone knew there was going to be trouble and that Mooney would be bringing a whole gang of people—the Bear among them—to do me. He was convinced that they were going to kill me. But I couldn't back out now. Besides, I had the dope for Johnny.

I don't know if Felix's suspicions were true, although it was the case that trouble had been expected. When the police arrived later to do their search and interrogation, they discovered that just about everyone was tooled up, with a blade or two secreted somewhere on his body.

I remember walking down Sauchiehall Street, very slowly, looking at everything, missing nothing. I had a blade up my sleeve, a new one, a twelve-inch Bowie knife. I kept fingering the handle, feeling its shape. I was making a picture for myself of what the pub would look like. It would be dark—the only light would be near the bar—and very crowded. Mooney wouldn't be far from Wee Joe. The Bear would be nearby. They'd be at the back, close to the exit. They would have made a point of being near the exit. At the Lunar Seven, the exit is through a swinging door, down some stairs and out on to the street.

My stomach was tightening into a ball. Sauchiehall Street was busy, with lots of people out, some already drunk.

As I walked into the pub I was aware of everything. The noise, the shadows, the smell of cigarettes and beer. It was very crowded, and I had to push my way to the bar, faces turning towards me as I did so, knowing, expectant. I spotted my friend Felix—he was standing next to Wee Joe—and the Bear. They were by the bar, at the back, near the swinging door.

'Collie,' the Bear shouted, arm outstretched to greet me. 'Over here! What're you drinking?'

Everyone was wearing a coat and drinking a glass of tomato juice: no alcohol. I stood next to Wee Joe. The scars on his face—like two railway tracks running down the length of it—still looked raw.

'Have you got the dope?' he asked.

'In a minute,' I said.

Mooney brushed my shoulder—not a word spoken between us—and I turned to follow him, watching him carefully. Then, as I turned back to the bar, a tumbler flew past my head. I twisted round, and there was Mooney, coming straight at me. Bottles were being broken and thrown, and someone was screaming. Instantly, the knife was in my hand. I slammed it into Mooney's chest just as he reached me. I could feel the fabric of his jacket on my knuckles from the force of the blow. He seemed stunned. I pulled the knife out, and my friend Felix grabbed me by the arms, trying to drag me away.

'Collie, you've done him. You've killed him.' He was whispering in my ear. 'Put the knife away and walk out quietly.' But I was staring at Mooney, who had only been stunned and was now reaching into his coat for the bread knife. He was coming back at me.

'Let me go, Felix.' He was holding on to my arms. Mooney was roaring now. 'Let me go.'

And then something snapped. It was as if my mind had liberated itself from my body, had floated up and away to the corner of the pub and, no longer able to control me, was watching what I was doing from a distance. Nothing was going to stop me.

I went for Mooney's arm and yanked it upwards, to give me a full, unobstructed view of his ribs, and then plunged the blade in between them. 'Fuck you,' I shouted. 'Fuck you, fuck you, fuck you.' I pulled out the knife and plunged it back into the ribs. 'Fuck you, fuck you, fuck you.'

But Mooney had me by the hair and threw me into the swinging door of the exit: down I fell, rolling down the stairs, pulling Mooney with me, clinging to my hair, my blade in his ribs. We hit the landing at the bottom, and he ended up astride me. Blood was pouring from his chest, but still he came at me. He had a beer tumbler in his hand, already broken, lifted it into the air and slammed it into the side of my head. I fumbled for my knife, gripped it firmly and plunged it into his throat.

He stopped and got off me, swaying. There was a gurgling sound, and he leaned back into the wall and slid down.

I got to my feet, exhilarated, covered in Mooney's blood, still warm, hot even, the knife in my hand. And then I stared at him, and realized what I was witnessing: these were his last moments; he was dying; I had killed him; he was dead.

'What the fuck have I done?'

I was dazed and staggered out into the street. I heard sirens and moved on, turned down a lane, dropping the blade in a dustbin along the way. I found myself in a fish and chip shop. What was I doing? I didn't want to eat. The people were staring at me. I was covered from head to toe with blood. I shuffled out and stopped. I had a view of the pub. The police had arrived and had cordoned off the area. I could see Mooney's legs sticking out.

I got the late bus home. It was packed with passengers. No one said a thing, but everyone stared at me.

'What the fuck are you looking at?'

Silence.

I got home, pulled off my clothes, got out my shotgun, put my chair in front of the door, and waited. When the police appeared, I would blow them away. I waited until dawn.

Hugh Collins was arrested the next day, 7 April 1977, and charged with the murder of William Mooney. He was also charged with three other attempted murders. Before he came to trial, he was impeached for two further murders. At the trial, three months later, the charges for the attempted killings and the two murders for which he had been impeached were found not proven. He was found guilty of the murder of William Mooney and sentenced to life imprisonment.

GRANTA

HENRY JOHN REID
BLIND RAGE

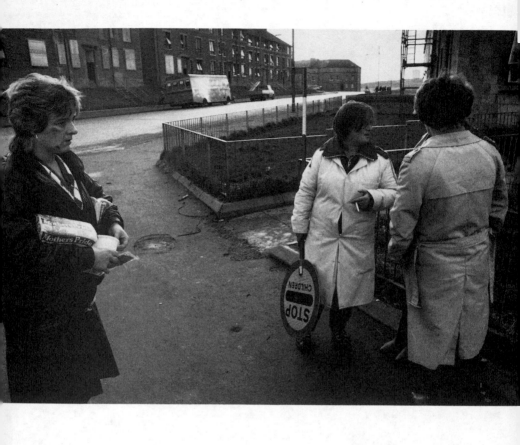

I was born in Dundee on 3 April 1951, of a mother who was not meant to bear more children and a father who had long before disappeared. The two never married, even though the man was my mother's one affair of the heart. She was crazy about my father, so crazy that she named me after him: Henry John Reid.

I never met my father, but I would dream of him: he was my hero, my myth, my everything, and I was sure that one day he'd return to me, disproving all the terrible things that were said about him. My mother would tell me endlessly how he had broken her arm, how he'd given her black eye after black eye, how he gambled away the housekeeping, how he sold anything for the price of a drink or a bet. My mother was always telling me that Henry John Reid, my father, my real father, was no good.

According to my mother, she should never have met him. I should never have been born. I was an accident, a mistake. My mother's other children—and there were four, all of them much older—never failed to remind me that I was an accident, a mistake. I was the step-brother: never fully a brother, never fully a member of the family. I was not allowed to use their name—O'Donnell. I had to be reminded that my father, a Reid, was different, and that I, also a Reid, didn't belong.

O'Donnell was the name of my mother's husband: Bobby O'Donnell, a good-for-nothing drunk, who left her years before but would turn up every now and again, needing money. His children by my mother included three girls and one boy, Bert. Of the girls, Alice was the only one I was close to. I always knew that Alice would listen to me and that she'd be fair. She tried to be hard—she had this tough manner—but she was a complete marshmallow on the inside, an utter softie. She was always, even on the day she died, a woman of great beauty—with jet black hair and very white skin. The other two sisters were Susan and Isa. Isa, ten years older than me, was the youngest. And there was Bert.

When I was four, the family moved from Dundee to Glasgow—to Bridgeton. Glasgow is a tough place, and Bridgeton was one of the tougher parts of it; I was picked on constantly—mainly because my accent, a Dundee accent, was different. I was never out of fights and would often go home in tears, only to be met by my mother who would take one look at me, give me the belt and then send me back out to fight, warning that if I returned crying again I could expect another belting.

I lasted three years at school, until I turned on the teacher as he was trying to punish me. I had been caught fighting, and as the teacher, an old, ugly man, went to give me the belt, I snatched it out of his hands and hit him across the face with it. I was dragged to the headmaster by my hair, held down and beaten. But I couldn't apologize—at least not properly. When asked to do so, I said: 'OK, I'll say I am sorry, but I hate your guts.' I was beaten again. Then I was expelled.

It was my last time in a normal school.

After that I ran away from every school they put me in. By the time I was eleven, I had been a truant far more than I'd ever been in a classroom. And that was when we moved again.

My sisters and Bert had married and moved out, leaving just me and my mum, who took me with her to a smaller house in Partick, another part of Glasgow.

I didn't like being the only one living with my mum. She treated me like a skivvy. While all the other lads were playing football in the yard, I'd be running her errands, sent to get the shopping at a place a mile off where the food was cheaper. On Mondays, my sisters appeared. Monday was the weekly visit to the pawn shop to make up for everything that their husbands had drunk or lost gambling over the weekend. They loaded me up with their husbands' suits or watches or both, or their wedding rings or some other piece of jewellery or one of their coats, and then sent me to the shop with a note. On Fridays I returned to get the things back. They sent me because they couldn't be seen in a pawnbroker's shop. An O'Donnell would never be seen in a pawnbroker's shop. But I wasn't an O'Donnell. I was a Reid.

It wasn't right. I ran away.

I found a second family in a Glasgow gang called the Tongs, and for two months I lived in a derelict tenement. I always had something to eat—my mates would steal food for me from their families—and then later at night we'd go out together breaking into shops and houses. It all came to an end when I was arrested. It was my first arrest.

My gang had smashed a big shop window, displaying expensive women's clothing, mainly fur coats. Two of us climbed inside and were throwing the coats out into the street to the others when someone shouted: 'Cops!'

We ran for it, but I slipped in the snow and was caught. I was charged, and when I wouldn't grass on my mates, was slapped around. When it was discovered that I had been missing for two months, my family was contacted. For two months, there'd been a big search for me—an eleven-year-old missing during a cold Glasgow winter.

My mother picked me up, and all the way home spoke only of the shame I, a Reid, had brought on this family of O'Donnells.

As I walked through the door at home, I was immediately knocked down. Bert had hit me across the face with his army belt, a great thick thing with a big brass buckle. He'd been there at the door, waiting for me to step through it. I got up and he hit me again, the buckle hitting me in the mouth. He picked me up, threw me against the wall and hit me over and over again. I thought he'd never stop. The next morning, my left eye was closed, and there was a welt down the side of my face. My arms, legs, face and back were covered with bruises, and there was a cut on my head. I could hardly move.

When Alice saw me she called Mum all the names under the sun and stormed out of the house saying that she was going to get the police and that Bert should go to jail. While she was out, my mother told me that if Bert got charged, she would disown me and send me to a home. She said that I was no good, just like my father, and that she should have flushed me down the pan at the first sight of me.

Years later, I learned that Alice really had brought the police back to the house to charge Bert. They even had a doctor with them.

My real family, I felt, was among the Tongs. They were my pals, my mates, my real brothers, and I preferred being with them to the aggravation I got from everyone else. It was around this time that I started drinking cheap wine and smoking.

When I was twelve, I was arrested for theft and sentenced to twenty-eight days in a remand home. Almost as soon as I got out,

I was caught stealing again and sent to an approved school called Lark Grove for three years. During my first year, I ran away at least a dozen times. I hated it. It was run by the Christian Brothers, and if you weren't praying or singing hymns, you were being beaten.

But by the second year, I had calmed down and was allowed home for weekends twice a month. That was when I realized that my mother had a hard life and was desperately unhappy. She couldn't pay her bills and had taken badly to drink. She was lonely, and I felt sorry for her. I spent my weekends out breaking into houses and shops and gave my mother the money I stole. I tried to give it to her on a Sunday, so she couldn't spend it straight away on drink. I had nothing to lose by stealing because all the courts could do was send me to the approved school, and I was going back there anyway.

Three months before my fifteenth birthday, I left school and got my first job, in a foundry. I had only been there two or three weeks when I started to get terrible stomach pains. I started vomiting—occasionally at first, but eventually every hour. I didn't know what was wrong with me and took a week off work. When I returned, I collapsed and was rushed to hospital. Over the next two weeks, I lost three stone. I had an operation, and the doctors told me that they had removed some of my intestine. They didn't tell me what was wrong.

I convalesced for six months. At the end, my weight dropped to six stone four pounds, and I had to have another operation. Again, they told me they had had to remove more of the intestine, but didn't tell me why. I would learn later that, because I was still under the age of sixteen, the doctors were not obliged to tell me what was really wrong: they were afraid to, for my sake. But the effect was to make my illness even more frightening and mysterious. What they did tell me, however, was that I could no longer work. At the age of fifteen, I was given a sick-book to take to the post office every week and collect my dole money like an old bloody pensioner.

I was terrified. I would get ill, be unable to eat or drink, lose massive amounts of weight in days and then have an operation, but I didn't know what was wrong with me. All I knew was that I couldn't do the things I enjoyed any more. I couldn't play football or do any sport at all; I was too ill to go out to the disco; I couldn't meet girls; I couldn't drink. For years, I had been looking forward to going out to work to support myself and my mother. Now I was on a permanent sick list. I felt I'd been thrown on the scrap-heap at the age of fifteen.

The hatred took me over. In Glasgow, we had something called a 'comeback': if you were beaten in a fight, you didn't slink off. If you wanted respect, you had to come back. I was now so small and skinny that all the boys I once fought were lining up for their comebacks. I had to show them that no comeback was possible. I learned to fight dirty; I felt I had to: if a lad turned his back I wouldn't hesitate to hit him with a brick or a piece of wood. I beat some people up so badly that I put the fear of God into them. I had solved a problem, but something in me had changed: I'd lost my respect for human beings.

For Bert, my illness merely confirmed that I was nothing but trouble. He was always there, at the small Partick house, if only because he was now drinking so much he needed to come round to pester money out of my mother. I remember lying in bed in the next room feeling poorly, listening to them arguing, when Bert said it would be better if I died, then everyone would get some peace. This was too much, even for my mother, and she tried to throw him out of the house. Bert was not going to be thrown out of his mother's house—not least for something he had said about me; he'd destroy the house first. Which was what he did. He started smashing everything. He moved from one thing to the next. He broke every ornament and vase, kicked in the television, took all the pictures off the wall, smashed the glass and the frames and ripped up the pictures inside. Then he moved into the kitchen where he smashed all the china and started breaking the chairs around the kitchen table. My mother was following him around, trying to get him to stop, without getting too close. Bert, at six foot three and twenty stone, was big, and my mother was only four foot eleven. But he wouldn't be stopped, and struck her and shoved her backwards over a chair.

I was holding a big, heavy bed bottle in case he started on me. When he shoved my mother, I hit him over the head as hard as I could. It stunned him and he stumbled. I was about to hit him again when my mother grabbed my wrist. She was terrified I'd scar Bert. In that pause, Bert caught hold of me. I was so light that he was able to pick me up and hurl me across the room against the wall. I rolled over in pain, and he kicked me in the ribs. And then he kicked me again—again and again and again.

He went off, leaving me on the floor. My mother was screaming and screaming; she'd become hysterical and was still screaming when a doctor appeared. He gave her an almighty slap and she stopped. He sent for an ambulance and I was taken to hospital. The police came to see me while I was there and told me that my mother had refused to press charges against Bert: she would have died before seeing him in jail. They said I could press charges by myself, but I had already made up my mind that Bert was due for a comeback.

A few months later, I went over to the tenement building where Bert lived, and hid on the landing. I had a cricket bat and had unscrewed the lightbulb overhead. I waited there for hours.

He came in drunk at one in the morning, cursing because he couldn't see to get his key in the lock. He began banging on the door and shouting for his wife to open it. I stepped out of my hiding-place and cracked him over the head with the bat. He fell to his knees. I cracked him on the side of the head, swinging the bat with all my strength. Then I went for his body—his ribs, his shoulders, his neck, his joints. I put everything into that cricket bat. Bert had crawled to the door and was clawing at it. He was bellowing to his missus to open the door. By the time she let him in, he was screaming for mercy. I ran off without either of them getting a look at me. Bert had his wife to thank that he was still alive, because if she hadn't opened the door, I would have killed him.

Although no one could prove it was me, everybody knew, especially Bert's wife. She heard the screaming but didn't open the door until she was good and ready. She had taken so many beatings from Bert that she wanted him to get a taste of his own medicine. Neither of us ever mentioned it.

Bert stayed out of my way after that. I had put real fear into him. Before then, he would always be ready to come back.

Afterwards, he wasn't so eager.

On my sixteenth birthday I learned that, by law, the doctors had to tell me what was wrong with me. I had Chrone's disease. It is like cancer of the intestine, a disease of old people. Normally a sufferer has one or maybe two operations, by which time either the disease will have been cured or he'll be dead. At the time, I was the youngest person in British medical history to have had it.

The doctors warned that if I carried on drinking it would kill me. But I think I really wanted to die. I had nothing to lose. I was more depressed than I have ever been.

I was caught stealing a load of televisions from a rental shop. But while in custody awaiting trial, the disease struck: I was rushed to hospital again, where I stayed for the next four months. The courts kept fixing a new date for the trial, but after a while I wasn't expected to live, and the charge was dropped.

Later, I was sent to Borstal for stealing, but after three or four months of my sentence I was taken ill and let out. Everyone was just sorry for me because of my disease. That was why they were letting me go. I couldn't even do Borstal.

My sisters were having problems of their own, and I tried to help. Isa's husband, John, was by now a complete alcoholic and could be very violent. I happened to drop round to her house one evening, and when no one answered the door, I looked through the letter-box and saw her kids standing in the passage—girls aged three and four. They said that Isa was asleep and tried to let me in themselves, but they couldn't reach the lock. I told them to go and wake Isa up, but they said that they couldn't, and that she'd been sick everywhere. Something was wrong, and so I broke the front-room window and got in that way. Isa was in the bedroom, and as soon as I saw her I knew what had happened: she had taken an overdose of sleeping pills. I phoned 999 and asked for an ambulance and the police.

Isa was taken to hospital, and the kids went to a neighbour. I stayed at the house to wait for John to return. He arrived home just before midnight, drunk and singing. It made me furious to see him in this state—hardly able to stand—while his wife was in hospital. I didn't even think about it; I acted. John needed to be punished; it was wrong what he was doing to my sister.

When Isa saw the state of her husband the next day, she told him he should press charges against me. He had a black eye, a broken nose and a split lip, and was covered in bruises. Isa, whose life I had saved, never spoke to me again.

In fact, few people were speaking to me at the time. Susan, my middle sister, was convinced that I was stealing the money from her gas and electricity meters and asked the police to charge me with the theft. When it happened again, she again approached the police, even though I was in Borstal at the time. How could I steal her money when I was locked away somewhere else? Three months later, she caught her son with the keys to the meters. For reasons I'll never understand, it remained my fault.

I tried to get away, to make a new start. I went to London and got some casual work. I returned to Scotland, where I got work as a waiter in a hotel in Glen Shee in the Grampians, near Balmoral Castle. It was probably the best job I've had, but it didn't last long. My illness had returned and no one understood why I was having to disappear into the toilet every hour. They thought I was having a smoke. And then I got caught with the day's takings and was dismissed.

I returned to Glasgow and on my first night back I fell in with my mates from the Tongs. I ended up spending the night in a police cell—I had got drunk and been arrested for a breach of the peace. That was the night my mother had a cerebral haemorrhage. No one knew where to find me, and she died before I could get to the hospital. I was drunk in a police cell while my mother was dying.

The family held a wake at Susan's house. I had to go, even though I wasn't speaking to any of them. Susan opened the door and didn't say a word. She just stared at me, icy cold. Finally she stepped out of the way and let me in. It turned out to be too much to bear. Everyone, even the neighbours, was there, drinking and talking about the good old days with my mum. I started shouting at them that this was no time to be having fun. I ran out of the house and went to a hotel bar, where I got drunk by myself. But however drunk I got, I couldn't forget that my mother had died without seeing me or saying goodbye.

I thought I might feel better if I went down to her little house in Partick. I sat there for a while, but the house felt very strange—cold and empty. I felt alone. I closed the windows and doors, turned on the gas and lay down on the floor with a couple of blankets.

The next thing I knew, the windows were open, and Alice's husband Jim was standing in the doorway. He had found me lying on the floor in the gas-filled house. The gas hadn't killed me because the meter had run out of money. I had been cheated out of death by a lousy shilling.

I left Glasgow—there was now nothing to keep me there—and went back to Dundee, the city of my birth. In Dundee, I met the most important woman of my life, Mary, the sister of a friend I had there. She was the eldest of six children. It hurts now to think back to that period with her. I hear through the grapevine that Mary is now dead—that she was struck down by cancer—but at the time she represented a new beginning for me.

We took a catering course together; there was a school in Oban. We got through the full four-and-a-half-month term, learning just about everything there was to learn: silver service, à la carte, wine, the works. We had this idea that we'd make a team, and that the two of us together would be a more attractive proposition to a possible employer than just one of us. I was hoping, I think, that we'd land a job in a small hotel, something out of the way, not unlike the place where I worked in Glen Shee. But when the course was finished and we returned to Dundee, Mary announced that she was pregnant.

Shaun was born on 19 November 1970.

Until then I had seen very little of Mary's mother. Connie was in her early forties and a very heavy drinker. Her husband had long since left her and she spent her time with her brother Watty, also an alcoholic. It was natural for Connie to help Mary with the birth, but afterwards she never seemed to leave. Every afternoon she and Watty arrived, completely pissed. It terrified Shaun. It made me very unhappy.

One day Connie appeared, in her usual drunken state, her drunken brother in tow, bearing a bowl of trifle for Shaun. As Connie started feeding it to him I noticed that the bowl was broken in places and tried to stop her, worried that Shaun would swallow some glass. I was always telling her what to do, she said. I thought I was better than everyone else; I was stuck up. I tried to make her leave. Then Watty started on me too, and I hit him.

The police arrived—the neighbours must have called them because of all the noise—and all three of us were put into the van. When Mary saw that they were taking me away she jumped on one of the policemen, screaming and scratching his face. So in the end, I got a hundred-pound fine and Mary got a fifty-pound one. Connie and Watty were fined ten pounds each.

We had no money. And neither did Connie: a week later, she was evicted from her house and asked us to take in her and the four children still living with her. I agreed to take the children—Connie could live with her brother Watty—and only because otherwise they would have been sent to an approved school. I knew what that was like.

But how was I to keep five kids and Mary? I went to the local convent and was given some tins of baby food, which wasn't much help, because as well as everything else, we were four weeks behind with the rent. I couldn't see any way round it; I had to get some money from somewhere, otherwise we would all be out on the street.

I went down to Ninewell, an area about five miles from where we lived, and broke into a house. I got £350 in cash, and some jewellery which I sold for £400. It put us right back on our feet. We paid off our debts and cleared the rent, and got some second-hand clothes for the kids to wear to school. It was bound to start again.

I entered into a partnership, of sorts, with my friend Jim Post. We made a point of getting out of Dundee. Sometimes we went to Edinburgh; usually it was Glasgow. Because of the redevelopment scheme, large parts of the Glasgow city centre were empty: tenements with unoccupied flats; sometimes whole buildings. But this was also where you found most of your pubs and off-licenses. What we did was called 'grafting' and consisted of entering a pub or an off-licence through the adjoining building or from the empty flat above it. All the places were wired for alarms, but only on the outer windows and doors. Sometimes we got cash; usually it was goods: cigarettes and whisky and beer, that we'd take back to Dundee to sell on.

The police were on to us eventually and arrested Jim Post. I discovered this only when they burst through the door one morning. The kids were at school, and Mary was in bed with Shaun. The police came rushing through the front door, pushing me all the way into the bedroom.

'Who are you?' the big cop said.

'I'm John Donachy,' I said. Donachy was Mary's family name. I introduced Mary, 'My sister.'

The big cop was taken aback. 'Where's Reid then?'

I didn't know, I confessed.

The big cop then turned to Mary. 'Where is he, Mary?'

It would have been just like Mary to say, 'Standing in front of you, you idiot.' But she didn't. 'Don't call me by my first name,' she snapped, 'and if you want Henry John Reid then get the hell out of here and go bloody find him.'

The big cop took me into the other room, leaving two other policemen with Mary. He urged me to co-operate, saying that my life could be made very difficult if I didn't. I told him that I'd get a battering if I told the police where Henry John Reid might be found, and that the police had to swear that they wouldn't reveal where they got their information. They agreed, and I confessed that Reid had gone off to get a van. I said something about Fintry, and within moments the police disappeared.

Within fifteen minutes, so too had Mary and I. We asked Connie to look after the kids, and we were on a train to Middlesbrough where I had some friends. From there we went to Scarborough where we got live-in jobs at a hotel. It was only when the tourist season was over that we thought it was safe to return to Dundee.

We had, for the first time in our lives, managed to save some money and used it to buy a terraced house for £250. We wanted to make a new start.

On Mary's twentieth birthday we were going out to celebrate, just the two of us. Then Connie turned up and insisted on coming as well. We went to the Angus Hotel and had a few drinks, but after a while the barmaid refused to serve Connie and called the bouncers to throw her out. Connie was only five feet tall and weighed eight stone. The bouncers weren't necessary. But when I tried to stop them, they tried to throw me out too.

I broke the nose of one with a bottle and gave the other a black eye, but they started punching me in the face. Mary hit the barmaid. We both got charged with assault and breach of the peace, and were fined a hundred pounds each. I think we would have got a jail sentence if it hadn't been for the mess my face was in—the judge commented that I couldn't have been the only one throwing punches.

It was clear that we'd never have a proper life together as long as Connie was anywhere near us. I suggested that we move. I thought Alice might take us in, even if only for a short time.

Alice was still the only one of the family who had any time for me. Her husband, Jim Cowan, was a poacher: a villain, true, but a successful one and not a bad man. Jim and Alice had three children and lived in a nice house—not big, but clean and comfortable and always something on the table.

Mary and I found jobs within a week. Alice was delighted to look after Shaun while we were at work and kept saying that she wished she could have another baby. She understood that I was trying hard to change my life and did everything she could to help.

One night, after we had been staying there for a couple of months, Mary and I decided to go out for a drink. As we left the house, Alice, who was lying on the settee watching the evening news, asked us to bring her some fish and chips on our way home. We had a good night out and were on our way up the street with Alice's fish and chips when we saw that the front door was open. A woman was standing in the doorway, looking out into the street. When we reached the house, she asked me if I was Alice's brother. Something terrible had happened, she said. Just after we had left, Alice had choked on something and died, right in front of her youngest son.

The family arrived the next day. That morning, I went out to the shops and when I came back, Susan was there. She opened the front door—Alice was still laid out there on the couch behind her because we couldn't get anyone to take the body away—and just stared at me. She asked me what I thought I was doing there.

Alice was my sister too, I said.

At the funeral, no one spoke to me. Bert was very still and withdrawn: he worshipped Alice, and now she was gone. Afterwards, Mary and I didn't go back to the house; we left town the next day.

Alice's death took something from me. I started drinking again. I lost interest in holding my life together. I stopped work. I started thieving. I didn't wash or change my clothes. Mary tried to help in her way but the moment she dared to say anything, I flew into a rage. I remember Shaun putting his arms out to me, asking me to pick him up. I ignored him.

I was tired of the whole bloody lot of my life and didn't know which way to turn. I was so desperate I went to see a minister, one who knew Mary's mother. I told him my story and asked if he could help us. But he treated me as though I was a tramp and told me he didn't help beggars. As he told me this, full of contempt and disgust, I sat quietly. When he finished, I remained sitting there. For some time, I didn't say a word. I couldn't. I was angry, very angry, and I wasn't going to be able to control this raw, terrible feeling welling up inside me. I could tell that it was going to be more than I could contain.

You can take your Christian charity, I said, and stick it up your arse. And then I exploded.

He was still conscious when I left him. He was covered in blood and moaning miserably. I wasn't sorry for what I did to him. To this day I'm not sorry. I never will be. He was the greatest hypocrite I ever met.

I had told him my name and where I lived. I knew the police would be coming round to the house to collect me. I sat and waited for them.

I was charged with grievous bodily harm and, to my surprise, was released on bail. I had no intention of waiting for the trial. That night we dropped off Shaun with Mary's mother and left for England. We never stayed in one town for longer than a week, mugging as we went, breaking into houses. We lived well or we roughed it, depending on how much money we had.

I'm surprised Mary went with me and stuck it out for so long. I was well back on the drink and was hitting her more and more often. We ended up in Doncaster on her twenty-first birthday. That night we got blind drunk and Mary started crying: she was missing Shaun and wanted to go home. I was feeling sorry for all I had put her through. I went out to get some money to send her back to Scotland and got caught breaking into a phone box. I was charged and put on remand in Leeds prison, then taken to Doncaster Crown Court and sentenced to eighteen months. I was returned to Dundee, where I appeared in court on the earlier charge and was sentenced to a further three years.

Three months later, my body failed. It rejected all forms of food and liquid. I had surgery, but the operation didn't work. I had another operation. It didn't work. The doctors tried to contact Mary—they believed I was going to die—but she didn't want to know.

Why didn't I die? Every time I got ill, I had another operation and another bit of my intestine was lopped off. What was left?

I had been in the hospital for six months when a doctor asked if he could help me. He said he would get me a job as a hospital porter and write to the parole board asking for me to be released into the hospital's care. He wanted me to undergo some experimental treatment for Chrone's disease.

Doctors are always trying to help me; to them, I'm a novelty, a new specimen. But I didn't want this doctor's help, or anyone else's. That night, still in my pyjamas and slippers, I ran away. I weighed only six stone two and was very weak. After three days, I got to Edinburgh, having walked across the Forth Bridge.

I ended up in Darlington, where I mugged and robbed a guy of his clothes and money. I used the money to go to Stockton-on-Tees. I stayed there for a few days, sleeping in a condemned house. I hadn't eaten for days and was vomiting blood.

By now I knew I did need help badly, and made up my mind that I would go and see a Catholic priest. Despite what had happened the last time, I was sure that if I told a priest the truth, he would have to help me. So I wandered around until I found a church, and when I did I went to the presbytery and rang the bell.

The priest answered the door and showed me into a waiting-room. We sat down, and I told him everything about myself: my real name, how I had run away from the hospital, my illness and my family life.

He listened to me, but once I was finished, he told me that he got five or six people begging at his door every day, all with some fantastic story, just for the price of a drink. He wasn't giving money to people like me, he said, and told me to go to the Social Security office. I said that if he couldn't give me any money, could he spare some food as I hadn't eaten for three days? No, he said, it was the housekeeper's day off and he was too busy. He told me to leave or he would call the police, and opened the door, taking my hand in his and saying, 'God bless you, my son.'

And then something terrible happened—something terrible in me. I have no recollection or image of my doing a thing. When I think back on those moments, even now, I see nothing. Only blankness. But something happened, and it was clearly done by me.

My next recollection is this: the room was a wreck, with chairs and tables overturned; the priest was on the floor, not moving. I was exhausted and shaking like a leaf. What had happened to me? What had I done?

I was arrested later in Harrogate after having collapsed with my illness. By then my face had been broadcast on television and had been pictured in all the papers, and I was recognized immediately. In court, everyone looked at me as though I was a monster. But the thing is this: I saw myself as a monster. Something in me had snapped, something I could neither recollect nor, evidently, control. For the first time in my life, I learned that I was dangerous—to other people and to myself. At my trial, I asked to be helped, to be put away in some kind of special hospital. But the judge ignored my pleas. He thought I was just trying to get out of a jail sentence. I was given seven years.

I was sent to prison in Liverpool, got caught trying to escape and was sent to Hull. I was frightened of losing my temper again and killing someone. I got bullied a lot but I never fought back, even to save myself—me, who had always been a fighter. I knew there was something wrong with me. Five times I asked to see a head shrinker, but they wouldn't let me.

Eventually I was sent to Grendon-under-Wood, a prison hospital in Buckinghamshire. I was kept there for weeks without being seen by anyone. Finally my temper went and I attacked an officer with a knife. I was tried and was going to be sent back to Hull. I told the magistrate that I'd been sent to Grendon-under-Wood to be cured of my tempers, and that it wasn't fair to be thrown out for doing what I'd come there to be cured of. I was given another chance, but it was no use. The officer I'd fought with believed I'd got off too lightly and made my life a misery from then on.

A week later, I slashed my leg wide open. The doctor wanted to stitch it, but I wouldn't let him near it until I had said what I wanted to say, which was that if they weren't going to help me then the next slash would be my throat.

They stitched up the wound. Two days later, they sent me back to Hull: to strong-boxes, padded cells and body belts.

I got parole in 1978, although I didn't want it. I had nowhere to go. The welfare people told me that they had found me a place in a hostel in London; at first I didn't want to go, because I thought it would be a dosshouse, full of drunks and jailbirds. But they told me that I would get my own room with a television and a bathroom.

When I got to London I found that I had got a bedroom and a television room—to share with 150 others. There I was, in my suit, wearing a gold watch and a gold ring, joining a queue just to get into the place. The queue was 500 yards long, and was full of old men with long beards, out of their heads on cheap alcohol. I felt sick at heart. I would rather have been in prison than shamed like this.

I wasn't supposed to leave the hostel—it was a condition of my parole—but I couldn't take it. I left after a couple of days and went down to the south coast to look for a job in a hotel.

But every place I went, I was asked to fill in a form saying where I'd been working before and what my last three jobs had been. I couldn't fill in the forms. After a week, my money had gone, and I was sleeping on the beach. By the following week, I was back to crime, breaking into a hotel in Bexhill first of all, where I stole a lot of jewellery, and then into several other places. When I had got enough money together, I went back to Scotland. I was going to look for my last surviving step-sister, Susan, but when I got to the place where her house used to be I saw that it had been knocked down.

I collapsed getting off a bus. With drinking and sleeping rough, my illness had returned.

I was taken to hospital in Glasgow, and a nurse helped me trace Susan through the electoral register. When I contacted her, she was kinder to me than I had ever hoped for. I think she was trying to make amends. She said she would put me up, and we would forget the past.

Within two days, I had got myself a job. And then I decided to go to the Prison Aid Society to see if I could be helped: I wanted my life sorted out. I told the man from the Society that I had broken my parole and that I was wanted by the police for stealing jewellery from the hotel in Bexhill. I explained that I wanted to work for nine months and would then give myself up. If people could see that I was trying to sort myself out, I thought I might be given another chance.

The man from the Society told me to meet him at six that evening and he would give me some clothes. But it was the police who turned up, not him. I was arrested, flown back to London and taken from there to Lewes Prison to finish my parole. Two days before my release date, I appeared at Brighton Crown Court and was given three years for housebreaking and three years concurrent for housebreaking and killing a dog.

I was sent to an open prison in Maidstone, and after I had served seventeen months I got a week's 'home leave', which meant that I was allowed to leave the prison and visit my family, unescorted. Home leave is a privilege, an exercise in trust, granted to prisoners as part of their preparation for freedom. I went straight to Susan's.

Things would have been all right if it hadn't been for Bert, who was still around and who still hated me. He kept coming round to Susan's and causing trouble, saying that I was a drunk and no brother of his, and telling Susan that she shouldn't have given me room in her house. In the end, Susan said that I had better leave—she knew that as long as Bert was around, her house would be a battlefield. I cried like a little boy. And then I left. I haven't seen Susan since.

I caught a train to Stirling. I didn't give a fuck what happened to me. My home leave was over, but I resolved not to return to Maidstone. I had no family, no wife, no friends. I had a child but no idea where he was, and knew, in any case, that his mother wouldn't let me near him. I had no home. I had nothing.

I lived by theft. I broke into a place, sold the goods, and then drank the proceeds. The next day, I did the same. And the next day, and the next.

One Saturday, I broke into a house in Dundee. I'd climbed in through the basement window. I had only been in there a couple of minutes when an old couple opened the basement door directly behind me. The old woman pointed her finger in my face—she was *that* close—and screeched for the police. I put my hand on her arm, trying to get her to calm down. And then the old man hit me with his cane. I told them both that I didn't want to hurt them, and the old man struck me again. My head was buzzing as I swung round and shoved him. The old woman carried on screeching and was pulling my hair, and I went crazy again, just like I had been dreading since I attacked the priest in Stockton-on-Tees. I hit both of them with anything and everything I could lay my hands on, screaming and shouting at the top of my voice. I have no idea how long it went on, but finally I came to, and they were lying on the floor covered in blood, their eyes staring into nowhere, not moving.

I couldn't stop shaking. I howled with laughter and sobbed at the same time. I was violently sick. I sat there on the floor in a daze for a long time, and eventually realized it was seven in the evening. I must have been there for two hours, just sitting. I got up, took some money and jewellery, and left.

I went down to the station. I was trying to get to Edinburgh, but made a mistake and got on a train to London. Every time I thought about the old couple I saw their eyes staring into nowhere, not moving, and I had to rush to the toilet to be sick.

Once in London, I got on a train to Brighton. I travelled all over the south coast for a few days and sold the jewellery I'd stolen.

One lunch-time, in Ramsgate, I was sitting by myself in a pub and overheard a conversation between a young man and woman at the next table. From the way they were talking, it was obvious that they were crooks. I got chatting with them; they were called Steve and Carol. I told them that I was on the run for drug-dealing and that I needed to get to France. They said they could get me out of the country and arrange for false ID, a cheque-book and a rent-book. I agreed to meet them again that same evening.

Before leaving the country, I felt I needed to see a priest and make a confession. A priest was the only person I could think of who wouldn't hand me over to the police, and even if he couldn't help, he would at least listen.

It took me a while to find a church, and when I did, it took me even longer to get up the nerve to knock at the presbytery door. But I had to confide in someone or I'd go crazy.

The priest turned out to be an old man, well into his eighties. He had white hair and a kind face. He took me into a room with a table and chairs, and sat me down, asking what he could do for me.

Before I started, I made him promise that whatever I said would be in complete confidence and that he would never repeat it to anyone. He promised that he would not, and added that if I didn't trust him then I shouldn't tell him anything.

There was a long silence. The pressure to tell the priest what had happened was boiling up inside me, but I still didn't know how to begin. I asked him for a cup of tea, which the housekeeper brought in along with some buns. She was old too, though not as old as the priest, and she also had a kind way about her. I asked if I could smoke. The priest said, yes, I could, of course. I lit a cigarette. I stared at the priest. He was frail, but warm, with clear and friendly eyes. He was patient and wanted to help.

'Father,' I said, 'I have killed two people in Scotland.'

Things happened very fast. He jumped out of his chair, shouting for the housekeeper. I hadn't been expecting anything like this and found myself unable to move. He was at the door and I knew I had to stop him, but I got to him just as the housekeeper

129

arrived. He was shouting at her that I was a murderer, and I grabbed his arms. The housekeeper was trying to get me off him, and I was trying to stop him getting to the front door, and at the same time begging him not to tell anyone. Then I snapped. It was as though a switch had been flipped. I wasn't thinking. I couldn't think. I wasn't conscious of anything except strength and anger. I don't know what I hit them with, or how many times I hit them, but I do remember coming to my senses and hearing my own voice shouting, 'You fucking bastard! Where's your God now? Tell me! Where is He?' And through the fog I could see the priest and the housekeeper lying on the floor, covered in blood.

I was overwhelmed by exhaustion, deeper than I had ever known. I was shaking uncontrollably, saying over and over again, 'What have I done? What have I done?' I left the room and wandered around the house, picking up money and jewellery, not really aware of where I was or what I was doing.

I was about to leave through a side door when I noticed that my white suit was covered in blood. There was a raincoat hanging on the back of the door, and I kept looking at it but I couldn't think straight. I finally managed to take it off the peg, but it was another five minutes before I could actually put it on. My body wouldn't do what I wanted it to do.

As I walked down the road, my mind was racing, and I was thinking, over and over again, 'I have killed four people. I must be out of my mind. I'm crazy. I can't have done this. God, what's happening to me? Why am I doing these things? Why?' I noticed people were staring at me and I tried to get a grip on myself. I went into a clothes shop; I wanted to buy a shirt and some jeans, but couldn't find my voice and ended up pointing to what I wanted. I went to a gent's toilet to get changed, but couldn't stop shaking. I sat in a cubicle for an hour.

That evening I met Steve and Carol at the pub to pick up my papers. I was first to arrive, and bought a double rum and drank it straight off, then bought another and a pint of bitter.

They appeared and gave me a rent-book and a cheque-book with a false name, and said they could get me over to France on a day-trip.

We had been in the pub for a while when Steve told us that he'd seen two CID in the public bar. 'There must be something on,' he said. 'One of them's a big noise, and you don't see him around here unless it's serious.'

My nerves were tearing at me. I gave Steve some of the jewellery I had stolen, and we decided to go on to another pub to sell it. As we left, two CID were coming in, and they moved out of the way to let us pass.

In the next pub, I drank rum after rum. Both Steve and Carol kept asking me if I was all right, and I told them that I was, but my body was screaming with fear. Steve went off to sell the jewellery, but came back after a couple of minutes. 'I can't sell these tonight,' he said. 'The whole town is crawling with cops. There's four at the bar I can see, and they're spaced out along it as though they're here on their own.' I knew I wouldn't be able to leave the country: all the ports would be watched.

Steve and Carol put me up that night, but I couldn't sleep. Every time I tried, I saw the same blank, staring eyes.

I smoked two packs of cigarettes waiting for morning. I was scared—not of being caught and going to prison for the rest of my life, but of what I might do to someone else. To this day, I don't know what made me kill those people. I only remember coming round, screaming and shouting, woken up by the sound of my own voice, and looking down and seeing the blood and the bodies. Doctors and psychiatrists tell me there is no such thing as a blind rage, but I know they're wrong. If a person's mind is completely blank, there is no limit to his strength, and he has no capacity for understanding hurt—either to himself or to others. The rage has no memory or sight. And doctors don't know how to talk about it.

I wanted to die. I wanted to dig a deep hole in the ground and bury myself.

Next day, I took a bus to Margate, another from Margate to Canterbury and then a train to London, where I spent the night. I then went to Brighton, to Hastings and Battle, back to London, then to Hornchurch and Southend, where I ran out of money.

I was walking around the town, trying to think what to do,

when I came to a Salvation Army hall where there were lots of people gathered, singing hymns. I went creeping around to the back and got into the offices. In one I found a briefcase and a big bunch of keys. One opened the safe, and I stole about £400. I caught a train to London that same night.

I went to King's Cross to get a train to Leeds. After I'd bought my ticket, I went to the bar, where one barman looked at me and said something to another barman. He was pointing at me, and I heard him say, 'That's him!'

I glared at him and said, 'You talking about me?'

He was in a terrible panic. He ran down the bar and picked up the phone. I got off my mark pretty quickly. I rushed down to the tube station and got on a train. After three stops, I got off and took a taxi to Bow. I sat in a pub for a while and then took a taxi to Liverpool Street station, then another taxi to Victoria, where I caught the last train to Brighton.

It was a bank holiday weekend, and Brighton was full of skinheads, so I shaved off my hair and bought some skinhead gear to fit in with the crowd. I read all the newspapers and listened to the news on the radio. After the bank holiday, my disguise was no use, so I dressed up like an American tourist in a flannel shirt, sunglasses and cap, with a camera round my neck.

I went to Eastbourne and booked into a bed and breakfast. I thought the woman who ran it looked wary of me, and then I overheard her saying, 'I'm sure that man is the one the police are looking for.' I didn't wait to hear more; I was out of the window and off. I didn't know where to go; if that woman had phoned the police, then they would be searching the bus and railway stations, so I booked myself on a one-day trip to Windsor.

On the tour bus, the woman sitting in front of me had a newspaper in her lap. On the front page was a large photograph of me, and the headline read CATCH THIS MAN. She was looking at the paper and then at my reflection in the bus window.

Once in Windsor, I immediately rushed into a public library to hide. I knew no one would think of looking for me there. I got a book and sat by the window, pretending to read. But really I was watching the activity outside: police cars were flying about everywhere. I sat there until the library closed.

I walked out but couldn't work out what was going on: the police cars had disappeared. There were no police at the railway station either. Later, I learned that there had been a positive sighting of me boarding a truck on the road to London, and so the police were sure I had skipped town.

I got a train to Slough and another from Slough to Reading. I then jumped on a train to York. I had no ticket and hid myself between the seats in an empty carriage. Two girls came and sat in the seats near me, and I listened to them chatting. At any other time, it would have been funny, because I got action replays of all their love affairs.

I got off the train in York, dodged the ticket collector and spent the night in a dosshouse. I had only five pounds left. The next day, I decided I'd ask people if their cars needed washing. That way, I wouldn't have to steal any more money.

The first house I went to was very posh. The woman who answered the door was nervous when I asked her if I could wash her car. She told me that her husband was out and that he always washed his own car anyway. It was obvious that she had recognized me: she couldn't get the door closed quickly enough, and as I walked down the drive, I looked back and saw her peering round the curtains.

That woman was stupid. I have read what she said in the newspapers, boasting about how she helped to catch me, but I could easily have killed her. She was stupid to tell me that she was alone. But I'm not a cold-blooded killer. I don't get a thrill out of killing, and I've never killed anyone while I was in my right mind. She should be grateful.

I was about a mile from the house when I saw a police van coming straight towards me. As it got nearer, I saw a copper reach for the door handle, and I thought to myself, 'This is it.' I couldn't move. I was shaking all over. Before I could do anything, the van had reached me and a sergeant got out.

He walked towards me, saying, 'Are you Henry John Reid?'

'Yes,' I said.

He seemed to relax then. He took hold of my cuff, said, 'OK, in the back,' and led me to the van. In those few moments, my mind was racing. Once we were round the back of the van, the copper was out of sight of the driver, with one hand on my cuff and the other on the door handle. That was when I made my move. I elbowed him in the stomach, pushed him to the ground and ran for it, faster than I've ever run in my life, right down the middle of the road.

Cars, buses and lorries were whizzing past me. I looked over my shoulder: the sergeant was running after me, fifty yards away and gaining. A lorry was coming at me, and as it went past I dived at the back of it. I clung on as it dragged me along the road, then got a better grip and pulled myself up. I was gasping for air.

I heard a whistle. This fucking sergeant was running after the lorry, blowing his bastard whistle at the same time. The lorry driver saw me in his mirror and slowed down. I tried to pull myself on more securely, but one of my legs cramped and I fell off.

I hit the ground and rolled over a few times. The sergeant was close now, not forty yards away. I jumped up and ran round a corner and across a bridge, but was only halfway across when a police car came straight at me. I crossed the road, straight in front of a bus, which had to brake hard and swerve to avoid me. I was gasping for breath and wanted to give up, but the fear in me wouldn't allow it.

Police were coming at me from both ends of the bridge. I shouted, 'I'm not going to give in!' and jumped from the bridge on to the railway line below. I didn't hurt myself at all, not even a scratch.

I ran along the railway line. My lungs were killing me and my breath was coming in great sobs. I couldn't go on much longer. I crawled up the embankment and on to a footbridge but just as I got to the other end, a police car drew up, blocking my way. I about-turned and ran back to the other end. I got on to the street and as I ran down it four police cars blocked my way, two behind and two in front. I swerved off the road and ran between buildings while a crowd of police chased me. I was on my last legs as I raced through a series of back lots and over some fences.

I started to climb over a garden wall but I was too exhausted to make it and collapsed over it on to the other side. The cops flooded over behind me. One gave me a kick in the ribs but I was too tired to feel the pain.

The depression I felt in prison, awaiting trial, was terrible. I honestly wished I was dead. Every time I fell asleep, a screw would wake me up and ask if I was sleeping. When I got my food, there would be gobbets of spit in it, and they would piss in my tea or put furniture polish in it.

And this is the most truthful thing I have ever said in my life: the only thing that has kept me going is the knowledge that I was mentally ill at the time of my offences. God alone knows the pressure I was under; He knows that I did not intend to hurt those people, let alone kill them. He knows the truth.

I was tried in Maidstone Crown Court in December 1981. Three doctors recommended that I be detained in hospital on the grounds of diminished responsibility. I went from the court to Wandsworth for a short while, and then I was sent to a special hospital, to be detained at Her Majesty's Pleasure.

Photo overleaf: Steele-Perkins/Magnum

HUGH BARNES
GLASGOW VICTIM

Five years ago I was the victim of a murder attempt. I ended up mangled and messed, but still alive. Unwittingly I made a sort of Houdiniesque escape from the would-be murderers just as they were about to throw my body into a river. For a long time the only thing I remembered about the incident was its mysterious, urgent frenzy, but in the last year or so I have begun to recapture a half-knowledge of my victimhood, whose deceitful images I have to rearrange in my memory like postcards.

I had left England a couple of years before and was living in Glasgow, trying to make a career as a newspaper reporter and, in between, hoping to write a book. The trouble was I had nothing to write about. I had only a vague knowledge of life, and in order to write, it seemed to me, a person had to know so many things.

I went to Glasgow to live out a fantasy. Its fluid, inconstant, nerve-wrung landscape had a claim upon my imagination. I liked being in a stone-built city of dark tenements and ornate public buildings. I liked the patter, the idiom, the tough, subtly nuanced language of the conversations I overheard in the street or in the pub.

I had a feeling of privilege, a sense of drama. I was interested—at times frivolously—in the working-class culture of Glasgow: a mixture of dog-eared romanticism with heroics and rough stuff, with false moves and failures and wasted lives. But my knowledge of Glasgow was incomplete. I had no understanding of the people who were boxed in, subtly victimized by a city that had nothing to offer its poor. The outlying districts had ceased to have any economic point, and those who lived there seemed to have fallen off the edge of the world: into a wilderness of crime and gangland violence and fearlessness. I was attracted to an old Glasgow of myth and legend, and was unable to grasp the one made up of the unemployed and the ill-employed, the people on the rim, the drifters, the layabouts, the punters.

In many ways I was living in a dream, and might as well have been sleepwalking, one night, on the way back from the *Herald* office, where I worked, to Maryhill, an unpromising district where I had two rooms on the top floor of a dim, wedge-shaped house. It was late, after midnight, and as I walked up Sauchiehall Street to Charing Cross and then down Woodlands Road, I saw few people.

As I turned into Belmont Street, I was struck by the thought that everything looked a little too sharply in focus. My house stood at the top of a hill, by itself, on the other side of a narrow bridge whose high, concrete, black walls hid the long drop to the rocks below. The road was empty and scattered with leaves. The number of them attracted my attention: I looked up at the overhanging trees, when, unexpectedly, two men emerged from the shadows into the lamplight fifty yards up ahead. They were brandishing the lids of rubbish bins, like cymbals, and my first impression was that they were like cartoon thugs. I stepped back to move out of their way, but my path was blocked by the taller of the two, a man with a long neck and a lean face, wearing black jeans and a striped jersey. He had stopped the percussion but I could tell that his body yearned to get back to work. There were awkward, slight, unexpected movements, and, as he paused to look about him, he flexed his fist, almost imperceptibly.

His companion was stocky and venomous in appearance, with a shiny face and wild eyes, those signals of aggression. My presence suddenly felt wrong. I was an intrusion. In the Merchant City, my office clothes—a suit, Burberry-trenched, polished shoes—were scarcely noticeable, but here they seemed provocative, foreign, wrong. The man with the long neck stopped abruptly and lowered his arms, and then, for no reason, began to punch me and to kick me violently.

The attack, so vivid at the time, became in my memory, and for a period of years, somewhat blurred: raw feeling and literalness. And there are still gaps in my recollections. I cannot visualize being dragged up the road, but I deduced it from a visit to Belmont Street a few days later where I observed the blood stains still visible on the kerb. In fact, the incident as a whole is jumbled, without sequence. The sequence I have given it here comes to me only because I am forcing myself to remember. Was it before my assailants seized hold of my arms and legs, or after they had begun to lift me over the parapet of the bridge, that I realized my crumpled body was about to be disposed of, in a rather prosaic and down-to-earth manner, like a sack of rubbish? I am still not sure.

I know that I began to beat my hands on the road. 'Let me go!' I said. The men laughed and kicked me sharply in the ribs.

139

The man with the long neck locked his arm about my throat, and twisted me in front of him. I recall that the corners of his mouth were pulled back by the effort.

I shouted with real pain, 'Stop!'

He tightened his grip and, as he hoisted me on to the parapet, looked at me with sullen downcast eyes, as though performing an unpleasant duty. I don't remember what happened next; I was told later that a police car, on a routine patrol, happened to disturb the aspiring murderers just in time.

After a while I was taken to a hospital, where I was cleaned up and stitched up and X-rayed and so on. Yet the blurring of a distinction between the real and my imaginary Glasgow gave me a feeling of helplessness, and I think I went to pieces after that. In bed the next day, propped up with three pillows but still sagging, I picked up a copy of the newspaper whose big black headlines—TWO FACE MURDER BID CHARGE—just made me depressed.

It seems to me that newspaper stories about murder always have a bias; in order to make sense of the crime they have to exclude some facts and highlight others; they develop a hero and a villain. Or, at any rate, there is some kind of struggle towards a resolution, a lesson or anomaly. They seem to say that horrors are a distraction in the order of things—as if there is a kind of metaphysical puritanism at work somewhere, a mechanical accountability that links transgression with violence.

In my case I could find neither lesson nor anomaly in the random attack. It was just random. I am in fact reluctant to investigate further for the fear of throwing the wrong things out and keeping the wrong things in.

I have a recollection of coming round in the back of a police van, drenched in blood, lying at the feet of one of my attackers. He was a disordered man. His eyes were red and blurred, one lid was half-stuck down. He sat handcuffed to a rail, but was otherwise docile and expressionless, in a kind of exaltation of uncomplaining discomfort. A bizarre encounter yet not unfriendly, and somehow appropriate: it contained no depth of feeling, no strong emotion of any kind. In that respect it was like the attack itself—almost perfunctory.

GRANTA

ANDREW SAVULICH
CRIME IN THE CITY

GRADE SCHOOl TEACHER PUSHES WOMAN iN FRONT OF TRAIN AFTER HAVING A DISPUTE WITH THE BOARD OF EDUCATION.

MAN DESCRIBING HOW HE STABBED AND KILLED THE GANG LEADER AFTER
GOING OUT TO BUY SHAMPOO FOR HIS GRANDMOTHER.

CRYing BABY RUSHED TO HOSPITOL — THE FATHER WAS ARRESTED AFTER HE ADMITTED TO
STRiking THE CRYing CHILD.

Police give neighbors cat & hamster found inside apt. containing double homicide.

BICYCLE MESSENGER AFTER BEING ATTACKED BY ANGRY MOTORISTS.

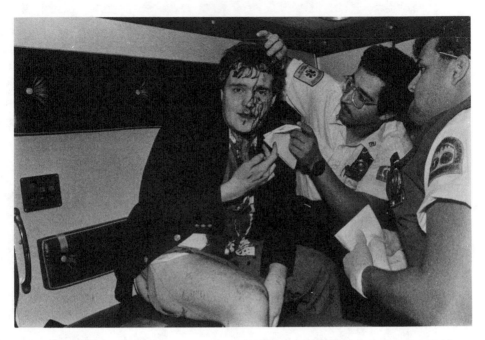

MAN complaining THAT HE WAS ATTACKED AFTER HE gave His money TO RObbers.

MAN SHOT in THE REAR END WHILE sleeping ON PARK BENCH.

TIM WILLOCKS
THE PENITENTIARY

A million man-years of confinement had burnished the surface of the granite flags to a greasy smoothness ingrained deeply with filth and despair. Here was the impacted stink of human waste and pain, concentrated, hyper-distilled and stored for decades beneath the high glass roof which rose in a great vault above the triple-stacked tiers of the teeming cell block. This was where men were sent to kneel and where those who didn't want to learned the way. Somewhere on the planet there were worse places in which to spend time. But this was the best that civilization could do.

Green River State Penitentiary had been designed by an English architect named Cornelius Clunes in an age when it had still been possible to combine philosophy, art and engineering in a single fabulous endeavour. Commissioned in 1876 by the governor of Texas, Clunes had set out to create a prison in which every brick was imbued with the notion of a power both visible and unverifiable. No dark dungeon was this. No squat, brutal box. Green River was a hymn to the disciplinary properties of light.

From a cylindrical core capped by a great glass dome, four cell blocks and two work blocks radiated away at sixty-degree intervals like spokes from the hub of a giant wheel. Beneath the dome was a central watchtower from which a spectator could enjoy a clear view down the central walkway of all four cell blocks. The block roofs were mounted on smooth granite walls and overhung the top tier of cells by twenty feet. The kingposts, tie-beams and rafters of the roof were constructed of wrought iron and covered with extravagant sheets of thick green glass. Light streamed through the glass: a permanent surveillance that induced in the cowering inmate a sense of permanent visibility, and ensured the automatic functioning of power. Looking outside from the window of his cell, the convict could see the encircling walls with their resident riflemen; from the bars of his door he saw the central observation tower with its cameras and guards. At night his cell was illuminated by a dim green bulb, and the walls and walkways by spotlights. A man entering Green River said goodbye to darkness for the duration of his stay. Darkness permitted at least the illusion of privacy and invisibility, places

Photo: Danny Lyon/Magnum

151

where a man might try to reconstruct some sense of his own individual existence. Light was discipline, darkness was freedom. Because the inmate was constantly visible he could never be sure whether he was being spied upon or not and thus became his own warder, perpetually watching himself on his jailer's behalf. Green River was an architecture of power built upon the paranoid fantasies of the guilty.

An hour before the 0700 lock and count, Dr Ray Klein opened his eyes and thought about the seagulls wheeling high above the outside walls. If Klein himself had been a gull he would've damn sure given this squalid grey shithole a wide berth. There had to be better garbage elsewhere.

He blinked and reminded himself that he was an asshole.

Freewheeling birds were a stupid image for a convict to hold in his mind, for they brought not a shred of comfort. Yet Klein thought about them just the same. And on this day, he had reason for letting the birds fly about the imaginary dawn landscape of his mind: after three years' hard time, there was a chance—a   *chance—* that the bastards who ran this place were finally going to let him go free. Klein exterminated the birds inside his head and swung his legs over the side of the bunk.

As he stood up, the stone flags were cool and dense against the soles of his feet. He squeezed the flags with his toes, then bent forward in the dim green aura of the night light and placed both palms flat on the floor, squeezing the stale blood out of his hamstrings and spine. He didn't really want to stand up in the semi-darkness and stretch his body. He wanted another hour of oblivion. Yet he spent a further ten minutes in a variety of painful contortions. He had long ago taken into his heart the words of William James:

> Be systematically ascetic or heroic in little unnecessary points, do every day something for no other reason than that you would rather not do it, so that when the hour of dire need draws nigh, it may find you not unnerved and untrained to stand the test.

So Ray Klein finished his stretching and knelt down, sitting back on his heels with his palms resting on his thighs. This part still made him feel kind of cool. He closed his eyes and inhaled sharply through his nostrils.

This was as quiet as it ever got in cellblock D, and it was Klein's Jamesian habit, every day, to get up earlier than he needed to and pretend that the hour was his own. He began with the *mokso*—the focused breathing to clear his mind—then went on to practise karate until the bell roused the rest of the block to the sullen and paranoid level of consciousness that, in Green River, passed for human existence.

This daily ritual helped to drain off the anger that the prison pumped into his blood. It neutralized the poison and kept him strong, kept him calm, kept him bound apart from all the rest; kept cold and hard the steelwork and ice he had constructed around his soul.

Since his plunge from grace, this architecture had proved a necessary blessing. In the River, a soul was a dangerous handicap, a personal torture chamber only to be visited by masochists and fools. The discipline and self-denial had come to him more easily than it had to most inmates, for his profession had prepared him for it. As an intern and as a resident and as a chief resident, he had hardened his heart against himself: against the endless hours on duty, against the intolerable and yet endurable lack of sleep; against alternating fourteen and twenty-four hour days, year upon year; against the pressure and the fear of making a mistake and killing or disabling a patient; against the horror of mutilated bodies and the naked grief of the bereaved; against the endless stream of examinations; against failure; against the unique dread of telling a man he was going to die or a mother that her child was already dead; against the pain he inflicted on himself and the pain he inflicted on others. By the time his life collapsed around him and he was sent up to the River, he had only needed to add a little ice to the steel and then he'd been ready.

On the street Klein had been an orthopaedic surgeon.

Now he was a convicted rapist serving his time.

Today he might be set free.

153

Klein turned in the narrow space and inflicted an elbow-strike-to-the-face/throat-lock/head-butt combination on an imaginary enemy standing just inside the steel bars of his door. The imaginary enemy's face collapsed and his body went limp as Klein strangled him. You're the *shotokan* warrior, he told himself, you hope for nothing, you need no one, you are free.

At first, Klein had felt kind of an idiot posturing this way and that in his cell. The inmates of neighbouring cells, in trying to explain the soft grunting noises he made, had accused him of jerking off, of threading a blunt instrument up his own anus, of unlubricated self-catheterization and other lone perversions both dangerous and obscure. At the time, telling them he was practising karate had seemed even more shameful than jerking off—and in addition much more likely to get him his face cut up. But before the mocking voices of his neighbours had become intolerable, Myron Pinkley had stolen Klein's dessert—lime-flavoured Jello—in the mess hall.

Ultimately, the brain damage Pinkley sustained proved irreversible. And Klein's neighbours had stopped asking what went on in his cell at each day's dawning, because they all understood thereafter that it wasn't any business of theirs.

The hammering of the bell and the bellowing of sour-faced guards marked the end of Klein's routine. Soaked in sweat, he wiped his face on a dirty shirt and stood at the front of his cell. There were six lock and counts every day and the first began when the lights came up and the cell block lumbered awake with a cacophony of coughs and hawked phlegm, of muttered obscenities and loud complaints about the stench of farting cell mates. Then came the mounting redneck blare of radios and cassette decks, and the shouts of the guards, ritually made and ritually ignored, to turn the goddamn music down. Finally came the count itself, the sullen litany echoing back and forth across the tiers as each man, six times a day, proclaimed his identity as a state-given number.

A screw appeared beyond the bars of Ray Klein's door.

'Eighty-eight-four-one-nine, Klein,' said Klein.

The screw nodded, checked his list, moved on.

Klein's feet slapped the sweat-spattered stone as he walked

to the back of his cell. He pulled back the hanging blanket that covered the toilet and took a piss. The cell had been built for one man, and since the private medical practice Klein had established in the prison had made him wealthy enough to afford it, he had lived there alone. Most of the single cells held two men and the doubles four. Everything had to be paid for, and living space was expensive.

Klein washed himself down at the sink and dried himself on a large bath towel, another luxury item. By the time he'd finished he was again drenched in sweat, such was the humidity in the cell block and the heat of his engorged muscles. He delayed dragging on his denims until his sweat had evaporated some into the stagnant air. He stood naked before his shaving mirror, the drone of his electric razor blending with that of hundreds of others. Blades were forbidden. On the lower edge of the mirror was a strip of grubby white adhesive tape. Written on the tape in black ink, where he could see them every morning and remind himself, were the words: NOT MY FUCKING BUSINESS.

This aphorism was the top and bottom of the moral, political and philosophical system necessary to survival in Green River State Penitentiary. Its importance had been impressed on Klein early on by Frogman Coley, the trustee superintendent of the prison infirmary. Klein had asked Coley how it was that one of the patients recovering on the ward had come to have both his testicles severed and inserted into his own rectum. And Coley had gripped Klein's shirtfront and told him:

'You don' ever wanna know, whitefish. You don' ever wanna find out 'bout nothin' goes down in here. You don' stick your pecker in. Anywhere. Look, say one day you passin' the shower room, you hear a guy bein' cut, or he gettin' his ass raped. Maybe he's your friend. Your best friend. Maybe you like to be in there yo'self, gettin' some. Or maybe like this po' sucker here they takin' his balls off with a blunt razor and you can hear him screamin' through the washrag they stuck down his throat. Walk on by, brother, 'cause there always a reason for it you don' know about. An' even if they ain't no reason at all, it's not your fuckin' bidness.'

And on a couple of occasions—rare but indelible—Klein had

155

witnessed atrocities and heard the screams of pain. And he had indeed walked on by.

He pulled on his regulation denims: long-sleeved shirt with two breast pockets, pants, a canvas belt. As he sat on his bunk and tied the laces of his training shoes a sudden rumble arose from all around him and climaxed in a teeth-jarring crash that echoed back down from the vaulted glass roof. The first count was complete, the machine was satisfied for another hour, and the 180 steel doors of D block thundered open in electronic unison. After breakfast, Klein and the other inmates would trail back to their cells, and the screws would lock them in again for the second count. Then they would be released again for morning work detail.

Klein stepped out on to the walkway, walked along the tier and clattered down the spiral stair. As he reached ground tier, Nev Agry passed him, walking towards the main gate. Agry was four inches shorter than Klein and about ten pounds heavier. His bulk was invested with the charisma of the tried and tested psychopath, and his potency enshrouded him like a forcefield. He was the barn boss of D block and the strongest of the white lifer crew chiefs. Klein had treated Agry a number of times for minor ailments and a series of recurrent chest infections resulting from three packs of Luckies a day. Klein was also good friends with Agry's wife, Claudine, but she was back on B block where she'd undergone another involuntary change of gender and, as plain Claude, was sweating it out under a lockdown. Agry nodded to Klein as he passed and headed off for the mess hall. A nod from Agry was considered a great privilege, but the only privilege Klein wanted now was parole. At ten-thirty this morning, he would find out from Warden Hobbes whether it was his or not.

Under normal circumstances Henry Abbott had a particular fondness for oatmeal. But the oatmeal sitting in front of him on the mess hall table was not good. Abbott knew. He pushed bowl away untouched. This oatmeal was full of ground glass.

From his shirt pocket, Abbott took a notebook and a black Shaeffer fountain pen with a gold nib. He opened the notebook to a fresh page and wrote today's number in green ink: '3083', then beneath it: 'Oatmeal not good—full of ground glass.'

The powdered eggs, on the other hand, Abbott found acceptable. He put his pen and book away, laced the eggs with ketchup and shovelled the mixture into his mouth with a plastic spoon. Things didn't taste so good off plastic. In the canteen, everything was plastic, and Abbott hated it. Now they had put plastic in his face too—packed it tight under his cheekbones to make it harder to smile, and down inside the canals of his teeth to make it harder to chew, and in and around the angles of his jaws and under the root of his tongue to make it harder to speak. They'd injected the plasticating chemicals into his left buttock yesterday morning. Now, twenty-four hours later, the chemicals had been processed by the liver while he slept and had worked their way into his face—as they were designed to do—and plastified so that he couldn't smile so good or talk so good and had to work hard at chewing and swallowing the rubbery breakfast eggs. Most of all, the chemicals placed a shroud of freezing fog around The Word, so that its voice became muffled and distant. Yet, despite the icy shroud, The Word remained always: beyond him, about him, above him. At The Word's suggestion, he had already documented the plastication in his book for the benefit of future generations, yet he rarely felt that his notes did The Word justice. Despite his continued failure as a scribe, Abbott tried. After all, they would have silenced The Word for ever if they could. And Abbott suspected it was this very motive that had compelled them to put ground glass in his oatmeal.

The Word knew and only The Word. And they knew it. And they would go to any lengths to prevent The Word's knowledge from getting out. If the oatmeal failed to make Abbott's inner organs bleed—and fail it would because he had been warned not to eat it—then the plastic in his face, distorting his speech, would ensure that no one would believe him. Abbott couldn't quell a certain admiration: they certainly knew their business. And yet they would fail, for The Word would be heard, at least by one. By him if by no one else. By Henry Abbott.

The canteen was busy, as Abbott had observed it always was at certain times of the day. Breakfast was one such time. The inmates queued up at a row of metal tubs. The tubs were suspended in a pool of hot water secretly concealed behind a polished steel partition. Behind the tubs, the cooks ladled lukewarm food into the plastic trays held out by the inmates. The cook who had laced Abbott's oatmeal with glass had been very quick: a wink to his partner, a smile at Abbott—he hadn't smiled at anyone else—and while the smile distracted him, the powdered glass: released from a concealed pouch up the cook's sleeve. Before Abbott had been quick enough to see the glass, it had dispersed, invisible and deadly, into his breakfast oatmeal.

Close, but no cigar.

Abbott looked up from his eggs and saw Doctor Ray Klein walking towards him between the rows of noisy, crowded tables. Abbott, as usual, had a table to himself. This wasn't something that he chose or even wanted; it was just the way of things. The Doctor carried over his tray and sat down facing him. The Doctor was just under six feet tall, and yet the top of his head was barely level with Abbott's collar-bone. The Doctor looked up. His face was lean, and behind the bones Abbott felt the flames of a pale, pentecostal fire that burned without warming and consumed without replenishing The Doctor's spirit.

The Doctor said, 'Morning, Henry.'

Abbott wiped his mouth on the back of his sleeve. 'Good morning, Doctor Klein.'

Abbott's voice sounded strange even to his own ears. No wonder. Plastication of the vocal chords. He held out his hand and The Doctor shook it. The Doctor's hand felt small, and Abbott was careful to be gentle. No one else ever shook Abbott's hand. He did not know why. And no one else called The Doctor 'Doctor Klein'. It was possible that that accounted for the handshake, but Abbott wasn't sure. It remained mysterious, and yet Abbott knew that it was significant.

'You're not eating your oatmeal,' said The Doctor.

The Doctor saw things. He observed more than most—but not everything. Abbott saw some things The Doctor did not. Since vice versa was also the case that was to be expected. It was something they shared: and so even when The Doctor missed the incredibly obvious, Abbott was there to point it out, and The

Doctor accepted Abbott's judgement as, of course, Abbott accepted his. It was mutual, then. And good.

'You're right,' said Abbott. 'It's full of powdered glass.'

The Doctor flashed him a look grave with concern. Abbott nodded. The Doctor pushed his own bowl towards him. 'This one's OK,' he said. 'Take it.'

Abbott hesitated. 'You'll be hungry. I can't.'

'You're a big man,' said The Doctor. 'You work hard. You need it more than I do.'

Abbott nodded. As usual, The Doctor's logic was irrefutable. Abbott took the bowl of congealed cereal and started to eat. As he ate he scanned the room with his eyes, without moving his head. He considered mentioning the plastic in his face, but The Doctor would only worry—that was the kind of man he was—and there were more important things to discuss. Between bites he held his hand in front of his lips and spoke from the side of his mouth.

'Don't look at me,' said Abbott. 'I have something to tell you.'

The Doctor concentrated on his eggs. 'Go ahead.'

'I've detected a vibe. An irruption.' Abbott took a swallow of his oatmeal.

'An irruption,' said The Doctor.

Abbott nodded. 'Someone is going to die.'

The Doctor nodded back. 'You?' he said.

'They tried, but I was too quick for them,' replied Abbott. 'Yesterday they added a plasticating compound to my injection to try to stop me talking. Today, powdered glass.' He paused while two inmates walked by the table. Abbott risked a look into The Doctor's eyes. 'It's incredibly obvious, isn't it?'

The Doctor nodded. 'Then who's the target?'

'I don't know yet, but I recommend you stay away from Nev Agry and his people.'

'Sounds like good advice,' said The Doctor.

Abbott wondered if The Doctor truly understood the risks involved. How could he without The Word? Abbott resolved to be vigilant on his behalf. The oatmeal was finished. Abbott sipped his coffee. It was cold.

'I advise,' he said, 'that you keep to your cell. To be absolutely safe, avoid all contact.' He lowered his voice. 'Especially with the coloureds.'

'I have to go to the infirmary,' said The Doctor.

Of course. Abbott understood. They needed him there.

'And I have an appointment with Warden Hobbes.'

'Be careful,' said Abbott. 'Warden Hobbes is a dangerous man.'

The Doctor stood up and put his hand on Abbott's shoulder. He squeezed firmly. For a moment Abbott felt the plastic in his face soften.

'You too,' said The Doctor.

Abbott looked up at him through the sense of softness now permeating his throat and liver. The Doctor's eyes were a pale blue, with a core of fierceness at their centre wherein burned the wasting fire.

The Doctor said, 'If you have anything else to tell me, any worries, I want you to come find me and tell me. OK, Henry?'

Abbott rolled his jaw. The plastic was hardly noticeable now. 'I understand.'

By the time second lock and count was over, a sharpening edge of nervous tension had scraped away the insides of Klein's viscera. Up there in his castle-keep above the main gates, Hobbes had the result of Klein's parole board review sitting on his desk. Klein checked his watch again: in ninety-four minutes he would get the verdict.

. He pushed the issue to the back of his mind, but it was hard to keep it there. He'd pushed a lot of things to the back of his mind during his imprisonment. As his meeting with Hobbes loomed before him, they had started to elbow their way back into his consciousness.

Deputy Prosecuting Attorney Henrietta Noades, for one, the prim, bespectacled bitch whose eyes had gleamed with unmistakable pleasure as the judge had sent him down for five to ten. Credited with bringing in the women voters in time for her boss's re-election she'd been promoted on the back of Klein's conviction. For another, there was the smoking rubble of his

Don't miss out on major issues

'With each new issue, *Granta* enhances its reputation for presenting in unequalled range and depth the best contemporary writers in journalism and fiction.' —*Sunday Times*

career. He'd never been any kind of academic hotshot. Working in the public hospital in Galveston where he could concentrate his energies on honing his skills and doing his job was all he'd wanted. That and his house with its view of the Gulf and his sailboat. All that was gone now, and Klein was long past the futility of mourning its passing. Or so, at least, he told himself.

The fact was that deep inside the ice around his heart was an unlanced abscess of pain: the thought that he would never be allowed to return to his work. Klein was a rapist. The law said so and the law had no taste for the ambiguities of human life. Klein was not guilty of the offence for which he had been sentenced. He was guilty of greater, more commonplace crimes—of selfishness and cruelty and stupidity—but not of that one. He had hurt a woman he'd once loved more than life, a woman whose name he no longer allowed into his consciousness. He'd hurt her more deeply than he could have imagined—that is, as deeply as he himself had been hurt, if he'd let himself feel it—and she had punished him savagely. And then she'd punished him again, more savagely still. But a man took whatever fate threw at him and he dealt with it. The way he did so was the only true measure of himself that he had.

Klein reflected that 'rapist' wasn't a word that had much of a ring to it. Armed robber, drug dealer, even murderer, were somewhat more respectable. In the River, the word that had been scrawled across his life meant little. Out in the world—well, he would find out when he found out.

He left his cell and made his way down the spiral stair of D block for the second time that morning. As he walked, he diverted his mind from his own maudlin thoughts by recalling Henry Abbott's warning at breakfast. He wondered what undercurrents the big man had picked up on.

The River contained a population of unusually paranoid men who were trapped against their will in a world where paranoia was the basic currency of existence for inmates and jailers alike. Here even the calmest and most trusting of souls was haunted day and night by suspicion and fear. This was the only rational reaction to the prevailing conditions. Beyond these rational paranoids, of whom Klein was one, was another group:

the clinically insane. Henry Abbott was a stand-out member of the latter, and by and large he was avoided and ignored by sane and insane alike. Almost everyone was content to write him off as a retard. But Klein knew that while the schizophrenic mind invested innocent phenomena with grossly delusional meaning, such a mind could also be abnormally sensitive to the actual, if unspoken, emotions of the people around it. With his overdeveloped, lopsided awareness, Abbott sometimes sensed real currents that Klein was unaware of.

Nine years before, on a balmy New Year's evening in the hill country west of Langtry, Henry Abbott had taken a heavy ball-peen hammer and with a single blow each killed all five members of his family—wife, three daughters and mother—as they slept in their beds. He'd then set fire to the house. The state troopers had found him standing in the yard watching it burn while singing a hymn that none of the troopers recognized. Up until that time Abbott had been a devoted husband, father and son, noted only for being—very probably—the most gargantuan teacher of high-school English ever seen in a state that prided itself on the size of its menfolk. The only explanation Abbott ever offered for his crime was that, 'The fires of Orc, that once did blaze with the smoke of a burning city, have been extinguished with the blood of the daughters of Urizen.' A number of interpretations of this statement had been offered to the court by expert psychiatric witnesses, but none of them was ever authenticated by Abbott himself. At no moment during the trial did anyone, least of all the jury, doubt that Abbott had been afflicted by a catastrophic psychosis and had acted without legal responsibility for his actions. Yet they'd brought in a unanimous verdict that he was legally sane and therefore fit to receive the five consecutive life sentences handed down to him by the judge. This was because the jury knew that the psychiatric services offered by the state for the treatment and care of the criminally insane were so primitive and inept that a legally insane Abbott might well have been out on the street within a few years, if indeed he did not escape within hours.

Once inside the River, Abbott was subjected to those special bigotries and punishments that are the usual lot of the mentally ill, but amplified—as were all bigotries in the River—by many degrees. He was insulted, he was shunned, he was cheated. He was deceived, robbed and exploited. And within the larger glass and steel cage of the penitentiary, he was trapped inside his own personal architecture of psychic pain: a cycle of isolation, psychosis, segregation, drugs, oblivion, neglect, more isolation, more neglect and more psychosis. Savagely punished from both within and without, Henry Abbott lived beneath the underdogs.

And yet Klein owed him. During those first weeks in D block, Klein had recognized the ability of the prison to turn a man's personality upside down. He felt the fear and deprivation perverting his thinking, warping his reason. NOT MY FUCKING BUSINESS. In the relative quiet after lights out, he would lie listening as the sounds of stifled weeping drifted through the bars. But that wasn't his business. Sometimes the sounds, shameful and small, were his own. Even then it wasn't his fucking business. Nor anyone else's. Klein, who wanted to live and survive and one day to leave, stifled the sounds of his own pain and ignored those of others.

But one night—just seven weeks into Klein's sentence—the voice of Henry Abbott would not be stifled.

'HELLO?'

The word had pealed around the stacked tiers of cells, echoing through the nightmares of light and heavy sleepers alike as if a damned and phantom soul were calling from the far side of creation. By the green cell light, Klein read his watch at 2.03 a.m.

'HELLO?'

And again.

'HELLO?'

And again.

'HELLO?'

With each repetition, the nature of the question changed and became more harrowing, more desperate, as if the whole vocabulary of this wounded creature had been stripped down to that single word.

In Abbott's cries, Klein recognized the vocalized half of the harrowing dialogue—by turns raging, threatening, pleading and cowed—that the psychotic person conducts with the torturer within himself. Klein had heard the half-dialogue before, in the chaos of the emergency room, but never from the same side of the fence. In cellblock D, the only attention Abbott provoked was a chorus of threats and obscenities that blended in with and exaggerated those already raging inside his skull.

It was an unpleasant scene. But it wasn't Klein's business, and he ignored it. Or to be more accurate, he ignored Henry Abbott.

Two days later, Abbott had still not been out of his cell. He had taken no food or drink, and had still found no more words with which to communicate.

'Hello?'

'Hello?'

On the third night, he subsided into a fragile and terror-stricken silence. When he was loud, the hacks had been reluctant to risk dragging him down to the hole for fear of one of them losing an arm or an eye, but when the bellowing of inmates complaining about the smell got angry enough and became an excuse for throwing burning rolls of toilet paper from the tiers, Captain Cletus turned up and gave the order to roust Abbott out.

When Klein saw them running a fire hose along the catwalk towards Abbott's cell, he realized that NOT MY FUCKING BUSINESS wasn't going to see him through his time here after all. During the three days in which Klein had left Abbott to suffer, he'd begun to feel himself dying—a rotting feeling in his guts, an ache in his pelvis and spine, a tightening band that cut into his brain. When he saw the fire hoses, he knew that they would wash Ray Klein away along with the excrement smeared over the inside of Abbott's cell. The burden on him was the burden of knowledge, his medical knowledge, and with that knowledge, obligation.

Klein had called Captain Bill Cletus to his cell and asked permission to go in and talk with Abbott. After a long pause, Cletus had said, 'You wouldn't be too smart a son of a bitch for your own good would you, Klein?'

'I hope I am not, Captain, sir,' replied Klein.

'Get yourself killed on my watch I'll have paperwork coming

out of my ass for weeks.'

'I could just do with some sleep,' said Klein.

Cletus considered him. 'OK, Klein. But it's your neck.'

Across the front of the stacked tiers there was a stir, a flurry of talk, a movement of faces to cell doors, of hands gripping the bars and ears pressed between them as the realization spread that the new guy Klein was going to go in there with the booby. Abbott, when steady, had the strength of three; when insane the strength of five, and they all knew that crazies didn't feel any pain. Why, the year before last one of them had sawn off his own cock and balls with a broken shaving mirror without making a fucking sound.

Abbott the giant sat crouched in a corner of his cell, covered in filth and mumbling incoherently while he picked at a sore on his face. Klein, mastering the urge to vomit and run, stood on the threshold of the cell door and introduced himself.

'Hi, Henry. I'm Ray Klein.'

When Abbott made no reply, Klein stepped inside and sat down on the bunk. A moment later the cell door thundered shut behind him.

Klein spent the whole night on Abbott's bunk, saying nothing. He ignored the obscene catcalls and shouts from neighbouring cells and just sat in silence, acclimatizing to the stench and trying to find a centre within himself that felt safe and that Abbott too might recognize and therein find some comfort. At some point in the early hours, Klein fell asleep. When he woke up to the bell at first lock and count, his head was pillowed on Abbott's shoulder and the big convict's arm was wrapped around him.

That day, Abbott accompanied Klein, without violence or persuasion, to a cell in the segregation block—the hole—and started on the drug regime that Klein recommended. Locking a man in the hole and giving him major tranquillizers wasn't Klein's idea of good treatment, but he was allowed to see Abbott four times a day, no one got hurt and Abbott had gradually recovered. Now he was on two-weekly intramuscular depot injections of slow-release phenothiazines to control his symptoms.

Abbott never quite made it to normality but he got by. He was given a job in the sewers that no one else wanted, and on the occasions he went crazy again, it was Klein who was asked to talk him out and take him to the hole. But there was one time that Abbott had gone to the hole when he wasn't crazy, when it had come down to Klein to stake out the other boundary of his life in Green River.

Myron Pinkley was a petulant, self-centred twenty-one-year-old sociopath with beefy shoulders and a bullet head who'd killed three strangers at a campsite in Big Bend National Park while on a mindless sex and murder spree with his girlfriend. Pinkley hovered sycophantically around the fringes of the Agry crew without any real hope of getting in and he was generally regarded as the kind of pain-in-the-ass jerk-off who would one day kill someone in front of a guard and spend the rest of his days in seg. One day—at a Sunday lunch-time not long after Klein had first drawn attention to himself by helping Abbott—Myron Pinkley had upped and stolen Klein's dessert.

Klein sat with dozens of eyes on him while his guts turned to lava. The little square of green Jello that Pinkley shovelled into his mouth with his fingers wasn't worth a shit to man nor beast, but it represented dignity, respect, power. For Klein it was still too soon, the values of this world still too alien for him to understand. To stop Pinkley would have required a violent scene and its consequences. The worthlessness of the Jello was so extreme, the price of retrieving it so absurdly out of proportion to its value, that Klein hadn't been able to bring himself to do anything. He just sat there blushing and trying to control his bladder while Pinkley sucked his fingers clean, grinned and walked away with his chest puffed out like a turkey. Klein passed the day in a torment. All the advice he received was to the effect that if he let Pinkley get away with it he was fucked. The evening of that same day Pinkley took Klein's chocolate pudding. This time Henry Abbott was sitting alone at the next table.

Abbott lumbered over and grabbed Pinkley's hand and Pinkley punched him in the mouth. Abbott didn't flinch and just stood there holding on to the hand. After a few seconds, Pinkley's face began to fold in on itself with pain. When he tried for Abbott's eyes with his free hand, Abbott squeezed harder and Pinkley fell screaming to his knees. Three guards, then four, then five, were unable to get Abbott to release Pinkley's hand. They threatened him, they kicked him and they bludgeoned him about the head. But Abbott silently refused to let go. Eventually they manhandled him to seg, Abbott dragging the shrieking Pinkley along the floor behind him like a recalcitrant teddy bear. When three hours later Abbott still hadn't let go of the hand, they put him under, first with twenty and then with seventy and then 180 milligrams of intravenous valium.

Pinkley lost his right thumb and index finger, hardly much better than losing the whole arm. He also lost credibility. Word got round that he had a shiv with Abbott's name on it for when Abbott got out of the hole. Big though he was, Abbott would be a sitting target. The prevailing mood was that Klein ought to do something about it.

When he came down to it, the problem was easy. Everything Klein had done since entering the River had been accompanied by a profound sense of helplessness and fear—taking a shower, pissing in the latrine, going to the gym, talking to a guard, not talking to a guard, choosing a table in the chow hall, whom to nod hello to, whom not. Every action, no matter how insignificant, carried a question with it: what will happen and whom might I offend if I do this? Can I speak with a Latino, can I afford not to hate the blacks, can I state a preference for Muddy Waters over Willie Nelson without getting my tongue cut out? Is it really this bad? He could never tell for sure. Finally enacting a piece of reality of his own was a relief. Klein purchased a six-inch nail from a man out of carpentry and a short length of broom handle from a Cuban cleaner. He drove the nail through the wood like a corkscrew. Then, finding Pinkley in the rear of the kitchens where, with his disabled arm, he'd fallen to the humiliating job of emptying slops, Klein punched the nail through the side of Pinkley's head, just behind the temple.

When Fenton, the head chef, found Pinkley an hour later, the young convict was still emptying slops as if nothing had happened, with four inches of galvanized iron piercing his frontal lobes.

Pinkley survived the repair of his middle meningeal artery with no memory of his accident, to which there were no witnesses. Nothing was ever proven or even seriously investigated. Nev Agry, a couple of days later, had bent down by Klein's ear just as he was about to tuck into his chocolate pudding and told him, 'Nice work, Doc.'

Captain Cletus had taken him to one side. 'Understand me, Klein, you fuckin' smart ass. Don't let this thing go to your head.'

If Klein's conscience had ever asked him if a crippled arm and permanent brain damage wasn't too severe a retribution for stealing four ounces of lime-flavoured Jello, its voice was drowned by the shouts of triumph and glee from every fibre in his body. As if by magic, a substantial wedge of fear disappeared from his life. For the first time, he found himself able to piss in the latrine while standing between two lifers. He assuaged any guilt he might have felt with the fact that Pinkley emerged from the affair with an altered personality which, even his mother agreed, was an immense improvement on the one that his creator had given him. Docile, obedient, almost irritatingly pleasant, Pinkley joined the Jesus Army—'Love, Faith, Power'—continued slopping out in the kitchens—a labour he was happy to offer up to God—and spent an hour twice a day in chapel redeeming his soul. If Pinkley had died—and the nail might have killed him—maybe Klein's conscience would have given him a harder time than it did, but hell, he'd had a fair notion of just how much the frontal lobes could take, and anyway, all that counted in the end was that for ever after his desserts were his own to dispose of as he chose. His habit was always to give his Jello away.

Klein's thoughts returned to the present as he approached the inner gate of the general purposes wing and saw the guard—Kracowicz—scowling at the prisoners walking past him. As Klein drew level, Kracowicz pulled a Latino from the line for a body search.

Outside, the sun was high and bright, and after the mixed effusions that permeated the interior of the prison, the air in the yard was sweet. Above the main gates rose a thick, squat turret that somehow managed to combine elegance and brutality in equal measure. Inside the turret, Warden Hobbes lorded it over his delinquent charges. The elaborate architecture spoke with the massive confidence of another age, and as a relic it was awesome, even beautiful, but to Klein it was a shitheap of misery. Under the gaze of the nearest rifleman, Klein turned away from the gates. That afternoon he would hold his private clinic in an underground room, where a stream of convicts would visit him with their ailments and infections, and pay him in cigarettes, porn mags, prison scrip, cash dollars or whatever other coin Klein decided was acceptable. Now he rounded a corner in the maze of wire mesh and headed towards the infirmary where he spent each morning.

The hospital was a two-storey structure built in the lee of the south-west wall. Klein jogged up the steps and through the big double doors which in daylight were usually wedged open. On duty at the second door, a barred gate, was the Korean guard, Sung. As Sung took him through and unlocked the third door, of plate steel, to let him into the wards, Klein wished him good morning. As usual, Sung did not reply. Sung had travelled halfway round the world to guard a bunch of killers in Texas and maybe didn't see the sense in wishing them good anything. Klein went down the corridor past the dispensary and into the sick bay office. The office had been painted mustard yellow fifteen years before, as if to remind the sick and their keepers that they weren't there to have a good time. The yellow paint now bubbled and peeled from the sagging plaster of the ceiling. Klein grabbed a white coat and a handful of lab reports and headed down to Crockett ward. When he got there, Frogman Coley raised his great grizzled head from examining a patient and walked down the aisle towards him. A stethoscope was slung from the nape of his neck and he wore rubber gloves.

'What's new, chief?' said Klein.

'Lopez is still shitting what blood he's got left in him. See what you think. I think Reiner's got PCP. Deano Baines's haemoglobin is up. And the Gimp tried to kill Garvey with a pillow.'

'He still alive?'

Coley raised an eyebrow.

'I mean the Gimp,' said Klein.

Coley nodded grimly. 'Let's check these mothers out.'

Coley snapped his gloves off, rolling them inside out, one into the other so that his skin didn't touch the outer surface and get contaminated. It was a habit he'd picked up from Klein, and Klein enjoyed seeing him do it. During the past three years, Klein had taught Coley most clinical medicine worth knowing, and Coley had been a sponge, soaking up knowledge with a passion that Klein envied. In Klein's mind there was no doubt: the black sharecropper had the gift of hands. Coley was a great natural physician. Bodies spoke their pain into his fingertips and he heard them. Klein had met a few such men in his profession and had always marvelled to see them work, but there were not many, and, much as he would like to, he did not count himself among them. Klein had never said any of this to Coley, never expressed his admiration and pride, for fear of mutual embarrassment. Yet before he left, he would like to tell Coley. Maybe that would be soon. Maybe this very day. A clatter of metal on stone rang from the end of the ward, and Klein put thoughts of freedom from his mind. He followed Coley to the foot of the first bed.

Klein sometimes thought of Green River as a Russian doll carved from increasingly dense layers of horror. And at the centre of the doll was a black void called AIDS. No one knew what proportion of the population was infected with HIV, but it was high. Large numbers of inmates brought the virus in with them. Once inside, continued addiction, the sharing of syringes, dangerous sex and a lot of spilled blood combined to raise the prevalence even higher. In Green River, the fear of contagion was so intense that it had disappeared from the surface of life—taboo, forbidden, unmentionable—and churned instead through dark cisterns hidden within the mind of every man. The infirmary was swamped with cases. Ray Klein and Earl Coley bore the brunt.

The official prison doctor was a local internist named Bahr who dropped by four times a week and stayed for an hour before heading off to the golf course, telling them to send anything they couldn't handle to the emergency room at the county hospital. His attitude was to lay heavy doses of sedatives on the AIDS guys and let them die in peace. Klein despised Bahr, not because this policy was unreasonable or inhumane, but because it was primarily designed to cut down Bahr's workload. Bahr collected a good fee from the Bureau of Corrections for his hour or two a week—money that would have been better spent on drugs and supplies. But Bahr wielded power. If he'd been so inclined, he could have had Klein and Coley removed from the hospital for good. In fact, they regularly broke so many prison regulations they could have been sent to seg for years. So they kissed Bahr's ass, kept most problems to themselves and only called him out of hours when there was a death to be certified, to which duty Bahr had never been known to object as it involved another generous fee.

Most guys opted for Bahr's tranquillizers, and, Klein thought, why the fuck not? But Vinnie Lopez, lying staring at the ceiling in a congealed mass of soiled sheets, was one of the fighters. A boxer. As Klein bundled the undersheet into a plastic bag, he glanced into Lopez's fevered eyes and saw the fiery defiance of terminal despair. For a second, the steelwork and ice around Klein's heart were shaken. Forbidden emotions assailed him. Before they could weaken him, before he could name them, Klein turned away. He snapped off his rubber gloves, bagged them and put on a clean pair. He shook out a fresh sheet. He avoided those dangerous eyes. He rolled Lopez to one edge of the bed and spread the sheet beneath him. As Klein rolled him back on to the sheet, the kid's face crumpled.

Lopez hid his face in the crook of his elbow and squirmed on to his side so that his back was turned to Klein. Klein's guts knotted inside him. Lopez, who boasted four slayings as leader of a San Antonio street gang and was taken seriously even in here, now looked like an eight-year-old child. Klein shook out the top sheet over the bed and let it drift gently down over Lopez's clenched figure. Klein knew that sometimes a man preferred to be alone with his pain and shame, and he knew that sometimes that was an excuse for not trying.

'Vinnie,' said Klein.

Lopez spoke from behind his elbow. 'Go 'way, man.'

Klein sat on the chair by the bed. Lopez's back was hunched towards him under the sheet.

'Vinnie,' he said. 'You can tell me to fuck off after this if you want to, but this is mine and Coley's outfit, and you've got to understand the way things are in here. The way things are is that there's no shame in tears, or in shit, or in the sickness infecting your body. Not in here. You understand?'

The thin body under his hand shook with grief.

'If I was sick maybe you'd do the same for me,' said Klein.

Lopez turned on him, his eyes hot with anger and contempt.

'I would spit on you,' said Lopez.

Klein shook his head.

'No,' he said quietly. 'You spit on yourself.'

The contempt in Vinnie's eyes dissolved into raw grief. His face trembled and he started to turn away again. Klein put his hand on his shoulder and stopped him.

'Die like a man, Vinnie.'

Vinnie stared at him, bewildered, his lips trembling. His voice was a whisper. 'I want to.' He struggled for his tears not to return. 'Tha's all I want. Tha's all, man. Tha's all.'

'This is how men die.'

Klein sat there in silence and let the ache fill his chest. He had learned that any comforting words he might have mustered would have been for himself and not for Vinnie. There was no comfort in rotting to death at twenty-two. Klein was suddenly possessed of a need, terrifying in its force, to cast some spell that made them all healthy. And happy and rich and free. And himself with them. And with that he was suddenly afraid that his parole application would be successful, and maybe understood why he had blown them out at his last year's review: if they let him go he would lose all this. Here he was still a doctor; out there he would be a bum. For a moment he wanted to go and break a chair over Captain Cletus's head and get himself sent to seg. The moment passed. He cleared his mind and held on to Vinnie's hand and listened in silence to the wasted lungs heaving quietly under the sheet. After what seemed like hours but was only a few minutes, Vinnie fell limp and quiet. A voice growled out from a few yards the other side of the curtain.

'Put that fucker out, Deano, we got oxygen in here. I tol' you before: you fit enough to smoke, you fit enough to drag yo' worthless ass down the TV room. We don't want to inhale your shit in here.'

Lopez stiffened and scrubbed his face with a handful of sheet. 'I don't want the Frogman to see me this way,' he said.

'Sure.' Like almost everyone else, Vinnie held Coley in awe. Klein nodded and stood up. 'I'll see you later.'

He slipped out between the screens and intercepted Earl Coley on his way in.

'Vinnie needs some time on his own,' said Klein.

Coley glanced at the screens then back at Klein. He hefted the bag of IV fluid in his hand. 'Guess this can wait till later.'

'Thanks,' said Klein.

Coley looked at his watch. 'Thought you had an appointment with great God Almighty, find out how sweet you sucked them stubby white dicks on the parole board.' He showed his watch to Klein.

Ten thirty-five.

Hobbes was waiting.

'Shit,' said Klein.

He dragged his white coat down over his shoulders and started at a run for the door.

K lein sat on a wooden bench on the ground floor of the admin tower and wondered if the big black patches of sweat on his denim shirt would piss off the warden. He'd sprinted the 400 metres from the infirmary to get here on time and of course he'd been sitting now for twenty minutes with the sweat from the run fucking up his shirt. Maybe Hobbes would figure he was sweating from tension. That would be bad. If Klein read Hobbes correctly the warden didn't like grovellers. Well, fuck him. It was out of Klein's hands anyway. A line from an old song ran through his head.

When I was just a little boy,
I asked my mother, 'What will I be?
Will I be handsome? Will I be rich?'
Here's what she said to me.

Klein found himself shaking inwardly with laughter. The

voice in his head belonged to Doris Day. It was perfection. He was sitting in the asshole of creation listening to a thirty-year-old Doris Day record stored from God knew where inside his skull. Will I be handsome? Will I be rich? He heard Doris take in a great breath and belt out: '*Que será será!* Whatever will be will be!' For its day, pretty subversive stuff, some kind of neo-stoicism maybe. Or even neo-Marxism. He wondered how many guys in their time had jerked off while thinking about Doris Day. Millions, probably. Klein considered trying it for himself some time. His sexual fantasy life needed a new angle. Doris Day. Klein was mildly shocked to find himself developing a hard-on.

'What the fuck's so funny, Klein?'

With a jolt, Klein straightened his face and looked up. Captain Cletus, lugubrious as ever, stood in the waiting-room doorway. At this late date, Klein's self-esteem did not depend on his daring to piss off Cletus. Because Cletus was widely feared and hated, he was an understandably, if excessively, paranoid character. He tended to interpret any laughter as being at his expense. Benson from A block had once spent a week in seg for using the phrase, 'as wide as the crack in Cletus's ass.' Klein could think of no better way of reassuring the Captain than to explain the true cause of his mirth. He stood to attention.

'I was thinking about Doris Day, Captain, sir,' said Klein.

Cletus walked over and stared at Klein from a distance of six inches for what seemed like a long time.

Finally, Cletus said, 'Doris Day?'

'Yes, sir,' said Klein.

Cletus continued his stare.

'I was thinking, "Whatever will be will be," sir,' said Klein. 'You know, *que será será.*'

'*Que será será,*' said Cletus.

'Yes, sir. Whatever will be will be, you know.'

'You are too smart a son of a bitch for your own good, aren't you, Klein?'

'I hope I am not, sir,' said Klein.

For the first time in three years, Klein watched a smile appear on Cletus's face.

'You're waiting to see the Warden.'

'Yes, sir.'

Cletus stared at him for another lengthy moment.

'Come with me,' said Cletus.

Klein, sweating harder than ever, followed Cletus up the stairs of the tower. As he watched the Captain's huge ass mounting the steps ahead of him, Klein cursed himself for letting his control slip, and Doris Day for infiltrating her voice so stealthily into his unconscious. At the top of the fourth set of steps, Cletus stopped at one end of a short wood-panelled corridor. At the other end was the door to Hobbes's office. Cletus turned to Klein.

'Sing,' said Cletus.

Klein looked from Cletus to the door of Hobbes's office and back again. He swallowed. 'Sir?'

'*Que será será*,' said Cletus. 'Sing it.'

'I don't remember the words,' said Klein.

'I don't know what the parole board has decided to do with your sorry ass,' said Cletus, 'but until you walk out them gates it's still mine. I put you on punishment, like, right now, the board will have to reconsider its decision.'

You cocksucker, thought Klein. He did not look at Cletus for fear of the thought showing in his eyes. He coughed.

'Listen,' said Klein, 'if I gave the impression of being a smart son of a bitch, it was not my intention to do so, and I apologize to the Captain unreservedly and without let or hindrance.'

'Sing,' said Cletus.

This time Klein let him have the cocksucker stare. Again, Cletus smiled. Klein took a deep breath.

'Loud,' said Cletus. 'So I can hear you all the way to he bottom of the stairs.'

Klein let the breath out. 'I've got to admit,' he said, 'I didn't think you had the imagination.'

Cletus put his lips close to Klein's ear. 'When I was a kid, I used to jerk off watching Doris Day movies.'

Klein looked at him. 'You're right,' said Klein. 'I'm too smart a son of a bitch for my own good.'

Cletus nodded. 'I still wanna hear that song.'

Then fuck you, thought Klein, and launched straight into it.

When I was just a little boy,
I asked my mother, 'What will I be?'
As Cletus disappeared, laughing, down the stairs, Klein
continued singing.
'Will I be handsome? Will I be rich?'
Here's what she said to me.
In the small corridor his voice echoed hugely. Damned, too,
if it didn't sound half bad. Klein inhaled deeply and gave the
chorus his best shot.

QUE SERÁ SERÁ!
WHATEVER WILL BE WILL BE . . .

As Klein took in another deep gulp of air, the door of
Hobbes's office erupted open. Klein's mouth snapped shut.
Hobbes stared at him from the doorway: massive balding
cranium, febrile eyes under heavy brows. If Klein had ever felt
more of an asshole he couldn't remember when. An excruciating
silence seemed like his only option.

'Klein?'

Klein's lungs were overfilled, and he felt unable to blurt out
all the air. His voice came out in a hoarse whisper. 'Yes, sir.' He
held on to the rest of the air.

Hobbes considered him with mild astonishment, as if Klein's
bizarre performance had just barely penetrated his consciousness
and distracted him briefly from matters of more profound
import. Something in Hobbes's bearing, his distance, his speech
patterns, gave him a quality of not being of this world, as if he'd
been catapulted into the present from some other time long past.
Like the prison itself: designed for the nineteenth century, now
floundering in the last days of the twentieth. In all modesty, or
maybe in all stupidity, Klein rarely found himself in the presence
of an intelligence he felt to be larger, deeper, more impenetrable
than his own. Hobbes evoked such a sense; a sense of the
unfathomable. If, now, Hobbes could not fathom Klein, it did
not seem to perturb him overmuch.

Hobbes said, 'Get in here.' He disappeared from view.

Klein let out the breath that was threatening to pop the
blood vessels in his face. He hauled his dignity back together and

strode down the corridor into the office.

The office spanned the width of the tower and was ascetically furnished: a bookcase, an old oak desk covered by a sheet of glass, three chairs. A fan with wooden blades turned in the ceiling above the desk. On the wall was a Ph.D. certificate from Cornell. Directly facing the door on a wooden plinth was a bronze bust of Jeremy Bentham. Klein closed the door behind him and stood to attention, staring at the glazed bronze orbs of Bentham's eyes. At that moment he imagined that his own eyes looked somewhat similar.

Hobbes's voice boomed across the room: 'The last mind of any real stature to devote itself to the problem of incarceration.'

Klein felt a fleeting vertigo. What was Hobbes talking about? Surely not Doris Day. Klein looked at him and said, 'Excuse me, sir?'

Hobbes inclined his head towards the bronze bust. 'Bentham.'

'Yes, sir.' Klein's wits suddenly fell back into place. He performed a rapid calculation and added, 'Panopticism.'

Hobbes's thick brows rose half an inch. 'You surprise me. Come and sit down.'

Hobbes indicated the chair facing him and Klein walked over. Under the sheet of glass on the desk was an old architectural blueprint of the prison and its walls. The south window at Hobbes's back threw his face into shadow. No doubt the effect was deliberate. As Klein sat down he saw a green cardboard folder on the desk with his own name and number printed on the front.

'So what does the concept of panopticism mean to you?' said Hobbes.

Klein looked up from the folder that contained his fate. He felt nineteen years old again, trying to remember the course of the phrenic nerve for the anatomy professor. 'Bentham was preoccupied with the idea that if you watched someone all the time, it would change their personality for the better. Force them to re-examine their souls. Something like that.'

'Something like that,' said Hobbes. 'What do you think of his theory?'

'I guess it depends who's doing the watching and who's being watched,' said Klein.

Hobbes nodded. 'How true.' He seemed pleased. 'Not all men are able to profit from the scrutiny of the panoptic machine. They cannot endure its light. Even less can they endure the light of self-knowledge.'

'Forcing people towards self-knowledge can be a dangerous business,' said Klein.

'How so?' asked Hobbes.

Klein didn't want to provoke Hobbes. Neither did he want to appear to be kissing his ass, if only because Hobbes wasn't the type to appreciate it, but what the hell. His fate was already decided. If Hobbes could tolerate Doris Day he wasn't going to be blown away by a little Plato.

'You remember the subterranean cavern in Plato's *Republic*? The dream of Socrates?'

Hobbes leaned forward. 'The Seventh Book,' said Hobbes. His brow was smoothed taut with excitement. He seemed to be holding his breath. 'Make your point.'

Klein swallowed. 'In the cavern men are chained, buried far away from the light of the sun. Their heads are fixed to stop them from seeing anything but their own shadows cast upon the wall by the flames of a fire. When challenged, the chained men violently defend their own dark ignorance. And Socrates asks: If they could seize hold of the man who tried to liberate them and lead them up into the light, would they not then kill him?'

Hobbes let out his breath, almost in a sigh. 'Would you kill him?' he said.

Klein looked at Hobbes for a long time. 'I don't know,' he said. 'You look at the sun for too long, you go blind.'

'Do you think we have a choice?' asked Hobbes.

In Hobbes's face was a yearning, a desperation that took Klein aback. He'd come here for five minutes' routine prison bullshit, either another year inside to rehabilitate himself further, or a paternal pat on the back and a firm handshake to send him on his way. Instead Hobbes's eyes were black pools swimming with a nameless inner horror that reminded Klein of madness.

'Again,' said Klein, 'only sometimes.'

'Even the man before the firing squad has a choice,' said Hobbes. 'He can fall whimpering to his knees, or he can refuse the blindfold and sing.'

Hobbes sounded like just such a man. Klein felt powerfully drawn to explore Hobbes's state of mind, like a Marlow to his Kurtz. But Klein was here as a convict hoping for parole. The convict warned him to back off.

'Yes, sir,' said Klein, 'You're absolutely right.'

Hobbes sensed the retreat. He blinked twice and sat back in his chair. He seemed shaken. He put his hand in his pocket and suddenly pulled out a pill bottle. He placed it on the table in front of Klein.

'My own doctor tells me I should take these three times a day. I consider him a fool. What do you think?'

Klein picked up the bottle and read the label. Lithium carbonate 400 milligrams. Klein suddenly felt empty of feeling. His mind registered without emotion the fact that Hobbes was taking a drug used almost exclusively for treating manic depression, the Arnold Schwarzenegger of mental disorders.

When swinging up into a manic phase of unhinged grandiosity and visionary disinhibition, such patients often stopped taking their medication, which was what Hobbes appeared to be saying right now. 'Maniac' was a word much and inaccurately overused. The implication of the little brown bottle in Klein's hand was that Hobbes was at least a contender for the real thing. A maniac. Unlike most maniacs, Hobbes wielded immense power over many lives. Klein looked up into Hobbes's eyes. Strangely, Klein felt calm for the first time since entering the office. It was simple now: instead of being everyday crazy, Hobbes was genuinely insane.

Hobbes nodded at the bottle in Klein's hand. 'You haven't answered my question.'

Klein put the bottle down on the glass-topped desk. 'I advise you to go back to your own doctor and ask him.'

Hobbes frowned.

'But if I was you,' Klein went on, 'I'd do whatever I felt I had to.'

Hobbes's eyes swam with emotion. He nodded. 'Any man

that doesn't do so isn't worth a damn.'

He grabbed the pill bottle and threw it into the aluminium waste bin under his desk. The bottle hit the sides of the bin with a dull clang. After the clang came a pause. Klein looked again at the green folder. Hobbes followed his gaze. He pulled the file towards him and opened it.

'The parole board was impressed by your performance,' he said.

Klein did not answer. Hobbes leafed through the file.

'As you know, they are morons to a man. A line memorized from the New Testament, preferably one that they'll recognize, is usually enough to get past them. Jesus always goes down well. That's why you failed last year. Wrong mental attitude.'

'Sir?' said Klein.

'Stubbornness,' said Hobbes.

'With respect, sir, I've been flexible enough to learn the rules in here.'

'Indeed. Your success, shall we say, has been remarkable. And yet every coin has two faces, is that not so?'

'Yes, sir.'

Hobbes glanced down at the file. 'For instance you are a healer, by all accounts a good one. Many inmates prefer to purchase their medical care from you rather than get it for free from Dr Bahr, not that I blame them. Yet contrast that with the case of Myron Pinkley's lobotomy.'

Klein kept what he hoped was a poker face.

'You get my meaning,' said Hobbes.

'If you mean am I aware of the duality of man's nature, yes, sir, I am.'

In a single beat of time Klein's mind was swamped with rage: a rage to know, a rage against Hobbes for fucking him around like this, a rage against himself for hoping, for sitting there, for breathing, for being too smart a son of a bitch to lean across the table right now and tear Hobbes's fucking head off. He shivered in the breeze from the ceiling fan. His shirt felt drenched. Across the desk, Hobbes snapped shut the green folder.

'You're free, Klein,' he said.

Klein sat staring at him. He didn't answer.

'The board concurred with my recommendation. You will be handed over to your parole officer at noon tomorrow.'

Hobbes rose to his feet and held out his hand. Klein stood up and shook it.

'Thank you, sir.'

'It's all right to smile, Klein.'

'Yes, sir.'

But Klein didn't smile. The emptiness remained. He knew, somehow, that if he allowed it to fill up it would not be with joy but with a terrible sense of loss, and he feared it. Hold on to it, he told himself, until you get somewhere safe. He let go of Hobbes's hand.

'Eighty-nine per cent of the men released from this institution return to prison,' said Hobbes. 'Don't be one of them.'

'I won't.'

'Is there anything I can do for you?' asked Hobbes.

Klein hesitated. All he had to do—all he had to do—was walk out the door and keep his head down for twenty-four hours, and he could drive down to Galveston Bay for a swim. The thought of wading out into that water and of how much he wanted to feel it against his skin made him frightened even at this late date—especially at this late date—of rousing Hobbes to fury. He remembered what Cletus said about his ass still being theirs until he walked out of the gates.

'Don't be afraid to speak your mind,' said Hobbes.

Klein looked at him. 'The way things are, Coley can't keep the infirmary running on his own. With respect, sir, that place is a disgrace to us all.'

Hobbes squared his shoulders. 'The prison infirmary is a disgrace to me, Dr Klein.' The madness in Hobbes's eyes was touched with fire. 'Your complaints, if not my own, have been noted. I assure you that events have been set in motion that will make the conditions in the infirmary an irrelevance.'

Klein wondered what the fuck that was supposed to mean. The thought must have shown on his face because Hobbes's expression suddenly became guarded. But his voice trembled with passion.

'You have my word that—' Hobbes searched for a word, '—improvements will shortly take place, not only in the hospital but across the whole of this correctional facility.'

Klein resisted the urge to take a step backwards. He nodded. 'I'm glad to hear that, sir.'

'Be glad, then, that you won't be here to see it.'

With that, Hobbes turned and walked across the room to the window. He stood with his back to Klein and stared out over the yard at the brooding megalith of the cell blocks. His hands trembled and he clenched them on the window sill. His body seemed to be straining to contain some immeasurable force.

Klein, watching him, didn't know whether he had permission to leave. Suddenly he was scared for more than just himself. Whatever the real extent of Hobbes's sickness, this behaviour was the merest of hints, the leakings from the psychic Pandora's box whose lid Hobbes was struggling to keep shut. What 'events' had he already set in motion? Should Klein ask him? Should he walk over and put a hand on his shoulder? It was none of his fucking business. Despite himself he took a silent pace towards Hobbes.

'Good luck, Klein.'

Hobbes spoke without turning from the window. Klein stopped in his tracks.

'And thank you for our conversation.'

In Hobbes's voice was a finality that somehow signalled more than just the end of the interview. Klein waited. If Hobbes turned to look at him maybe something would happen. But Hobbes did not turn.

'Good luck, Warden,' said Klein.

Hobbes, still staring through the window at his prison, nodded slowly, twice.

Ray Klein stepped silently to the door, opened it and left the Warden's office without another word.

GRANTA

ALLAN GURGANUS
LOCAL MAN HAS SEX WITH CORPSE

John Bill Whitehead

SEX-WITH-DEAD
Suspect

RALEIGH—A former funeral home employee charged with having sex with a body he was transporting pleaded guilty Wednesday after a psychiatrist testified that the man had sexual problems and that the incident probably was an isolated one.

Superior Court Judge Davis Cashwell sentenced John Bill Whitehead, 60, of Falls, NC, to two years in prison, then suspended the sentence and placed him on five years' probation. Cashwell also ordered Whitehead to serve 30 days in the Person County Jail, to undergo a psychiatric evaluation and to complete 100 hours of community service.

'There is not a single thing I can possibly do to make it hurt any less,' the judge said before handing down the sentence.

Whitehead, a thin man with carefully combed brown hair and thick glasses, said nothing during the proceedings other than answering 'Yes sir' or 'No sir' to Cashwell in a near whisper.

On Feb 22, Person County sheriff's deputies said they found Whitehead in a funeral home station wagon several hundred yards off US 401 in southern Person County. In the vehicle with Whitehead was the body of a 40-year-old woman he had picked up at Dorothea Dix Mental Hospital and was supposed to deliver to Nowell-Johnstone Funeral Home of Falls.

'There was a man kneeling over what appeared to be a stretcher in the back of the hearse and covering up a body with a funeral home blanket,' Person County Assistant District Attorney Howard Chalmers told the judge. 'They noticed that his pants were in disarray and his zipper was found, I'm afraid, down.'

Whitehead told deputies that the cot 'became loose and was rocking back and forth,' and he had gone into the back of the vehicle to secure the body. He later admitted that he had sex with said body, Chalmers said.

The victim, Deborah Jo Hartman, had spent most of her life in state institutions and was transferred to Dix for treatment of a heart condition. The mother, Donna Coleman Hartman, said her daughter had the mental capacity of a three-year-old child. When Deborah Jo died, she weighed 72 pounds and stood less than five feet tall.

The victim's family and others in the courtroom shook their heads and muttered when Attorney Ryland R. Smith, also of Falls, claimed that he had no reason to think that Whitehead had done anything similar in the past.

'I believe this was a spontaneous, isolated event and not a pattern,' Smith affirmed.

Smith described Whitehead as 'non-assertive, timid and compliant.' He said that in 1970, at the age of 38, Whitehead had an inflammation of the spinal cord that paralyzed him briefly from the waist down. Since then, Whitehead had had 'impaired sexual function' and 'limited sexual activity', Whitehead's lawyer said.

Smith claimed Whitehead may have been seeking a sexual encounter with a person or 'non-threatening object'.

The prosecutor said he was satisfied with the sentence. If Whitehead had been given the standard two-year sentence for the charge, he likely would have been released after serving only two months and would not be on supervised probation.

Whitehead, who worked at the funeral home for 17 years and was fired shortly after the incident, chose not to speak in court, explained his attorney.

'This case is one that from the very beginning had sadness written all over it for everyone involved,' Smith stated.

'This ranks up there,' Smith said. 'This moment on 401 South, in the dark of the night, hurt this woman's family deeply, it hurt Mr Whitehead's family, and it hurt Mr Whitehead himself. This was an awful night, but he has owned up to it.'

Patty Holden-Thorp, Staff Writer, the *News and Observer*, Raleigh, North Carolina, 21 May 1992.

Deputy Sheriff Wade Watson Cutcheon, Jr, fifty-seven: his unedited tape-recorded testimony, taken at the County Courthouse, Falls, NC, 5.37 a.m., Feb 20, four hours after apprehending suspect Whitehead.

A person thinks he's seen pretty much everything. Babies we all are, when it comes right down to it. We ain't got clue number one, now do we?

Betty? I will talk it all out. Please trim the rougher stuff and make it to sound official, OK, honey? I feel so lucky, knowing that my beloved wife is the finest legal secretary in Person County. Helps steady me, knowing it's you my voice is going to.

OK, so me and Rocky get a call saying Mrs Wembley's greenhouse is being broke into. Again. The call comes every few weeks in cold weather, anonymous, and we guessed who'd made it. But you got to check things out or folks will eat your ass alive if somebody really does steal 1,500 geranium seedlings.

I always use the five-battery flashlight you gave me, Betty. Shined it into the greenhouse (locked up tight as a tick, of course). I remember light scooting over all those baby plants. Little did I know what that good beam'd have to clamp on to not nine, ten minutes later. There was most of a moon out, everything in it looking orderly at present. Eleven forty-nine, we're talking.

So we was coming down old 401 South, eating your own very excellent cheese straws. Rocky having finally quit smoking, we been keeping the baggie in our Cruiser's (clean) ashtray. Some kind of good eating. I remember we'd just got serious about the upcoming Police Benevolent Barbeque Fundraiser at the firehouse—how many trestle tables we'd be needing—when Rocky says, 'Wait one, Wade bud. Now, who'd be having a funeral at the edge of Old Man Martin's peanut field on to midnight with it being a February this cold?' Of course, in any town where folks call the police to check their geraniums, a hearse misparked after the witching hour is bound to draw at least a second glance. There'd been some drug smuggling over in Castalia and Red Oak. Private airstrips in tobacco fields, leather knapsacks still tainted with white powder. FBI got into it. A local deputy found three apple-red BMW 730s, keys, everything, abandoned in one ditch. Sure snagged him quite some glory. So . . .

We pulled the Cruiser over—and I played my five-battery wand across the hearse bumper and read Nowell-Johnstone's gold-lettered crest: at least the funeral home is local. Some comfort. According to procedure, we split up and approached from opposite sides of the aforementioned vehicle. My light showed me a single set of tiny (probably human) shoeprints, leading from the driver's door to the rig's tailgate, tracks crawling right on up in there as unto the grave itself. Honey? My small hairs knew before I did.

Long, black limo-wagoneer, waxed, moonlight softsoaped all over and aimed at an angle like it'd been run off the road or had car trouble. Strange thing: if the hearse had been parked correct, we might not have noticed.

'Lookee,' Rocky goes. That's when I saw some crawling and scrambling in the back. First it appeared to be one large, weird, busy animal. A full moon lit separate parts of it, all moving like a pale bug, rowboat-sized, with maybe too many legs hooked on it and struggling to get upright off its back. Yuk. Moon kept making everything prettier and therefore considerably creepier.

Our lights caught a face behind the car window, a pair of eye-glasses. Blinking, it was. Flat-white, and under the blue-green of the hearse's tinted glass, it looked like drowning, mouth opening, mouth closing. What seemed to be a man, looked to be kneeling, over what appeared to be a stretcher, in the back of what was sure as hell a hearse. The man was trying to cover the body with a blue blanket. I stopped cold. Even my flashlight tried to look the other way. Babies we all are when it comes right down to it. We think we know decency, but we ain't got clue number one, now do we?

I recognized the thick spectacles. Hadn't I known John Bill Whitehead all my life? In school, had he not been considered book-smart, even if doughy and kind of a runt? Hadn't I given him a ten-dollar tip after he'd done everybody so nice at Momma's funeral and her looking so 'natural', plus a fiver for old maid Aunt Mary that won't a real aunt but we called her that?

Yes.

'What you got ahold of back there, John Bill?' Rock hollered, jolly, not knowing what a mouthful he'd done asked. Our lights held Whitehead's specs, glaring. Such a yanking up of breeches. Such wrestling, Jacob and his angel, Jacob winning right on top.

I think it was Rocky went around, opened the back of the hearse-wagon. Out spilled Whitehead, white as the wax on fig preserves. Kept fumbling with his belt buckle and zipper, with more manhood than you might expect from somebody so outwardly wimpish.

Maybe if he'd just buttoned his black suitcoat over the problem area, we wouldn't have thought too much about it. Maybe I am wrong. Her being completely naked—I mean, the corpse—was, I'd say, prominent among our first early-warning tip-offs.

Here it was, late February, quite the cold snap. In the moonlight, our breath showed plain, cut through by flashlight crossbeams. A little fog was rising off the peanut field like the stubble peaks, Betty, on your lemon meringue pie: like witnesses watching. Odd. We had to help hold John Bill up some, none too sure on his legs. Never what you'd call a big man nor a gruff one. Our off-duty mortician then whispered: 'Everything under control, boys. Routine matter really, everything covered, boys. I should know what I'm doing here, but can't thank you enough, boys, everything cov—' Then Rocky's light found much that wasn't . . . covered.

It looked to be a child, spread-eagled, not real secretly: a girl-child. That much even Sherlock's Dr Watson could have picked up at a glance. Only when we'd seen it was a girl-one did we understand about the shapes we'd spied earlier, flung up on his shoulders. I ain't going to say Whitehead was a-pushing into her like shoving a wheelbarrow, with the handles of her legs to guide him, but something like that—under oath, in however crowded a courtroom—is what I'm going to have to spill. SohelpmeGod.

Whitehead tried explaining how the straps had slackened and she'd come a-loose. Due to speed bumps. Out here? Rocky, always a joker but with that gentle streak you find in most men his size, laughed one mean-spirited snort, 'She's probably come a-loose OK, John Bill.' Babies we all are when you get right down to it. We think we know decency and what local folks will do to other locals, but the majority of us good Christians ain't got clue number one concerning what goes on 'behind closed doors', now do we? It was only about then, Betty, that I begun to glom on to the full extent of it.

If Mrs Wembley—at least we think it was her—had not phoned in that anonymous tip as how somebody was busting into her glass geranium house; *if* we hadn't then swung over to 401 South instead of our usual route past Millie's Diner (it being so late that even Millie would be closed), Rock and me might not have noticed how crookedy that hearse was parked at a dead-end road where the high-school kids like to go to smooch (but usually earlier). It wasn't that original or clever a spot for John Bill to pick, not a whole hearse. And then we might not have caught him with the poor little Hartman girl.

Whitehead kept trying to block the open tailgate with his body, arms out and fingers spread so as to make for a better screen. But we had viewed enough to where it seemed we'd best go on and check further.

'Stand aside, John Bill. Look at you—and you a family man.' It was then he drew both hands up over his face. It was only then I noticed the white rubber gloves. Those scared me the worst so far: on hands way bigger and stronger than all the rest of him combined, rubber pale as roots. They forced me to step back one. If it hadn't been for them gloves, and the lowered zipper he'd had such a hard time drawing up (be*cause* of those slippery rubber gloves?), the man might have got away with it for another seventeen years and at the best white funeral home in Falls.

'John Bill,' I said in a style that was stern but human, like a law officer but one who'd known him coming and going all these years. 'John Bill . . . Why?'

Here, way off the record, I need to say that Rocky acted inappropriate. It was nerves, I believe. Referring to Whitehead's heavy-set wife—and with John Bill being such a jumpy, bent soda-straw of a man, not much taller than five-four would be my guess—Rocky says: 'What, Doris holding out on ye?'

That wasn't funny for anybody concerned (little Hartman girl least of all) and Rocky regretted it, hearing the lack of response. But I want to cite it, not to get poor Rock in trouble, just to show how mixed up and end-over-end we were, all of us. Sex after death. It's not something you bump into with the frequency of, say, Saturday jay-walking downtown. Lordbepraised.

'Well, sir,' I told John Bill, 'I reckon we need to see . . . the condition of the . . . of her . . . of the accessory . . . '

I was righter than I knew.

When Rocky lifted one handle of the stretcher, John Bill grabbed the other, maybe thinking if he co-operated we wouldn't tell? And up to that point, I got to admit I was considering not— telling.

Because I didn't rightly know how to. Words never were my strongest suit. Betty, you know what I can do and what I can't. But, hey, a person needs college to explain this mess. Needs medical school.

In my mind I test-phrased it: 'Guess what? You know that mousy John Bill Whitehead who has the rock-thick specs, and is one-third the size of his nice but humongous wife, and with a high-school daughter who's just been tapped into the Honor Society? Well . . . And you know the Hartmans' Mongolian idiot child who has lived longer than anyone expected and has been in homes except for Christmas and Easter, when her folks dress her up like a doll in frills the color of bad cakes and punish everybody local by bringing her to church (at her age, twenty-five or forty, still carrying that same blue, stuffed toy, long-since too old to wash)? You know how her folks just spite everybody who criticizes them for not keeping her at home and doing and caring for her and ruining their lives because they slipped up and had a child too late in life and there won't enough left in either of them to make a whole person? Well . . . And you'll never guess what . . . '

No, I could not bring myself even to put these two unlikely people in one sentence, much less stuff them in a single midnight hearse.

191

But here was the other odd part. Odd, past its being so late, and past its being a girl I'd never seen but on major holidays and only then in pinafores, and even past its being a body naked as day. Maybe oddest of all, atop the pile of oddness already heaped up, was—I've got to say: the beauty of her.

'What a body!' Rocky sighed, then caught himself, giggled but sounded punished. See, it made me know: beauty is odd, always. Odd like death—and nearabout as surprising. Once you come to know how to see both death *and* beauty, why they start fetching up pretty much everywhere. Betty, don't be going thinking I've flipped. This is how it reached your Wade out yonder. Out beside a field whose crop was moonlit fog with headlights scooting through it. Very beautiful out there. And a total spook show.

See, honey, it was the beauty of her body that first made Rocky and me look at each other, and then look across it, and then look it over, and then check back with each other before turning shoulder-to-shoulder and staring afresh at John Bill. It was an ideal, miniature midgety body. Freeze-dried perfect, like a small, white, naked old-timey statue. I think it was Debbie Jo's unexpected below-the-neck perfectness that told us that we had not a lick of choice except to turn poor John Bill Whitehead in. I felt my stomach fist all up. Babies we each are when it comes right down to it, and not having clue number one as to what-all some folks'll try when nobody's around. Not the first hint do we got, nor do we want it, either, right?

But Rocky and me both understood: we both could almost imagine it. Sure, we'd just seen the deed in progress. Which was rough. But imagining was very rough. Know why? Because, that puts you into it. Her. Her coolish ankles mashed up humid near your ears. Sorry.

Our lights were aimed down on one pert chest. Strange, but her tiny nipples drew to my mind my favorite boyhood candy, little purple discs with a nice mediciny taste. The flashlight then found her small reddish pubic brush, and her legs as tapered and strong, if a little more bowed, than Sonja Henie's. Of course, Rock and me are Veterans of Foreign Wars members, him from Nam, me from that overlooked Korean expeditionary mistake.

But us two strong fellows studied each the other and knew; and then spun around and, as if trained in this at the Smithfield Police Academy Brush-Up Weekend Law Enforcement Seminar, both vomited.

The orange from certain recent cheese straws made the act a mite more dramatic—out there in the blue mud and the brown fog and the clear moon. It was only then, I believe, that John Bill gauged our seriousness, once he seen us upchuck (or heard us, because, mercifully, we both aimed our lights elsewhere, though Rocky couldn't resist, once it was over, from doing a quick check on his—only human).

A trained professional, I at least checked my watch throughout. It was 12.07 a.m. when we first seen the bad parallel park that hearse had made, as if 'the Moleman' (as we used to call weak-eyed John Bill at school) had been barely able to resist stopping. Maybe he drove slower and slower till, four miles from surrendering her to Nowell-Johnstone's funeral parlor, John Bill saw this muddy moonlit road and temptation activated the turn signal.

At 12.09 our flashlights first found the facts I'd rather not have lodged into this so-so local brain (too much for somebody like me with a big heart but just a high-school education).

At 12.11 we got John Bill, refastening his own unzipped lower body, off her and out of there. My clipboard report states plain how both officer Rockford Suggs II and yours truly 'Retched, copious, 12.14.' Which must mean it was about 12.13 sharp when we started understanding, to the full extent of the law, what had gone on.

By then we'd seen her body, the opened crotch just perfect, and we knew that in some small, unlawabiding, ugly yet beauty-loving part of us, we too, on looking at her (the face still covered), felt a teentsy bit of, if not desire, then . . . imagination. Yoosch!

Forgive me, Betty?

And John Bill, cleaning those big smudgy eyeglasses (God knows where they'd been) on his shirt-tail without even needing to yank it out, and Rocky noting (with a little help from his three-battery flashlight—gift of his wife, but not near so good as

the one you gave me) that just a bit of the said shirt-tail was
pooching forth out through the quickly-shut, snaggle-toothed
zipper of John Bill's black pants. Well, plainly, some deed from
yours truly was now required. It was hard, though. I mean,
haven't I known Whitehead for as long as I've been knowing I
am alive on earth? Yes. So . . .

Yours truly was forced to approach the Cruiser, take up the
handset and risk reporting it. But in what language? Whose? In
my head, I am Winston Churchill doing the 'Blood, Sweat and
Tears' speech. It's only when my mouth opens do I hear a piss-
poor used-car's carburetor coughing. Still, here goes, thought I.
In some way, your Wade already knew his life was changing. I
hope I never have another case like this. I reckoned I would
never again enter Bob Melton's Barbeque without getting pointed
out by somebody's toothpick as the man that caught the
undertaker doing an undertaking not exactly family-authorized.

'Twelve-eighteen and over, Edna?'

'Read you, Smoky. How many geraniums did that pot-
smuggling gang swipe from a certain selfish Wembley woman,
not to name names on air, ha, over?'

'Edna, tonight we got us something a little different. I need
the rules and regs, need chapter and verse on somebody's trying
to . . . no, somebody managing right well, seems like, to have
sexual congress, Edna, with, Edna?—with a corpse, Edna.'

'Who is this?'

'It's me, it's Officer Cutcheon. It's me, just Wade, dummy. I
mean it. Look it up, the law, because I need a citation, I need to be
official, because I am feeling so damn harem-scarob out here . . . '

'You should have Millie pour you all black coffee, but she
closed early on account of her step-daughter's birthday. So you
just hightail it back here quick, hear me? You do that, I swear I
ain't going to write this up and ruin you boys' next fitness
reports.'

I had to tell her everything. And the second I said, 'An
employee of Nowell-Johnstone's Mortuary Arts,' Edna said, 'It's
John Bill Whitehead.'

I swallowed hard once.

'I knew it,' she gloated. Edna does that. She gloats. 'It is that

John Bill, ain't it, Wade? Because, just before Mother's funeral, he had me in for the viewing. And . . . I don't like to announce this on the air, Wade, but it was something—about Momma's mouth. I can't say it. But, in some way, I've known. Whoever he's got out there at the edge of a dark peanut field—I believe Mr Martin put in peanuts last year?—I swear to you, Wade, it ain't his first. Who *has* he jumped?'

'The little Hartman girl.'

There was a pause. It may be the first time I ever did (or will) hear a decent, blinky, gulping, human pause from veteran police dispatcher Edna 'Mouth City' McCabe.

She recovered. No surprise. And finally went: 'The child is thirty-eight if she's a day. IQ of a collie, they claim.' Then I could hear Edna inhale a full one-third of her Camel at a gulp. 'Still, you know, Wade? It's something about his pickin' a person that slow: like he knew that even if Debbie Jo woke up, she *still* couldn't squeal on him. It's something even way nastier 'bout that. Me, I can abide anything but a sneak. Ten-four, over and out. Bring the scuzz in wearing cuffs, leg irons—hop him up the front center courthouse steps, and don't let him pull a windbreaker or nothing over his bald ole head. I got to get off this line, boy. I got people to talk to, Smoky. I got people to wake. You know what this is, Wade?'

'Nome.'

'This is History.'

'Well, I reckon . . .'

'Wade? I'm three years from retirement. So I best to thank you now, because you finally brought me one that's . . . well, this un's national, Wade. Love you to pieces. Overandout.'

Edna had mentioned her dead mother's mouth. She'd said nothing more. Edna never spelled out what she meant by 'it was something about Momma's mouth.' But I rushed in and imagined how, if you know a person real good, and especially if you've been with them during their hard dying (is there any other kind?), and you've seen them wheeled out of the hospital room and you've known them through and through, and then you turn up at the home for the viewing not two days later and you can just tell from the look of them, from some relaxing of the face, some tightening, some twist or angle of the closed eyes, that something extra has got hold of them. As if Death ain't enough! I mean something besides embalming. I mean, before embalming. I mean, a more familiar type of embalming, easier to administer, harder to detect.

Somebody like me yelled, 'What'd you do to my Momma and Aunt Mary, you?' And before I knew it, I had Moleman flung up against his own hearse. Did. I had that John Bill pretty much by the throat and him suspended mostly across the roof of it, pointy black shoes dangling—the guy weighs that little.

'Look, ah, Wade?' Rocky was behind me rapping on my shoulder like a door.

'Oh, sorry,' I said, 'But, Rock, did John Bill lay out any of your people?' I let the undertaker settle back on his feet.

'Only my brother, my kid brother that drowned, the pretty one that we . . . ' I heard how Rocky, a little slower, got my drift.

'Why, you little . . . '

I had to hold Rocky back.

Edna being always on the job, it's in less than eighty seconds we commence to hear the sirens growing more and more out our way. And more. Why she sent the fire department is not clear, beyond her owing several fellows there a favor.

I hated that. I didn't want others looking at the Hartman child. Not yet. Or, as far as that goes, studying myself either. I leaned forward, pulled at the blue blanket part-covering Deborah Jo's face, planned to ease it down, cover her whole slender body. (You know me, Betty, regular Sir Walter Raleigh.) In such a high-octane of a moon, her amazing little carcass shone white as a lit forty-watt white bulb. But soon as I tugged at the blanket, oops, her whole face was exposed. Rocky's light was trailed right on it, with me hunkered not twelve inches above the thing. Its eyes were opened, see. I just kept staring down at her. Her face had this look—with its extra lids and the little mouth curled up at either end. 'Poor thing,' I said. 'Poor pretty little thing.' I never knew where beauty could seep up from. Then I heard Whitehead, back of me, whimpering, 'No,' like I was planning to cross-examine her. 'Leave her be.' His voice hoarse, him without an overcoat, and it fifteen degrees out there.

Next, with sirens building, Rocky, interested as some kid touring the Merita Bread Plant, asked, 'Ain't it cold, John Bill?' (I figured Rock meant Whitehead's lack of muffler or coat.)

'Only at first,' the mortician answered, voice gone all soft and mothy.

'Oh,' thought I. 'Uh oh,' thought I.

By 12.40 we'd got Whitehead secured in holding cell no. 4. By 12.43 we had United Press International on the phone asking about hotel accommodation and Edna referring them all to her late husband's aunt's three-room boarding house.

Our jail's narrow cell-side hall is lit by twelve green-glass hanging lamps. Like the kind over pool tables. Cells are mercifully cut off from tonight's busy-ness out front by a swinging port-holed door (left over from the Chief's last kitchen remodelling). This door now muffles TV spots and the miked question-askers. I've never before seen such flashbulb blaze, what us bass fishermen call 'a feeding frenzy'. Never, except on TV.

I am right glad to hang back here. I sit studying John Bill—'suicide watch', him stripped of belt, his good black Parker fountain pen, two shoe-strings, one skinny black tie. (Most of your prison suicides happen in the first three hours of incarceration, for what it's worth.)

I feel like half a fugitive myself. I just know that future strangers will come right up to me on the street and grill me about tonight for as long as I live. Betty, I remember your hints about how nice Florida is, and for the first time ever, I've considered not living—in Falls.

From the public waiting-room, I hear blabbering: 'Outrage', 'Final Taboo', 'Some people sure are sickies.'

Out yonder, we already had us the Raleigh *News and Observer*, the *Greensboro News and Record*, *Rocky Mount Evening Telegram* and, of course, late but finally here, despite needing all of forty seconds to stroll across Main Street, our own *Falls Herald Traveler*. Plus, double-parked out front on Courthouse Square, with nobody bothering about its being illegal, CNN, with two ferry-sized trailers spiked with antennas enough to supervise the moon walk.

Concerning TV, and being on it or not, it's strictly Us and Them. Your National Power seems measured by how often you get on it. Or else stay off by choice. Well, our Edna sure feels qualified. She earns the title 'dispatcher' hands down. (You want to tell 'Mouth City' only your good news.) Her married daughters—all four—arrived by 3.30 a.m., toting garment bags containing Edna's five best Sunday dresses, plus a portable hair-burner. By 4.45 (huddled in that unlikely beauty parlor, cell no. 1), they'd done major home improvements to Edna's entire head and person.

By now, out there, holding forth behind a flannel board commandeered from the Second Baptist's Sunday School and made into a map with an X marking the 'Hearse Locale (Actual [presumed] Sexual Act Crime Scene)', Police Spokeswoman Edna McCabe is part Welcome-Wagon Hostess, part cold-front Weather Anchor Woman, part Jackie Kennedy in the bloodied suit on the Dallas cargo plane back to DC, part sweet ole apron-lady Aunt Bea. 'Any further clarifications, coffee, doughnuts, required, boys? Because, given the gravity of all this mess, you got you instant access, I mean, whatever . . . ' Suddenly, chain-smoking, chain-talking, chain-charming, Edna perches out yonder high behind the bailiff's desk, hair sprayed half-stiff as a cycle-patrolman's helmet, acting prim yet bossy in her suit all Jackie-pink: our Edna is sounding at least . . . semi-national.

Meantime, back here in shadow, in the guarded quiet, I'm still hunched outside our body snatcher's holding pen, gaping in at John Bill Whitehead—the homely, blinky, half-blind mortician, a mild town-joke till now. Suddenly he's Falls's most famous native since the oldest living Confederate soldier died here (possible homicide). Whitehead grins back, handcuffed, having arranged a white handkerchief just-so in his black jacket pocket. ('How can he hang hisself with a one hundred per cent cotton hankie?' I asked Rock, pleading on behalf of Whitehead's pitiful vanity.)

There was so much I longed to ask him, I became tongue-tied. Only jokes dawned on me, rude, crude salesman-type jokes: 'Was it as good for you as it was for her?' 'Did you, a gent, let her go first?' Stupid things. But my questions are real ones. What had scared me into losing supper was the idea that . . . if I let myself I might . . . I could, know why he did it.

I wanted to ask so many questions, but feared good guesses. Dear Christ, I mean, all this unseals all these possibilities.

The way I see it, sexual desire is surely the most living part of being alive, right? But to think of it in, actually inside, *the dead*: that sure put me off a week's feed and religion. What kind of God lets this stuff happen, then arranges it so's I'll be the one who comes upon it whilst on duty and holding that caliber of flashlight!

Dead folks? In my line of work, I see them bi-weekly, and battered besides. You try, but you never do get accustomed. You can't be vaccinated against the slow Novocaine shock that comes from glimpsing Old Death new again. How casually it stuns you! It's like the jolt of seeing 'skin', what boys here call 'full-out beaver'. Your mouth goes cotton. Without asking, your breath signs on for time-and-a-half. 'Aha' and 'Uh oh' blend. Your legs feel lead. Your mind, all of a sudden, is just so much blowaway thistledown. But tonight's? Debbie? She seemed different.

I used to make out Death to be a man. Poppa Time, ragged beard, bad sandals, sickle, attitude problem. But now Death means Female. And that's what's shook me so. Death can screw us pretty much any time she chooses. Astride, she can bear down on us, hard, and that, I reckon, I've long known. But now I had to consider a new possibility. You know, screwing her *back*.

Maybe I'm making no sense here.

I keep scanning John Bill Whitehead. But I never do ask Whitehead all that much. He just smiles, a milky smile, blinking out at me. Still has no idea.

'You thirsty? How's it going?' I say, to be nice. Somebody has to.

Folks hereabout have always known which single thing to remark about a tragedy over coffee at Millie's. It's like they vote on just one line, a show of hands, then stick with that.

Till now, it's always run maybe: *At least there were no children, that's one thing.*

Another oft-times goes: *If only they hadn't turned back to check if that gas stove was still running they'd be alive and happy today.*

Or: *It would've been worse if he hadn't already lived seventy-nine years and had him a full life. Still, it was a rough exit.* (This about poor old Cyril Mangum whose Chevy pick-up hit a 160-pound white-tail stag that was tossed into the air, came back down through the windshield and seven of whose ten-point antlers stabbed poor Mangum right there in the cab in his safety-belt.) *If just this single time he'd left the seat-belt flap unfastened, why, even as we speak, he'd be out playing golf. Loved his golf, that Cyril.*

And now, salted back here, safe from the world press, I wonder: what will we say about John Bill and his little victim girlfriend?

Does poor Falls, North Carolina, get more than its fair share of this grim stuff? Or is it that we're all bored and so far from Action Central, we just remember it longer?

And how will Whitehead ever explain it? If this loser ever tries, then your Deputy Wade Cutcheon sure wants to be right there.

I know it's way past me. But I can tell you, not seven hours after my 'career find', I understand at least this much: no fire or knifing, no stalker, no wicked if married Scout leader, not nothing's ever going to get inside me like this one tonight. Nothing. I bet no local act's ever likely to breed more rumors or sadness or more of this strange excitement. Just wait till every citizen of Falls who's buried a lady loved-one out of Nowell-Johnstone's hears about this over breakfast, then starts making mind-pictures that cannot be easily erased.

I'm slumped here, elbows on my knees, big chin propped in palms, remembering how school-smart we'd always figured weak John Bill to be. The principal's secretary told my sister that Whitehead was the only one for years with near a genius IQ. He was a couple of grades in front of me at school, from a family of dirt-poor mill-workers. He was always considered good at pinning up hall bulletin boards: TRAFFIC SAFETY WEEK SAVES

LIVES; PLANET OF THE WEEK; polite but panicky-acting, unable to take the slightest joke, and wearing glasses thick as the bottoms of Coca-Cola bottles when there *were* glass Coke bottles. His science-fair project—a working model of the solar system—one hooked to bicycle pedals, and him sitting at the center of these tinfoil moons and worlds, little feet cranking, smiling, watching what he made spin and orbit around him, the school's main laughing-stock.

My thought's a jumble. I have not slept. You probably hear that in my tone. It only just happened. But, Betty, hon? Already I suspect I know who's waiting for me in my very next dream. There, on ice, ahead, she is, so white. It feels like a date, a blind date, prearranged.

I didn't choose this.

I'm looking in at Whitehead. I get a little case of the shakes. He is not four feet away and grinning through the bars, combing his hair, just so, but with both wrists still cuffed. His white rubber gloves make his hands seem like ten separate condoms, busy digits each in need of being curbed. Seated on the metal bunk, his pointy shoes can't even reach the floor.

'Don't tell my wife?' he asks.

'Pardner, it's way past that now.' I feel sorry for him. But when I recollect my own lady kin, and the folded cash money I slipped him, honoring what-all he'd done on their behalf, and with them being female and buck naked and not bad looking for their age and state, and all too trusting and dead and totally alone with him . . . only then do I want to reach in through the bars, slap him, maybe bash his head against the concrete wall over the lower aluminum-frame bunk where he waits, legs swinging back and forth, like some boy dreading the principal's paddle. I admit I imagine slamming him till he is stretched out there, unconscious, and then . . . then what?

'Rocky, pal?' I holler. 'Want to come on back in here, spell me, please? Cause I'm starting to see things. All this brings up stuff a person'd rather keep . . . '

'Buried?'

'Buried.' I'm in pretty much total agreement. Rocky scuffles towards me from the blinking flash of the media-type-carnival out yonder. But as he moves nearer, I see that the boy is weaving. Dragging like somebody older. Young Rockford, a nice-looking, lanky fellow, doesn't act real happy to leave the reporters. He's coming through the low, green lights. Me, I rise to offer him my folding chair. It's only then that I see that this fine, big, rosy boy I've known all his life—excepting his Marine years—is crying. Rocky stands before me, his veiny hands a heavy load at either side of him. And he's sobbing like some kid too tired to know why he's cranky and can't admit to wanting sleep. Deputy Rockford Suggs II keeps on, right in front of Whitehead. Rock's nose is running, his eyes a sudden mess. Even John Bill quits swinging his legs. It's the guiltiest I've seen him get so far. First real guilt I've seen out of him.

I hug Rocky, in plain view of our town's overnight celebrity corpse-screwer. I hug Rocky and hear myself say, not knowing how I know, 'Makes you think of Nam, don't it?'

I feel the boy nod against me.

Rock speaks into my shoulder, arms up hard around me. 'Women not much bigger than our children here: but dead. Little women. We seen them all over. Some sitting up, by the side of the road, not a mark on them, like still expecting something.' And sobs.

A bit, I cry with him, in my way.

It's while I'm patting Rock and him pretty much boo-hooing, glad that no reporter will pry or know, I look back through the bars. At Whitehead. He is zooed like he deserves, I guess. And he's crying too, snuffling, and, with his rubber gloves, wiping his face. Tears for him will always be a turn-on. Tears'll always be a part of it—babies we all are. When it comes right down to it, we think we know decency and what local folks will do for other locals, but we ain't got clue number one as to what-all lurks in any human heart, much less lower-down especially, now do we? Ever?

Betty, hon, please tidy this up to sounding semi-official and keep it from seeming just personal.

As to the question: guilty or not guilty?

I am forced to say: guilty. If anybody is. Guilty of anything.

Whitehead, over the Hartman girl, allowing himself to: I got to say, yeah, Whitehead's guilty.

So 'The End'. Only, when is it, the end? If a live man, put in charge of a dead girl, can manage to fall in love with her and believe he's fallen hard enough to try stuff without notarized permission, then dear Lord, God, the possibilities.

I don't have the experience to judge any of this with.

Well, tonight only one thing is sure: Deputy Wade Watson Cutcheon here has plainly earned his keep. And now I'm heading home. To catch what helpful winks I can, and dream whatever scary dreams a person must.

I swear: the longer I live, the more of nothing, bigger percentage of nothing do I most firmly know.

Except, of course, one single saving fact.

I love my wife.

PEREGRINE HODSON
FOREIGN BODIES

It was our last day. We'd been in Morocco for a couple of months, travelling around, staying in cheap hotels where the walls were too thin and the taps didn't work and the sheets on the beds were patched and grey. Now we were in Rabat, and we didn't want to be there. It was different from Marrakesh: less African, more European, a place of white concrete buildings and office blocks—somewhere to wait for a flight, nothing more. We'd reached the end of the journey: a day and a night and then home. Perhaps that was our first mistake. We forgot where we were.

Amanda had already left: she couldn't get used to the dirt and the flies, and she missed her dog. Roddy had stayed on with Jane and me. His presence seemed to help. He could make Jane laugh when she didn't want to talk to me. Sometimes I wondered if he wasn't half in love with her.

Morocco had come between Jane and me. She found the attentions of Moroccan men oppressive. Each time she went into a bazaar, it happened: in the slow-moving crowds, everyone pressed close together, invisible hands pinched and pulled at her flesh. Once, she managed to grab someone's hand, and before the man could pull away, she wrenched the fingers back, and he gave a cry of pain. People laughed as he slid among them, holding his hand to his chest.

If I tried to explain the Moroccan men's behaviour in terms of Islam, we argued. Eventually we stopped talking about it. Instead, we spent hours in our hotel room reading, or avoiding the silence between us by making love. We had been together for almost three years, but we knew it wasn't going to last, and neither of us wanted to make the first move.

Our last afternoon in the hotel bedroom we lay on the metal-framed bed, smoking hashish, the fan in the ceiling spinning above us. We were naked, and our bodies were smooth with sweat. I'd read all the books we had with us except some poems by Pope, which the hashish made impenetrable. In the street below, a caged bird was singing, on and on. The sun-bleached sky through the half-open shutters was a colourless glare, alien and frightening. I moved towards Jane and she took me in her arms.

It wasn't Jane's fault. I don't think it was my fault either.

207

We were together, but she could have been anyone; so could I. Two strangers fucking in a Moroccan hotel.

When we woke up, the diagonal of sunlight had disappeared, and the room was darker. We took turns washing under the tepid trickle of water that was the shower. We both knew what had happened, but we'd been lovers long enough to pretend. Jane was thirsty and went downstairs to the café to drink some mint tea. I said I would be with her in an hour or so.

I sat on the rusty balcony and watched the sun setting over the city. It was Ramadan; and once it was dark, the lights of the mosque near the station were switched on, the muezzin began the call to evening prayer and the streets filled with people. They had been fasting since dawn—the devout had not even allowed themselves to swallow their own saliva. But during the hours of darkness, the fast was suspended. The night was carefree and permissive, and the crowds in the street below seemed to have a hectic, almost carnival energy.

Men walked hand in hand along the roadside, nudging each other to look at unveiled tourist women window-shopping, their grey-looking husbands walking uncertainly behind them. People in djellabas, women in veils, police with pistols and machine-guns, groups of young men in sharp silk shirts—all of them poured through the narrow streets. The mass of people had a strange electricity: I wanted to be part of it.

I went downstairs, left the key at the desk and walked among the passers-by. The endless succession of faces was hypnotic, and I lost track of time as I wandered through the lanes near the bazaar. It was after eight o'clock when I got back to the hotel.

I found Jane and Roddy at a restaurant on the corner of the square a few minutes walk away from the hotel. They were already eating, and Jane was annoyed that I was late. I had been lulled by the anonymous movement of the crowds and felt only half awake. Her anger exaggerated the distance between us.

The lights on the ugly cement fountain in the middle of the square changed colour from ambulance red, through sodium yellow to horror-movie green and blue, then back to red. The different colours caught our faces in turn as we watched a man with no legs, propped on a little wooden trolley, his hands in clumsy leather pads, pushing himself around the fountain. Roddy made a heartless joke, which fell flat, and ordered another bottle of wine. A man went by, lashing a donkey with a whip of jagged black rubber, cut from an old car tyre. Jane turned away. Some boys playing in the gutter noticed her reaction, and one began lashing a smaller companion with a bit of rope, whooping and laughing in Jane's direction.

We left the restaurant around eleven. Roddy and Jane walked together, while I followed a few paces behind. I didn't want to avoid their company but I couldn't think of anything to say. The trip was over, and we were going home, back to the real world.

Roddy and Jane stopped, and Jane pointed upwards, beyond the silhouettes of the buildings and the dazzle of the neon signs, towards the moon—a silver sphere misted by cloud, floating in the west. We decided to walk to the beach and watch the Atlantic waves breaking against the shore in the moonlight.

It was good to get away from the flashing signs and the smell of low-grade petrol. As the noise and the lights receded, we came to a field of white rocks and boulders. We walked among them for a while, towards the moon and the sound of the sea, until we came to some stone tablets overgrown by thorns and realized we were wandering through a graveyard.

Some of the gravestones had inscriptions. I stopped to decipher the sinuous Arabic lettering. Roddy and Jane went on ahead, their voices fading into the darkness and the roar of the waves.

I knelt down clumsily by one of the graves and let the sand slip through my fingers. I was drunk in a Muslim graveyard. The dead seemed indifferent to my sacrilege. It was a good place to be buried, I thought, with the heartbeat of the Atlantic reverberating in the stones, and the wind blowing from Africa.

As I lay propped against a gravestone, waiting for my head to clear, voices came towards me from the direction of the town, and two shadowy figures appeared among the white rocks. They were walking down to the sea. They didn't see me, and I watched them go by without saying anything.

It seemed to be getting colder.

I got up and followed the path that Jane and Roddy had

taken. The graveyard ended a short distance from the sea wall. The shoreline stretched away in a great curve, framed by the darkness of the sea and the night sky. I called out, and Roddy's voice answered me.

He and Jane were sitting together, two dark shapes on the luminous sand between the sea wall and the waves. I sat down beside them, and we watched the long white crests emerging from the darkness, one after another, vanishing against the shore.

'Every seventh wave,' said Jane. 'It's true. Every seventh wave's larger than the rest.'

I asked why.

'I don't know,' she said. 'I read it somewhere. It's just the way it happens.'

We counted the waves for a while.

'How far is America?' asked Roddy. 'Thousands of miles away. Each wave's travelled thousands of miles to get here.'

No one challenged what he said. Even if it wasn't true, it seemed the right thing to say. Then there was a shooting star.

We waited for another. It was the end of August, and we hoped it might be the beginning of a meteor shower.

'*Salaam!*' A figure silhouetted against the moonlit surf came towards us. He asked us in French what we were doing.

'*Eh, oui.*' He turned to look at the sea. '*La mer est belle.*'

He squatted down in the sand beside us, his back to the sea, and took out a packet of cigarettes. Did we want to smoke some *kif*?

The moon was almost directly overhead, and the man's face was in shadow. The wind had dropped. I asked Jane what she wanted to do.

'I don't mind,' she said. 'But we've got an early start tomorrow.'

As we passed the smouldering cigarette between us, two more figures emerged out of the darkness. Our companion shouted a greeting and invited them to share the remains of the cigarette. They were friends of his. They didn't understand us when we spoke to them in French, and after a minute or so they began talking softly to each other in Arabic. The man with the *kif* rolled another cigarette, and Jane said how good it was to be in a group of strangers, sharing *kif,* all looking at the same moon.

210

Even if there weren't any more shooting stars.

Two more men appeared from behind us. They were wearing uniforms. I was nervous until I saw that they weren't police. They were soldiers and everyone in the army smoked *kif*. One was tall and solid-looking; the other's uniform looked too large for him. They all began talking to each other in Arabic, and then the man with the *kif* turned to us: the soldiers wanted to know if Jane was married, and, if so, who was her husband?

We'd been asked the same question all over Morocco. I gave the usual explanation: things were different in the country we came from, women preferred to get married later, some didn't even want to get married at all. We were simply friends, travelling together.

The soldiers' boots squeaked as they squatted beside us in the sand.

'Busy place,' said Roddy. 'Rabat on a Saturday night.'

Jane and Roddy laughed, and the man with the *kif* asked why they were laughing. I said they were surprised how many people there were. The man took the cigarette from his mouth and threw it towards the ocean. Then he spat on the ground. The soldiers were whispering with the other two men. I heard the word '*bint*'—Arabic for 'woman'—and saw one of the soldiers glance towards Jane. Something wasn't right. Maybe it was too much wine and hashish. I got up. Jane asked what I was doing.

'I don't know,' I said. 'I think we'd better go.'

The man with the *kif* was already on his feet. He stretched out his hand towards me. Jane was asking if there was anything the matter.

'We've got to go,' I said. 'Now.'

Jane and Roddy began to get their things together, but it seemed to be taking them an age. The man was standing between me and the sea wall. The moon was bright as an arc light. Everything was turning into something else.

The man grabbed at my shirt. Jane screamed. Roddy shouted, 'Fuck off!' I pulled away. The two soldiers came at me. The big one bent down, and a handful of sand hit me in the face, blinding me. A fist smashed against the side of my head. I got one eye open as someone kicked at my crotch. I managed to catch the leg and twisted the man over. Then I saw the knife. The big one had a knife. A flash in the moonlight.

'Knives!' I shouted. 'They've got knives!'

Someone whistled, and another shrill whistle answered from the shadow of the sea wall. There now seemed to be six or seven of them. A trap. I was in front of Jane, Roddy was beside her. The men were in a circle around us. The soldier with the knife shouted something and waved his arm at me—the blade was invisible in the dark. Someone lunged at Jane.

'Get help, Roddy!' I shouted. 'I'll stay with Jane!'

They wouldn't want a witness. Some would follow Roddy. He could lose them in the dark.

The soldier with the knife said something to the others, and the shadows in front of us spread out.

Roddy darted forwards, turned and ran towards the sea wall. Two shadows ran after him, then another. The man with the *kif* whistled over his shoulder and turned towards us.

'*L'argent!*' He pointed at Jane's bag—it was still on her shoulder. In the darkness further along the beach, I could hear shouting.

'*L'argent!*'

His voice had a sharp edge. He was nervous. Jane started to give him the bag, but, as she lifted it over her head, the man snatched at it, jerking her neck. Some of the bag's contents fell on the sand, the man grabbed at them and ran off into the dark. The soldier with the knife took a step forwards.

'*La fille,*' he said.

A shadow moved to the right of me. A fist slammed into my face. The big soldier was pulling Jane's hair, yanking her head back, holding the knife at her throat. He tugged at her hair, hard, and she screamed. He let go, grabbed her skirt and slit it from the hem to the waist.

Everyone else had gone. Now there were just the two soldiers, Jane and me. I could manage the soldier in front of me, but the big one had the knife and he was pointing it at Jane's face. His other hand was under her skirt.

Jane cried out. The soldier slapped her, grabbed at her waist and cut the elastic.

The knife was at her belly.

'Stay alive,' I said.

The man gestured with the knife, and Jane lay down on the ground. He pulled up her skirt and waved her legs apart with the knife, then handed it to the soldier in front of me, who held the blade at my throat. The big soldier undid his trouser buttons, knelt down and spat between her legs.

'It doesn't matter,' said Jane. 'It doesn't mean anything.'

The man pushed her legs further apart and got on top of her.

The soldier jabbed the knife at my face.

'Let them do it,' said Jane. 'It's not important. I want to get out of this alive.'

It was the first time I saw someone fucking another person.

It didn't last long, maybe a couple of minutes. Then he stood up and took the knife, and the other soldier started. Jane began to laugh, on the edge of hysteria.

'He can't get it up. It's a pathetic little thing.'

The soldier slapped her and pressed her hands to the ground. He lay on top of her for a while and then got up. The soldier with the knife at my throat muttered something and moved towards Jane. I guessed they would kill me first, then her.

The big soldier kicked her legs apart, undid his trousers and began masturbating. If I rushed him, I might get the knife, I might not. If they killed me, they would kill her. I measured the distance between me and the man in front of me.

The soldier with the knife was now lying on top of Jane. I called her name softly.

'Sshhh!' she said. 'I'm OK. He's got the knife at my throat.'

I was less than ten feet away. I could see Jane's hair in the moonlight. The soldier was moving about on top of her. I could see the rhythm of his body, the steady, instinctive motion of his hips. I could hear him breathing through his nostrils. I caught the ammoniac smell of sex. The bright, silver-blue light of the moon shone over everything.

His breathing was getting louder, little snorts of air that turned into deeper, heavier grunts of effort.

We were caught in a place where it seemed we were the only people alive, moving and breathing under the stars.

The sky disappeared, as a fist slammed into my eyes.

The soldier was still on top of Jane. He was breathing

213

heavily, he was about to come. I could predict the moment. He grunted, and the air in his throat gurgled into a final gasp.

He pushed himself up from Jane's body. He was still holding the knife. He stood up and said something to the soldier in front of me. I called out to Jane.

'The bastard,' she said. She was crying. 'The bastard.'

'*L'argent!*' The soldier with the knife pressed the flat of the blade under my chin; the metal was cold and smooth. I lifted my head slightly. Someone's hand found the money belt at my waist. The man behind me clutched my hair and pulled my head back, while the soldier with the knife tore my shirt open.

Fingernails scratched my stomach. There was a sharp tug at my waist, and the soldier stepped back with the money belt in his hand.

Jane had got to her feet. Her bag was still hanging from her neck. She took it off and threw it on the ground. The soldier holding my hair let go and picked up the bag.

They were going through our things. We had a chance. If Jane was OK, we could make a run for it.

'It hurts,' she said. 'The bastard hurt me.'

She could hardly stand and began to sob. If we tried running, she wouldn't make it.

The big one shouted something in Arabic and spat on the ground. Suddenly they were gone.

I held Jane in my arms.

The waves were still breaking on the shore in the moonlight. We walked towards the sea and stepped into the milky surf. She washed herself, and the water glowed and sparkled with phosphorescence.

We stood in each other's arms, not saying anything, the sea gently rocking us.

A beam of light flashed on the top of the sea wall and swung across the water. We held each other closer. There were men's voices. Another beam of light raked the empty beach. Someone was calling our names.

I kissed her and tasted the salt on my lips. We let go of each other and walked towards the shore.

214

PAUL AUSTER
DIZZY

One sultry August afternoon I went out to Arlington and put a thousand on a long shot to win the third race. I did crazy things as a matter of routine back then, and when the colt came in by half a length at forty to one, I knew there was a God in heaven and that he was smiling down at my craziness.

The winnings provided me with the clout to do the thing I most wanted to do, and I promptly set out to turn my dream into reality. I requested a private counsel with Bingo Walsh in his penthouse apartment overlooking Lake Michigan. Bingo was right-hand man to Boss O'Malley, who had one of the largest setups in Cook County. Gambling parlours, numbers operations, whorehouses, protection squads, slot machines—Bingo managed all these enterprises with a firm hand, accountable to no one but the boss himself. I was lucky to have him as my mentor.

Once I laid out the plan to him and he got over his initial shock, he grudgingly gave me the green light. It wasn't that he thought the proposition was unworthy, but I think he was disappointed in me for setting my sights so low. He was grooming me for a place in the inner circle, and here I was telling him that I wanted to go my own way and open a nightclub that would occupy my energies to the exclusion of all else. I could see how he might interpret it as an act of betrayal, and I had to tread carefully around that trap with some fancy footwork. Luckily, my mouth was in good form that evening, and by showing how many advantages would accrue to him in terms of both profit and pleasure, I eventually brought him around.

'My forty grand can cover the whole deal,' I said. 'Another guy in my shoes would tip his hat and say so long, but that's not how I conduct business. You're my pal, Bingo, and I want you to have a piece of the action. No money down, no work to fuss with, no liabilities, but for every dollar I earn, I'll give you twenty-five cents. Fair is fair, right? You gave me my chance, and now I'm in a position to return the favour. Loyalty has to count for something in this world, and I'm not about to forget where my luck came from. This won't be any two-bit cheese joint for the hoi polloi. I'm

Opposite: Jerome ('Dizzy') Dean playing for the Chicago Cubs, September 1938.

talking Gold Coast with all the trimmings. A full-scale restaurant
with a Frog chef, top-notch floor show, beautiful girls slithering
out of the woodwork in skin-tight gowns. It'll give you a hard-on
just to walk in there, Bingo. You'll have the best seat in the house,
and on nights when you don't show up, your table will sit there
empty—no matter how many people are waiting outside the door.'

He haggled me up to fifty per cent, but I was expecting some
give-and-take and didn't make an issue of it. The important thing
was to win his blessing, and I did that by jollying him along, steadily
wearing down his defences with my friendly, accommodating
attitude, and in the end, just to show how classy he was, he offered
to kick in an extra ten thousand to see that I did up the place right.
I didn't care. All I wanted was my nightclub, and with Bingo's fifty
per cent subtracted from the take, I was still going to come out
ahead. There were numerous benefits in having him as a partner,
and I would have been kidding myself to think I could get along
without him. His half would guarantee me protection from
O'Malley (who *ipso facto* became the third partner) and help keep
the cops from breaking down the door. When you threw in his
connections with the Chicago liquor board, the commercial laundry
companies and the local talent agents, losing that fifty per cent
didn't seem like such a shabby compromise after all.

I called the place Mr Vertigo's. It was smack in the heart of
the city at West Division and North LaSalle, and its flashing neon
sign went from pink to blue to pink as a dancing girl took turns
with a cocktail shaker against the night sky. The rhumba rhythm
of those lights made your heart beat faster and your blood grow
warm, and once you caught the little stutter-step syncopation in
your pulse, you didn't want to be anywhere except where the music
was. Inside, the decor was a blend of high and low, a swank sort of
big town comfort mixed with naughty innuendos and an easy,
roadhouse charm. I worked hard on creating that atmosphere, and
every nuance and effect was planned to the smallest detail: from
the lip rouge on the hat-check girl to the colour of the dinner
plates, from the design of the menus to the socks on the
bartender's feet. There was room for fifty tables, a good-size dance
floor, an elevated stage and a long mahogany bar along a side
wall. It cost me every cent of the fifty thousand to do it up the way

I wanted, but when the place finally opened on 31 December 1937, it was a thing of sumptuous perfection. I launched it with one of the great New Year's Eve parties in Chicago history, and by the following morning Mr Vertigo's was on the map. I was there every night, strolling among customers in my white dinner-jacket and patent leather shoes, spreading good cheer with my cocky smiles and quick-tongued patter. It was a terrific spot for me, and I loved every minute I spent in that raucous emporium. If I hadn't messed up and blown my life apart, I'd probably still be there today. As it was, I only got to have those three and a half years. I was one hundred per cent responsible for my own downfall, but knowing that doesn't make it any less painful to remember. I was all the way at the top when I stumbled, and it ended in a real Humpty Dumpty for me, a spectacular swallow-dive into oblivion.

But no regrets. I had a good dance for my money, and I'm not going to say I didn't. The club turned into the number-one hot spot in Chicago, and in my own small way I was just as much a celebrity as any of the bigwigs who came in there. I hobnobbed with judges and city councilmen and ball players, and what with all the showgirls and chorines to audition for the flesh parades I presented at eleven and one every night, there was no lack of opportunity to indulge in bedroom sports. Dixie and I were still an item when Mr Vertigo's opened, but my carryings-on wore her patience thin, and within six months she'd moved on to another address. Then came Sally, then came Jewel, then came a dozen others: leggy brunettes, chain-smoking redheads, big-butted blondes. At one point I was shacked up with two girls at the same time, a pair of out-of-work actresses named Cora and Billie. I liked them both the same, they liked each other as much as they liked me, and by pulling together we managed to produce some interesting variations on the old tune. Every now and then, my habits led to medical inconveniences (a dose of the clap, a case of crabs), but nothing that put me out of commission for very long. It might have been a putrid way to live, but I was happy with the hand I'd been dealt, and my only ambition was to keep things exactly as they were. Then in September 1939, just three days after the German army invaded Poland, Dizzy Dean walked into Mr Vertigo's and it all started to come undone.

I have to go back to explain it, all the way back to my tykehood in St Louis. That's where I fell in love with baseball, and before I was out of diapers I was a dyed-in-the-wool Cardinals fan, a Redbird rooter for life. From April to October I never missed a box score, and I could recite the batting average of every player on the squad, from hot dogs like Frankie Frisch and Pepper Martin to the lowest journeyman scrub gathering splinters on the bench. This went on during the good years, and it continued during the bad years that followed. No matter how dark things got for me, I still kept up with my team. They won the pennant in '30 and '31, and those victories did a lot to buck up my spirits, to keep me going through all the trouble and adversity of that time. As long as the Cards were winning, something was right with the world, and it wasn't possible to fall into total despair.

That's where Dizzy Dean enters the story. The team dropped to seventh place in '32, but it didn't matter. Dean was the hottest, flashiest, loudest-mouthed rookie ever to hit the majors, and he turned a crummy ball club into a loosey-goosey hillbilly circus. Brag and cavort as he did, that cornpone rube backed up his boasts with some of the sweetest pitching this side of heaven. His rubber arm threw smoke; his control was uncanny; his windup was a wondrous machine of arms and legs and power, a beautiful thing to behold. By the time I got to Chicago and settled in as Bingo's protégé, Dizzy was an established star, a big-time force on the American scene. People loved him for his brashness and talent, his crazy manglings of the English language, his brawling, boyish antics and fuck-you pizzazz, and I loved him, too, I loved him as much as anyone in the world. With life growing more comfortable for me all the time, I was in a position to catch the Cards in action whenever they came to town. In '33, the year Dean broke the record by striking out seventeen batters in a game, they looked like a first division outfit again. They'd added some new players to the roster, and with thugs like Joe Medwick, Leo Durocher and Rip Collins around to quicken the pace, the Gas House Gang was beginning to gel. 'Thirty-four turned out to be their glory year, and I don't think I've ever enjoyed a baseball season as much as that one. Dizzy's kid brother Paul won nineteen games, Dizzy won thirty, and the team fought from ten games back to overtake the Giants and win the pennant. That was the first year the World Series was broadcast on the radio, and I got to listen to all seven games sitting at home in Chicago. Dizzy beat the Tigers in the first game, and when Frisch sent him in as a pinch runner in the fourth, the lummox promptly got beaned with a wild throw and was knocked unconscious. The next day's headlines announced: X-RAYS OF DEAN'S HEAD REVEAL NOTHING. He came back to pitch the following afternoon but lost, and then, just two days later, he shut out Detroit 11–0 in the final game, laughing at the Tigers hitters each time they swung and missed at his fastballs. The press cooked up all kinds of names for that team: the Galloping Gangsters, River Rowdies from the Mississippi, the Clattering Cardinals. Those Gas Housers loved to rub it in, and when the score of the final game got out of hand in the late innings, the Tiger fans responded by pelting Medwick with a ten-minute barrage of fruits and vegetables in left field. The only way they could finish the series was for Judge Landis, the commissioner of baseball, to step in and pull Medwick off the field for the last three outs.

Six months later, I was sitting in a box with Bingo and the boys when Dean opened the new season against the Cubs in Chicago. In the first inning, with two down and a man on base, the Cubs' cleanup hitter Freddie Lindstrom sent a wicked line drive up the middle that caught Dizzy in the leg and knocked him down. My heart skipped a beat or two when I saw the stretcher gang run out and carry him off the field, but no permanent damage was done, and five days later he was back on the mound in Pittsburgh, where he hurled a five-hit shutout for his first win of the season. He went on to have another bang-up year, but the Cubs were the team of destiny in 1935, and by knocking off a string of twenty-one straight wins at the end of the season, they pushed past the Cards and stole the flag. I can't say I minded too much. The town went gaga for the Cubbies, and what was good for Chicago was good for business, and what was good for business was good for me. I cut my teeth on the gambling rackets in that series, and once the dust had settled, I'd manoeuvred myself into such a strong position that Bingo rewarded me with a den of my own.

On the other hand, that was the year when Dizzy's ups and downs began to affect me in a far too personal way. I wouldn't call it an obsession at that point, but after watching him go down in the first inning of the opener at Wrigley—so soon after the skull-clunking in the '34 series—I began to sense that a cloud was gathering around him. It didn't help matters when his brother's arm went dead in '36, but even worse was what happened in a game against the Giants that summer when Burgess Whitehead scorched a liner that hit him just above the right ear. The ball was hit so hard that it caromed into left field on a fly. Dean went down again, and though he regained consciousness in the locker-room seven or eight minutes later, the initial diagnosis was a fractured skull. It turned out to be a bad concussion, which left him woozy for a couple of weeks, but an inch or so the other way and the big guy would have been pushing up daisies instead of going on to win twenty-four games for the season.

The following spring, my man continued to curse and scuffle and raise hell, but that was only because he didn't know any better. He triggered brawls with his brushback pitches, was called for balks two games in a row and decided to stage a sit-down strike on the mound, and when he stood up at a banquet and called the new league president a crook, the resulting fracas led to some fine cowboy theatre, especially after Diz refused to put his signature on a self-incriminating formal retraction. 'I ain't signin' nothin',' was what he said, and without that signature Ford Frick had no choice but to back down and rescind Dean's suspension. I was proud of him for behaving like such a two-fisted asshole, but the truth was that the suspension would have kept him out of the All-Star Game, and if he hadn't pitched in that meaningless exhibition, he might have been able to hold off the hour of his doom a little longer.

They played in Washington, DC, that year, and Dizzy started for the National League. He breezed through the first two innings in workmanlike fashion, and then, after two were gone in the third, he gave up a single to DiMaggio and a long home run to Gehrig. Earl Averill was next, and when the Cleveland outfielder lined Dean's first pitch back to the mound, the curtain suddenly dropped on the greatest right-hander of the century. It didn't look like much to worry about at the time. The ball hit him on the left foot, bounced over to Billy Herman at second, and Herman threw to first for the out. When Dizzy went limping off the field, no one thought twice about it, not even Dizzy himself.

That was the famous broken toe. If he hadn't rushed back into action before he was ready, it probably would have mended in due time. But the Cardinals were slipping out of the pennant race and needed him on the mound, and the dumb-cluck yokel fool assured them he was OK. He was hobbling around on a crutch, the toe was so swollen he couldn't get his shoe on, and yet he donned his uniform and went out and pitched. Like all giants among men, Dizzy Dean thought he was immortal, and even though the toe was too tender for him to pivot on his left foot, he gutted it out for the whole nine innings. The pain caused him to alter his natural delivery, and the result was that he put too much pressure on his arm. He developed a sore wing after that first game, and then, to compound the mischief, he went on throwing for another month. After six or seven times around, it got so bad that he had to be yanked just three pitches into one of his starts. Diz was lobbing cantaloupes by then, and there was nothing for it but to hang up his spikes and sit out the rest of the season.

Even so, there wasn't a fan in the country who thought he was finished. The common wisdom was that a winter of idle repose would fix what ailed him and come April he'd be his old unbeatable self again. But he struggled through spring training, and then, in one of the great bombshells in sports history, St Louis dealt him to the Cubs for 185,000 dollars in cash and two or three warm bodies. I knew there was no love lost between Dean and Branch Rickey, the Cards' general manager, but I also knew that Rickey wouldn't have unloaded him if he thought there was some spit left in the appleknocker's arm. I couldn't have been happier that Dizzy was coming to Chicago, but at the same time I knew his coming meant that he was at the end of the road. My worst fears had been borne out, and at the ripe old age of twenty-seven or twenty-eight, the world's top pitcher was a has-been.

Still, he provided some good moments that first year with the Cubs. Mr Vertigo's was only four months old when the season started, but I managed to sneak off to the park three or four times to watch the Dizmeister crank out a few more innings from his battered arm. There was an early game against the Cards that I remember well, a classic grudge match pitting old teammates against each other, and he won that showdown on guile and junk, keeping the hitters off-stride with an assortment of dipsy-doodle floaters and change-ups. Then, late in the season, with the Cubs pushing hard for another pennant, Chicago manager Gabby Harnett stunned everyone by giving Dizzy the nod for a do-or-die start against the Pirates. The game was a genuine knuckle-biter, joy and despair riding on every pitch, and Dean, with less than nothing to offer, eked out a win for his new home town. He almost repeated the miracle in the second game of the World Series, but the Yanks finally got to him in the eighth, and when the assault continued in the ninth and Harnett took him out for a reliever, Dizzy left the mound to some of the wildest, most thunderous applause I've ever heard. The whole joint was on its feet, clapping and cheering and whistling for the big lug, and it went on for so long and was so loud, some of us were blinking away tears by the time it was over.

That should have been the end of him. The gallant warrior takes his last bow and shuffles off into the sunset. I would have accepted that and given him his due, but Dean was too thick to get it, and the farewell clamour fell on deaf ears. That's what galled me: the son of a bitch didn't know when to stop. Casting all dignity aside, he came back and played for the Cubs again, and if the '38 season had been pathetic—with a few bright spots sprinkled in—'39 was pure, unadulterated darkness. His arm hurt so much he could barely throw. Game after game he warmed the bench, and the brief moments he spent on the mound were an embarrassment. He was lousy, lousier than a hobo's mutt, not even the palest facsimile of what he'd once been. I suffered for him, I grieved for him, but at the same time I thought he was the dumbest yahoo clod on the face of the earth.

That was pretty much how things stood when he walked into Mr Vertigo's in September. The season was winding down, and with the Cubs well out of the pennant race, it didn't cause too much of a stir when Dean showed up one crowded Friday night with his missus and a gang of two or three other couples. It certainly wasn't the moment for a heart-to-heart talk about his future, but I made a point of going over to his table and welcoming him to the club. 'Pleased you could make it, Diz,' I said, offering him my hand. 'I'm a St Louis boy myself and I've been following you since the day you broke in. I've always been your number-one backer.'

'The pleasure's all mine, pal,' he said, engulfing my little hand in his enormous mitt and giving a cordial shake. He started to flash one of those quick, brush-off smiles when his expression suddenly grew puzzled. He frowned for a second, searching his memory for some lost thing, and when it didn't come to him, he looked deep into my eyes as if he thought he could find it there. 'I know you, don't I?' he said. 'I mean, this ain't the first time we've met. I just can't place where it was. Way back somewhere, ain't I right?'

'I don't think so, Diz. Maybe you caught a glimpse of me one day in the stands, but we've never talked before.'

'Shit. I could swear you ain't no stranger to me. Damnedest feeling in the world it is. Oh well.' He shrugged, beaming me one of his big yap grins. 'It don't matter none, I guess. You sure got a swell joint here, mac.'

'Thanks, champ. The first round's on me. I hope you and your friends have a good time.'

'That's why we're here, kid.'

'Enjoy the show. If you need anything, just holler.'

I'd played it as cool as I could, and I walked away feeling I'd handled the situation fairly well. I hadn't sucked up to him, and at the same time I hadn't insulted him for going to the dogs. I was Mr Vertigo, the downtown sharpie with the smooth tongue and elegant manners, and I wasn't about to let Dean know how much his plight concerned me. Seeing him in the flesh had broken the spell somewhat, and in the natural course of things I probably would have written him off as just another nice guy down on his luck. Why should I care about him? Whizzy Dizzy was on his way out, and pretty soon I wouldn't have to think about him any more. But that's not the way it happened. It was Dean himself who kept the thing alive, and while I'm not going to pretend we became bosom buddies, he stayed in close enough contact to make it impossible for me to forget him. If he'd just drifted off the way he was supposed to, none of it would have turned out as badly as it did.

I didn't see him again until the start of the next season. It was April 1940 by then, the war in Europe was going full tilt, and Dizzy was back—back for yet another stab at reviving his tumbledown career. When I picked up the paper and read that he'd signed another contract with the Cubs, I nearly choked on my salami sandwich. Who was he kidding? 'The ol' soup bone ain't the buggy whip it used to be,' he said, but Christ, he just loved the game too damned much not to give it another try. All right, dumbbell, I said to myself, see if I care. If you want to humiliate yourself in front of the world, that's your business, but don't count on me to feel sorry for you.

Then, out of the blue, he wandered back into the club one night and greeted me like a long-lost brother. Dean wasn't someone who drank, so it couldn't have been booze that made him act like that, but his face lit up when he saw me, and for the next five minutes he gave me an all-out dose of herkimer-jerkimer bonhomie. Maybe he was still stuck on the idea that we knew each other, or maybe he thought I was somebody important, I don't know, but the upshot was that he couldn't have been more delighted to see me. How to resist a guy like that? I'd done everything I could to harden my heart against him, and yet he came on in such a friendly way that I couldn't help but succumb to the attention. He was still the great Dean, after all, my benighted soulmate and alter ego, and once he opened up to me like that, I fell right back into the snare of my old bedevilment.

I wouldn't say that he became a regular at the club, but he stopped by often enough over the next six weeks for us to strike up more than just a passing acquaintance. He came in alone a few times to eat an early supper (dowsing every dish with gobs of Lea & Perrins steak sauce), and I'd sit with him shooting the breeze while he chomped down his food. We skirted baseball talk and mostly stuck to the horses, and since I gave him a couple of excellent tips on where to put his money, he began listening to my advice. I should have spoken up then and told him what I thought about his comeback, but even after he muddled through his first starts of the season, disgracing himself every time he stepped on to the field, I didn't say a word. I'd grown too fond of him by then, and with the sad sack trying so hard to make good, I couldn't bring myself to tell him the truth.

After a couple of months, his wife Pat persuaded him to go down to the minors to work on a new delivery. The idea was that he'd make better progress out of the spotlight—a frantic ploy if ever there was one, since all it did was support the delusion that there was still some hope for him. That's when I finally got up the nerve to say something, but I didn't have the guts to push hard enough.

'Maybe it's time, Diz,' I said. 'Maybe it's time to pack it in and head home to the farm.'

'Yeah,' he said, looking about as dejected as a man can look. 'You're probably right. Problem is, I ain't fit for nothin' but throwin' baseballs. I flunk out this time, and I'm up shit's creek, Walt. I mean, what else can a bum like me do with hisself?'

Plenty of things, I thought, but I didn't say it, and later that week he left for Tulsa. Never had a great one fallen so far so fast. He spent a long miserable summer in the Texas League, travelling the same dusty circuit he'd demolished with fastballs ten years before. This time he could barely hold his own, and the rinky-dinks and Mickey Mousers sprayed his pitches all over the lot. Old delivery or new, the verdict was clear, but Dizzy went on busting his chops and didn't let the rough treatment get him down. Once he'd showered and dressed and left the park, he'd go back to his hotel room with a stack of racing forms and start phoning his bookies. I handled a number of bets for him that summer, and every time he called we'd jaw for five or ten minutes and catch up on each other's news. The incredible thing to me was how calmly he accepted his disgrace. The guy had turned himself into a laughing-stock, and yet he seemed to be in good spirits and as gabby and full of jokes as ever. What was the use of arguing? I figured it was only a matter of time now, so I played along with him and kept my thoughts to myself. Sooner or later, he was bound to see the light.

The Cubs recalled him in September. They wanted to see if the bush-league experiment had paid off, and while his performance was hardly encouraging. it wasn't as dreadful as it might have been. Mediocre was the word for it—a couple of close wins, a couple of shellackings—and therein hung the final chapter of the story. By some ditsy, screwball logic, the Cubs decided that

Dean had shown enough of his old flair to warrant another season, and so they went ahead and asked him back. I didn't find out about the new contract until after he left town for the winter, but when I did, something inside me finally snapped. I stewed about it for months. I fretted and worried and sulked, and by the time spring came around again, I understood what had to be done. It wasn't as if I felt there was a choice. Destiny had chosen me as its instrument, and gruesome as the task might have been, saving Dizzy was the only thing that mattered. If he couldn't do it himself, then I'd have to step in and do it for him.

Even now, I'm hard-pressed to explain how such a twisted, evil notion could have wormed its way into my head. I actually thought it was my duty to persuade Dizzy Dean that he didn't want to live any more. Stated in such bald terms, the whole thing smacks of insanity, but that was precisely how I planned to rescue him: by talking him into his own murder. If nothing else, it proved how sick my soul had become. Maybe it wouldn't have happened if he'd pitched for some town other than St Louis. Maybe it wouldn't have happened if our nicknames hadn't been so similar. I don't know. I don't know anything, but the fact was that a moment came when I couldn't tell the difference between us any more. His triumphs were my triumphs, and when bad luck finally caught up with him and his career fell apart, his disgrace was my disgrace. I couldn't stand to live through it again, and little by little I began to lose my grip. For his own good, Dizzy had to die, and I was just the man to urge him into making the right decision. Not only for his sake, but for my sake as well. I had the weapon, I had the arguments, I had the power of madness on my side. I would destroy Dizzy Dean, and in doing so I would finally destroy myself.

The Cubs hit Chicago for the home opener on 10 April. I got Diz on the horn that same afternoon and asked him to stop by my office, explaining that something important had come up. He tried to get me to come out with it, but I told him it was too big to discuss on the phone. If you're interested in a proposition that will turn your life around, I said, you'll come. He was tied up until after dinner, so we set the appointment for eleven o'clock the next morning. He showed up fifteen minutes late, sauntering in with that loose-jointed stride of his and rolling a toothpick around on his tongue. He was wearing a worsted blue suit and a tan cowboy hat, and while he'd put on a few pounds since I'd seen him last, his complexion had a healthy tint after six weeks in the Cactus League sun. As usual, he was all smiles when he walked in, and he spent the first couple of minutes talking about how different the club looked in the daytime without any customers in it. 'Reminds me of an empty ballpark,' he said. 'Kinda creepy like. Still as a tomb, and a helluva lot bigger.'

I told him to take a seat and fixed him up with a root beer from the ice box behind my desk. 'This will take a few minutes,' I said, 'and I don't want you getting thirsty while we talk.' I could feel my hands starting to shake, so I poured myself a shot of Jim Beam and took a couple of sips. 'How's the wing, old timer?' I said, settling back into my leather chair and doing my best to look calm.

'Same as it was. Feels like there's a bone stickin' out of my elbow.'

'You got knocked around pretty hard in spring training, I heard.'

'Them's just practice games. They don't mean nothin'.'

'Sure. Wait till it really counts, right?'

He caught the cynicism in my voice and gave a defensive shrug, then reached for the cigarettes in his shirt pocket. 'Well, little guy,' he said, 'what's the scoop?' He shook out a Lucky from his pack and lit up, blowing a big gust of smoke in my direction. 'From the way you talked on the phone, it sounded like a matter of life and death.'

'It is. That's exactly what it is.'

'How so? You got a patent on a new bromide or somethin'? Christ, you come up with a medicine to cure sick arms, Walt, and I'll give you half my pay for the next ten years.'

'I've got something better than that, Diz. And it won't cost you a cent.'

'Everything costs, fella. It's the law of the land.'

'I don't want your money. I want to save you, Diz. Let me help you, and the torment you've been living in these past four years will be gone.'

'Yeah?' he said, smiling as if I'd just told a moderately amusing joke. 'And how you aimin' to do that?'

'Anyway you like. The method's not important. The only thing that counts is that you go along with it—and that you understand why it has to be done.'

'You've lost me, kid. I don't know what you're talkin' about.'

'A great person once said to me: "When a man comes to the end of the line, the only thing he really wants is death." Does that make it any clearer? I heard those words a long time ago, but I was too dumb to figure out what they meant. Now I know, and I'll tell you something, Diz—they're true. They're the truest words any man ever spoke.'

Dean burst out laughing. 'You're some kidder, Walt. You got that wacko sense of humour, and it don't never let up. That's why I like you so much. There ain't no one else in this town that comes out with the ballsy things you do.'

I sighed at the man's stupidity. Dealing with a clown like that was hard work and the last thing I wanted was to lose my patience. I took another sip of my drink, sloshing the spicy liquid around in my mouth for a couple of seconds, and swallowed. 'Listen, Diz,' I said. 'I've been where you are. Twelve, thirteen years ago, I was sitting on top of the world. I was the best at what I did, in a class by myself. And let me tell you, what you've accomplished on the ball field is nothing compared to what I could do. Next to me, you're no taller than a pygmy, an insect, a fucking bug in the rug. Do you hear what I'm saying? Then, just like that, something happened, and I couldn't go on. But I didn't hang around and make people feel sorry for me, I didn't turn myself into a joke. I called it quits, and then I went on and made another life for myself. That's what I've been hoping and praying would happen to you. But you just don't get it, do you? Your fat hick brain's too clogged with cornbread and molasses to get it.'

'Wait a second,' Dizzy said, wagging his finger at me as a sudden, unexpected glow of delight spread across his face. 'Wait just a second. Now I know who you are. Shit, I knowed it all along. You're that kid, ain't you? You're that goddamned kid. Walt . . . Walt the Wonder Boy. Christ almighty. My daddy took me and Paul and Elmer out to the fair one day in Arkansas, and we seen you do your stuff. Fuckin' out of this world it was. I always wondered what happened to you. And here you are, sittin' right across from me. I can't fuckin' believe it.'

'Believe it, friend. When I told you I was great, I meant great like nobody else. Like a comet streaking across the sky.'

'You were great, all right, I'll vouch for that. The greatest thing I ever saw.'

'And so were you, big man. As great as they come. But you're over the hill now, and it breaks my heart to see what you're doing to yourself. Let me help you, Diz. Death isn't so terrible. Everybody has to die sometime, and once you get used to the idea, you'll see that now is better than later. If you give me the chance, I can spare you the shame. I can give you back your dignity.'

'You're really serious, ain't you?'

'You bet I am. As serious as I've ever been in my life.'

'You're off your trolley, Walt. You're fucking looped outta your gourd.'

'Let me kill you, and the last four years will be forgotten. You'll be great again, champ. You'll be great again, forever.'

I was going too fast. He'd thrown me off balance with that Wonder Boy talk, and instead of circling back and modifying my approach, I was charging ahead at breakneck speed. I'd wanted to build up the pressure slowly, to lull him with such elaborate, airtight arguments that he'd eventually come round on his own. That was the point: not to force him into it, but to make him see the wisdom of the plan for himself. I wanted him to want what I wanted, to feel so convinced by my proposal that he would actually beg me to do it, and all I'd done was leave him behind, scaring him off with my threats and half-baked platitudes. No wonder he thought I was crazy. I'd let the whole thing get out of hand, and now, just when we should have been getting started, he was already standing up and making his way for the exit.

I wasn't worried about that. I'd locked the door from the inside, and it couldn't be opened without the key—which happened to be in my pocket. Still, I didn't want him pulling on the knob and rattling the frame. He might have started shouting at me then to let him out, and with half a dozen people working in the kitchen at that hour, the ruckus surely would have brought them running. So, thinking only about that small point and ignoring the larger consequences, I opened the drawer of my desk and removed the gun. That was the mistake that finally did me in. By pointing that gun at Dizzy, I crossed the boundary that separates idle talk from punishable crimes, and the nightmare I'd set in motion could no longer be stopped.

But pulling out the gun was no more than a desperate attempt to save face. I talked him back into the chair, and for the next fifteen minutes I made him sweat a lot more than I'd ever intended to. For all his swagger and size, Dean was a physical coward, and whenever a brawl broke out he'd duck behind the nearest piece of furniture. I already knew his reputation, but the gun terrorized him even more than I thought it would. It actually made him cry, and as he sat there moaning and blubbering in his seat, I almost pulled the trigger just to shut him up. He was begging me for his life—not to kill him but to let him live—and it was all so upside down, so different from how I'd imagined it would be, I didn't know what to do. The standoff could have gone on all day, but then, just around noon, someone knocked on the door. I'd left clear instructions that I wasn't to be disturbed, but someone was knocking just the same.

'Diz?' a woman's voice said. 'Is that you in there, Diz?'

It was his wife, Pat; a bossy, no-nonsense piece of work if there ever was one. She'd come by to pick up her husband for a lunch date at Lemmele's, and of course Dizzy had told her where she could find him, which was yet another potential snag I'd neglected to think of. She'd barged into my club looking for her henpecked better half, and once she collared the sous-chef in the kitchen (who was busy chopping spuds and slicing carrots), she made such a nuisance of herself that the poor sap finally spilled the beans. He led her up the stairs and down the hall, and that was how she happened to be standing in front of my office door, pounding on the white veneer with her angry bitch knuckles.

Short of planting a bullet in Dizzy's head, there was nothing I could do but put away the revolver and open the door. The shit was sure to hit the fan at that point—unless the big guy came through for me and decided to play mum. For ten seconds my life dangled from that gossamer thread: if he was too embarrassed to tell her how scared he'd been, he'd keep the imbroglio to himself. I put on my warmest, most debonair smile as Mrs Dean stepped into the room, but her snivelling husband gave the whole thing away the instant he set eyes on her. 'The little fucker was gonna kill me!' he said, blurting out the goods in a high-pitched, incredulous voice. 'He was holdin' a gun to my head, and the little fucker was gonna shoot!'

Those were the words that knocked me out of the nightclub business. Instead of keeping their reservation at Lemmele's, Pat and Dizzy tramped out of my office and headed straight for the local precinct to swear out a complaint against me. Pat told me they were going to do as much when she slammed the door in my face, but I didn't stir a muscle. I just sat behind my desk and marvelled at how stupid I was, trying to collect my thoughts before the bulls showed up to cart me away. It took them less than an hour, and I went off without a peep, smiling and cracking jokes when they put the cuffs around my wrists. If not for Bingo, I might have done some serious time for my little stab at playing God, but he had all the right connections, and a deal was struck before the case ever came to court. It was just as well that way. Not only for me, but for Dizzy too. A trial wouldn't have been good for him—not with all the flak and scandal-mongering that would have gone with it—and he was perfectly happy to accept the compromise. The judge gave me a choice. Plead guilty to a lesser charge and do six to nine months at Joliet, or else leave Chicago and enlist in the army. I opted to walk through the second door. It wasn't that I had any great desire to wear a uniform, but I figured I'd outstayed my welcome in Chicago and that it was time to move on.

Bingo had pulled strings and paid bribes to keep me out of the can, but that didn't mean he had any sympathy for what I'd done. He thought I was nuts, ninety-nine-point-nine-per-cent nuts. Bumping off a guy for money was one thing, but what kind of dimwit would go after a national treasure like Dizzy Dean? You had to be stark raving mad to cook up a thing like that. That's what I probably was, I said, and didn't try to explain myself. Let him think what he wanted to think and leave it at that. There was a price to pay, of course, but I wasn't in any position to argue. In lieu of cash for services rendered, I agreed to compensate Bingo for his legal help by signing over my share of the club to him. I was nobody special now. Just my old ordinary self again: Walter Claireborne Rawley, a twenty-six-year-old GI with a short haircut and a pair of empty pockets. Welcome to the real world, pal. I gave my suits to the busboys, I kissed my girlfriends goodbye and then climbed aboard the milk train and headed for boot camp. Considering what I was about to leave behind me, I suppose I was lucky.

By then, Dizzy was gone, too. His season had consisted of one game, and after Pittsburgh shelled him for three runs in the first inning of his first start, he'd finally called it quits. I don't know if my scare tactics had knocked some sense into him, but I felt glad when I read about his decision. The Cubs gave him a job as their first-base coach, but a month later he got a better offer from the Falstaff Brewing Company in St Louis, and he went back to the old town to work as a radio announcer for the Browns and Cardinals games. 'This job ain't gonna change me none,' he said. 'I'm just gonna speak plain ol' pinto-bean English.' You had to hand it to the big clodhopper. The public went for the folksy garbage he spewed out over the airwaves, and he was such a success at it that they kept him on for twenty-five years. But that's another story, and I can't say that I paid much attention to him. Once I left Chicago, it had nothing to do with me any more.

GRANTA

Tibor Fischer
The Getaway Lunch

Montpellier

I found a seedy hotel not far from the station, where you would expect to find one. France has some of the finest seedy hotels in the world. Elegance tends to be uniform: seediness surprises. I like three or four different types of wallpaper in the same room, and not knowing which fixture isn't working or is going to come off in your hand.

I explained at reception that I just had my money stolen on the train, and that I'd like a cheap room. They understood. It was obvious that they dealt with much more outlandish customers than grimy philosophers in grave difficulty with their world ranking, and that weird and deleterious as I thought I was, they had handled odder oddities.

A passport seemed to satisfy the receptionist. 'The English are always welcome here,' he said, as if there was a reason. It didn't seem any way to run a business. I'm not sure I would have let myself in, but the place didn't seem burdened with customers. A lanky youth in a cheap black leather jacket and half a haircut was slumped in an armchair, waiting openly, as if he was paid to sit there to heighten the disreputability of the establishment.

I went up to my room, opened my suitcase (in the mechanical way one does, although I had nothing that needed unpacking) and lay on the bed. I find I can think better this way, and a horizontal position makes you more streamlined for life. Nearly all the trouble in life comes from standing up.

There was a tapping at the door.

'Who's there?' I asked, perplexed at my sudden social attractiveness.

'You forgot to sign something,' said a voice.

What greeted me when I opened the door was not an unsigned document, but a large gun, pointed at me by the quintessential dangerboy from downstairs.

'Your money!' he demanded with admirable succinctness, a quality much lacking, I feel, in modern philosophy. Untutored as I am in firearms, I could see with the merest of visual licks that this was enough gun to kill me and three or four major philosophers. It has to be declared that moments like this are an excellent justification for decades of gross intemperance. Imagine how great my distress would have been if I had spent my early mornings gasping around jogging, abstaining from wine and beer, shunning patisseries, dodging rotundity by one square meal a day, only to be plugged like a fairground bull's-eye in a cheap hotel.

I unpocketed my four francs and held them out. The corridorman pushed me back into the room and closed the door to give a little privacy to the robbery.

'Don't mess around. Give me your money.'

'That's it,' I replied.

'But you're a tourist.'

'Yes, but a tourist without any money.'

'There's no such thing as a tourist without money.'

'Well, you've met one now. You're welcome to have a look,' I said indicating my worldly possessions of the moment.

'But you're a tourist,' he insisted, though I was relieved to hear with a tone of incredulity rather than menace.

But

His tone of voice reminded me very much of Tanizaki's, 'But you're a philosopher.' Tanizaki's Japanese brain had been ripping at the seams trying to fit in the concept of a philosopher who could defraud. He was a decent soul, and I sympathized with him at that moment. Tacked on to the general Japanese inability to understand anything more than five miles offshore of Japan was a quite common misconception of philosophy as moral callisthenics. He had confronted me in the hope that I might have some inconceivable but all-embracing explanation to turn a prolonged and messy embezzlement into idiosyncratic bookkeeping. I didn't lie; because (a) it was before lunch and therefore too much effort, and (b) it would have shoved the nastiness away for only a few days or weeks.

I got away with defrauding the foundation much longer than I thought I would. For years, Tanizaki's predecessors had come over, nodded approvingly at my administration and directed their energies

237

to acquiring the correct brands of golf clubs and whisky. Ironically, Tanizaki would catch it for being more efficient than they were.

I might have acted more honourably in my earlier years. Idealism shackled to faith in my trade went overboard as soon as I went pro; dedication and decency decisively overtaken in the last lap by a desire to look out on the world from a balcony of cash. Perhaps if I had retained any hope that there was a great deal left in the way of pathfinding in the biz, I would have reined in my ignobility. But for years the distant rumbling—that as a thinker all I was doing was acting as a museum flunkey, dusting off a few thoughts, shifting around some of the exhibits—had grown to a deafening roar.

I would be delighted to be proved wrong; it would be splendid if some genius were to come along and tidy up the history of thought, to wow us by showing how all the pieces click together. But I fear that all that's left is some bitter skirmishing in the footnotes, shoving around some punctuation, shoot-outs in the letter-pages.

Years ago, I noticed some areas that no one had done any work in, but the thing about areas in which no one has done any work is: (a) there's nothing to be done, or (b) it's extremely difficult to do something, or (c) the work's been done but you didn't know about it. In addition, as a specialist in the history of philosophy, I can tell you that there isn't a thought that the Greeks didn't copyright; they corralled all concepts, long before Christ. That's a position you could defend comfortably. And any cranial creations that you might maintain weren't spotted by them have certainly been mopped up by the French, German and British crews.

Still, if you think abusing a position of trust is so easy you should try it. Dishonesty can be hard work.

Blocking others?

There will be those who will say I was blocking those with talent from furthering the cause of philosophy. Good. I'm glad, as the politicians say, that you mentioned that. That's exactly what I was doing. Three years at university doing philosophy is enough for any healthy individual.

Hmmmmm

So, a warning against any assumptions about philosophers' morality and tourists' funds.

'You're a tourist,' my armed assailant summed up for the third time, as if this datum was a bulky parcel he was trying to push through a narrow letter-box, 'and you haven't got any money.'

I apologized, I would have liked to have had some money for him to purloin, but there it was. Thankfully there was no hint of violence, just the murmuring irritation and sulky resignation people demonstrate when they discover they've got on the wrong train.

The gunman didn't threaten me, but neither did he leg it. He sat down and leaned forward to rest his forehead on his palms, making his head look like a mutant golf ball on its tee. 'No, no, no,' he said. Slowly. With equal spacing. I didn't know what to do. Another lamentable gap in our education system. The gun was perched at an unsupervised angle in his lap.

'Shouldn't you be careful with the gun?' I offered.

'There aren't any bullets,' he said very quietly, in the tone of a man whose entire family has just perished in a car crash (a family that he loved).

'I couldn't even afford the bullets,' he elucidated.

I was going to say he had outstayed his welcome, but since he hadn't had a welcome in the first place, I suppose more accurately, he was outstaying his barging-in. How does the well-brought-up philosopher deal with a failed armed robber? These days I tend to keep quiet about my profession because there is something about the way it's perceived that prompts disclosure; the unloading of confidences, most of which you'd rather not hear. However, even without the incentive of a known philosophical audience, the gunman proceeded to tell all.

'He didn't want to sell me the gun. I had only half the money,' he revealed. '"But," he said, "Hubert, since you've just got out, and since half a gun is as much use as no gun, I'll give you credit, as a favour."'

Without any expression of interest on my part, I proceeded to get a generous helping of his life story. He had been released from prison that morning and had used his start-up money to buy what he described as a disappointingly small gun. He had then looked around for a suitable victim, nothing personal.

'I'm pleased to think I look so affluent,' I interjected, to show there were no hard feelings.

'I've got a lot of catching up to do,' he said, but there were none of the signs traditionally associated with the process of leaving, and he didn't budge. I wanted to offer him a drink—now that the attempted robbery was over and we were getting down to the tale-bearing; I wanted to offer myself one, but alas the room was drinkless.

He gave me an appraising eye, and I noticed that what I had thought was a squint was a glass left eye.

Then his right hand fell off and hit the floor with a hand-sized clunk.

'It's always doing that,' he said, not making any attempt to retrieve it, or committing any other action that amounted to preparing to leave. His getaway was as flawed as his intended brigandage.

'And you,' he said, 'you speak good French. What do you do?'

I steeled myself like a pro. 'I'm a philosopher,' I said, pondering the present tense. It was going to be very late before he left.

'Ah. Is there any money in that?'

'Depends.'

'Depends on what?'

'On what sort of philosopher you are.'

'You're not the rich sort? Or did someone rob you before I got to you?'

I led out the less embarrassing parts of my day.

'You had parents, I suppose?' he asked, jumping theme.

'People tend to.'

'Not me.'

We indulged in a silence, which I didn't want to break by professing curiosity as to his family tree.

'And how do you like France?' he resumed, finally the good host.

I aimed for a nutshell account, but his attention boomeranged back to himself. I got the one-hour performance of the Meet Hubert show. Clearly there was nowhere Hubert was expected.

Hubert: a short criminal, but a long penal career. Strong on misfortune, weak on working anatomy.

'I came into this world short-changed,' he said, 'a hand short. Or so they tell me.' His childhood: he had been found abandoned, inexplicably, in a dustbin and taken into care. 'They always like to remind me about the dustbin.' An infection removed the left eye. He was sparing about the details of care, assuming I would take it as read that it was infernal.

As I mentally noted that it was a pity I couldn't find a way of making money out of listening—I seem to give good ear—he skipped a bit to eighteen and his criminal début in the big time.

He and an accomplice more senior in the felonious hierarchy had stalked and ambushed a well-known local miser and entrepreneur, whose first reaction had been one of utter terror as they waylaid him in his flat and trussed him up, believing Hubert and his partner to be an active service unit of the tax authorities. When he realized they were common breakers of the law, he just chortled as they kicked him around and threatened him with their knives in an effort to get him to reveal the combination of the safe.

'I won't talk,' he had said gleefully. The can of petrol that Hubert had been instructed to bring along was then poured over the bound curmudgeon. Hubert's *confrère* then ostentatiously lit a cigarette and mimed confusion as to what to do with the match still bearing a head of flame.

The miser talked. He talked so fast Hubert and his mentor couldn't take down the details as he furiously repeated them before keeling over, cardiac-ed out.

'This is an interesting legal point,' Hubert's chum had remarked, 'I wonder what they'll charge us with?' They left empty-handed apart from some postage stamps Hubert had noticed on the kitchen table.

Hubert then reflected it might be a good time to go solo. He went up to the *arrière-pays* to do some grape-picking and live in a barn, and to brood about his fingerprints being all over the petrol can they had left at the scene of the crime. 'And,' he observed, 'I'd had to pay for the petrol with my own money.'

After resting up, Hubert studied a nice, small but fat, bank, where the staff had been powerfully snooty to him when he had tried to get a loan to buy a prestigious firearm (one that would get him noticed).

He expertly stole a car for getaway purposes. Carrying a gun that represented most of his grape-picking wages, he entered the bank and found robbing easy, as easy as breathing (easy if you don't have a medical condition that makes breathing difficult, or some blockage in the windpipe, in which circumstances, I concede, breathing can't be easy—as it can't be, on reflection, if you should find yourself submerged in a great body of water with a block of concrete round your feet; and, if you can forget the ordeal of respiration at high altitude, not to mention the struggle to inhale at low altitude if it transpires you're in the middle of being strangled).

Hubert, thinking he had found his calling, got the money, cleared his throat and announced to the small gathering of bank employees and two Algerian plumbers: 'Ladies and gentlemen, your attention please. You have been privileged to witness my début performance. Your grandchildren will think all the more of you for having been here; this alone will make them cherish and respect you.'

And then he hoofed it out of the bank with his haul to find that his stolen getaway car had been stolen.

He had left the door open and the ignition key in. Of course, with some calm, he could have found an alternative means of absenting his sense-data from the scene of the crime—hijacking another car or whatever. But: 'I flipped.' He started running. The police followed a series of pointing fingers which led them to the frozen food section of a supermarket where Hubert was huddled amid frosty peas in a futile attempt to reduce the visibility of his surface area. He surrendered on demand, dropping his gun, causing it to fire a bullet into a policeman's leg.

Here, Hubert insisted his luck changed drastically, because they didn't shoot him. He got ten years instead. Prison was better than the children's home. 'No one pretended you were free.' And: 'I knew I was going to get out. I knew I was going to get another chance.'

Night. I offered to go out and find something to eat for four francs. The brotherhood of hunger. Hubert accepted. He gave me his franc and suggested I borrow the pistol if I wanted. 'I'm not risking another flop tonight.' There was a late-night grocery which was willing to trade some baguettes for five francs. We ate them, and, having distracted his hunger, Hubert (after politely asking permission) grabbed some bedcovers and a cushion and gave up verticality for the day.

More consciousness

Hubert was lying sedately on the floor, almost making it look comfortable. I could tell from his breathing he was awake too, but not eager to confront the day either. Why endure verticality when you can be horizontal?

The day had slipped a sample of its wares through the curtains on to the ceiling. I wasn't impressed by the sunshine. I wasn't falling for that old trick.

Bits of Hubert adorned the room. His hearing-aid was enthroned on his leather jacket. The artificial leg, in a manner that didn't speak well of its legness, leaned against the alleged chair. The hand was on the basin, with a head start as it were, awaiting the order to turn on the tap for morning ablutions. With an assemblage like that, I could see why Hubert wasn't bounding off the floor: he was no doubt pondering how to scrape his world ranking off the ground.

I was deeply bogged too. My plans to dissolve myself out of life were scuppered without reasonable, if not inordinate, amounts of cash. There comes a time when you consider yourself entitled not to have to worry about money any more. (A little struggle in one's youth, OK, that looks good.) I had reached that point.

Some Universals

I may be wrong on this, but it seems to me that there are certain impulses of a non-fleshy nature that occur to everyone, or nearly everyone, in a minimally developed civilization.

In no fixed order: the book. I go along with the view that most people have one book in them. Many are kind enough to keep it under skull arrest. It might be memoirs, fiction, love effusions or a guidebook, but most people toy with leaving their brainprint behind. Mercifully for publishers and those of us constrained to read for a living, only a fraction actually go the full road authorially. (Some people succeed in making a career out of the one book by changing the title on a regular basis.)

Another common brainwave: the restaurant. Who wouldn't like a tenner for every occasion an associate chimed in at a meal with the idea of opening a restaurant, café or some species of catering service?—(a) it looks not too difficult; (b) we all like food; (c) you tend to see the better side of people when they're at the table.

The third unfulfilled recurrer: bank robbery. The charms are obvious. Almost all of us, most of the time, find ourselves short, or painfully short, of dosh. The solution: the dosh-houses rarely more than a few minutes walk away. You saunter in and run out with handfuls of remedy in its most naked form. A U-turn of fortune. The financial peep-show, just glass between you and those thin, coloured slices of freedom. A couple of pounds of pounds, a few kilos of the local figureheads, those pocket portraits, and you're on your way to wherever you want to go.

Then, as lawbreaking activities with long jail sentences go, bank robbery seems fairly blameless. Banks seem to have more money than they need—it's just lying about all over the place. And everyone hates (a) banks and (b) bankers, so it looks rather victimless. Of course, the people who aren't doing the bank robbery pay, but they do so in a hard-to-notice fashion. Furthermore, because of (b), the idea of sending a wave of terror down the lower reaches of bankers' digestive tracts is appealing.

What stops us in the main is not a belief in order or a palliness with ethics. No, we are shackled by the likelihood of punishment—fear's bilboes. On top of which, pragmatically speaking, it's unlikely that one bank job would set you up for life; whatever its benefits, they're short term. You can't get rich robbing banks. The big money and the shorter sentences naturally lie in fraud, where with a bit of luck no one will even notice that a crime has been committed. But fraud lacks the directness, the plain beauty of bank robbery.

At various thin-walleted junctures of my life, the temptation had swung through, but now, abetted by Hubert's presence, I invited it in for a drink, to sit down and tell me all about it. Bank robbery's other merit is that it scores highly in the I-can-do-that stakes. Great bank robbery might demand some talent and dedication, but not bank robbery.

Apart from a need for wonga, there was also curiosity . . . and there was no alternative I could think of to make or acquire money. There wasn't much call for blubberous English philosophers with a six-figure world ranking on a Friday morning in Montpellier. My chums were out of convenient reach, and anyway I didn't want to gash my friendships with unwarranted demands. I wanted to keep as much of my address book as possible in good shape.

The Ultimate Truth: On the Blag

Like water swirling round the plug hole, my speculations wound into the idea. There's nothing like death on the horizon for shrinking inhibition. And the zetetics were prodding me to check the still unexplored corners of existence.

My main objection to poverty is that it's boring and just sands you away; I've done my share of that. Being poor is the same everywhere. I'm not sure being rich is; my embezzling only trampolined me fleetingly into those heights. But I was willing to investigate further. I had little to lose. I was looking at a stretch inside anyway, and if I was out, I wanted to spend.

Gear

I was lucky in that misfortune had provided me with the hardest-to-get ingredient of a bank-robbery kit: a gun.

'Pass the gun, Hubert. I think I'll go out and rob a bank.'

'It isn't that easy, Prof.'

Demarcation. Closed shop. Initiates don't like outsiders to think you can just decide yourself in.

'I didn't say it was easy, but there comes a point in life when you've got to go out and rob a bank.'

'You can't get money somewhere else?'

'No, I haven't got a penny. And I'm on the run.'

'On the run? From the bobbies? Scotland Yard? Prof, I knew when I set eyes on you there was something agreeable about you. And it's much more agreeable to rob agreeable people, you know.' Hubert fixed on his leg, stirred by my proposal. 'I haven't had much success, that's true, but I recommend starting with some tourists. Not succeeding with a tourist is better than not succeeding with a bank. Or can't you philosophize or something? How have you made your living so far?'

'I could philosophize, but I don't think we'd get any lunch.'

Hubert tried dissuading me all the way to the bank (the receptionist said, 'Double room rate,' as we left); he insisted on accompanying me although I indicated association with me in my bank-robbing capacity wouldn't do his liberty any good.

'What would you say to me, Prof, if I decided to be a philosopher just like that, eh?' Hubert repeated, stressing my lack of background. I certainly was unsure what the signs of an eminently robbable bank were; I was tempted to sound out Hubert for his advice, but I didn't want to expose anything that looked like irresolution. I circled around, scrutinizing banks, Hubert quietening and showing approval that I was taking the trouble to appraise the merchandise.

But I realized that I would always find grounds to hesitate; the ideal bank certainly didn't exist in Montpellier. Or, as Plato would maintain, anywhere in this world. I could have chosen a bank further away from the hotel, I could have waited till the afternoon when there was less custom, I could have pandered to a dozen other considerations, but thinking about bank robbery doesn't make it any easier, and I couldn't face lunch-time without lunch.

I plumped for a branch of the bank where they had been the most offensive and most unhelpful. What do you do if a bank is rude to you? Go to another bank. Which will have the same rates, same services, same rudeness. Bankers have a cartel of disdain, an agreement to treat like dirt all customers who are not markedly rich, their revenge, no doubt, for having to go through life as bankers.

With bank robbery, the first decision you have to make is where to hide your gun: in an act of tremendous symbolism, I had emptied my suitcase of its books and placed the gun inside. The second decision you face is whether to make an entrance or to join the queue. Inside the bank, three harried, badly dressed figures with hairstyles a decade or two out of fashion who looked like teachers were taking time out from their crises to carry out some financial transactions.

One woman with a number of small infants was letting them crawl and invade all the space around them—her air suggested that she wouldn't be unduly bothered if she lost one. Hubert did some tricks for a couple of them with his detachable hand. One looked up at me with curiosity; perhaps he was expecting me to be interested in him (as young children tend to assume everyone must be, not long having lost the twenty-four-hour attentions of the womb), or perhaps he had never seen a philosopher revving up for a bank robbery.

I decided to let the customers go about their business; I didn't see why I should ruin their day. There were two tellers. One was a grizzled veteran who was going badly into baldness, over-indulging the few, scattered strands left, letting them grow long into absurd squiggles which merely underlined the shortage of pileous action. He moved briskly, with contrived jollity, as if he were trying to convince us and himself that he really enjoyed being a banker, that he was doing what he wanted to do.

The other teller was a woman. She had that look.

I know. It's wretched. Still a slave. There I was: skint, fallen off the edge of middle age, a career careered off the road, undertakers eyeing me up, about to wallow in villainy. And yet I took the time to think about the possibility of getting work for my jubilation specialist. Instead of concentrating on my blag, I found my sentient space becoming crowded with amorous plans.

I stood in the queue and prayed that I would get the strand master and not the belle. I've often thought that locating the seat of thought in the head is wrong: in men it's closer to the seat, down there in the soft head that dangles, with its loose hemispheres, the secret capital. What sits on our shoulders is a front.

For the male, you only lose interest when you're (a) dead, or (b) very nearly dead. Boxed in the gonad's monad. It's always been a good rule of thumb for judging how ill I am—if the concept of a young blonde wearing nothing much doesn't make the blood chuckle, I know it's time to call the doctor.

It was odd; I wanted to board her acquaintance, but at the same time I couldn't help surmising that robbing her bank wouldn't be the best way of presenting myself.

Also, as a reason handler, I was nudged by the notion that I should be able to convince people that this was a bank robbery without the banal aid of a gun. As a nod to my world ranking. There was, I noted, a video camera. Hubert waved at it with a big smile. The teller a few hairs' breadth from baldness copped the extended family.

I walked up to her.

'Good morning, Madame,' I said. 'This is a bank robbery.' I wouldn't have been surprised to have been told I was at the wrong counter.

'A bank robbery?' She wasn't bothered. Not lackadaisical, not shrill: a stoic. I could have been asking the time. That look was still there, like jam smeared around the mouth. Past the years deemed to be the best for female beauty, but there are women who can make a mug of time, especially when they have that look, a constituent of which might be prosified as *hard to shock*.

'You're sure about this?'

'I'm sure,' I said, opening my over-large holster to reveal the cash-hungry maw and the gun. She started plunking wads of money into the suitcase, not slowly, not fast. I rested the gun on the counter.

'Do you want the change as well?'

'No thanks,' I said.

'Yeah, leave something,' said a tetchy voice behind me. 'I drove in this morning especially to make a withdrawal. Some people have to earn a living, you know.'

Quasi-baldy next door hadn't grasped it was a robbery. He

was arguing some technicality of money orders with the much-reproduced woman.

My dispenseress packed all the visible cash in, then added a small slip of paper she had scribbled on. 'That's it. My colleague has some more.'

'No, don't bother him,' I said. That would have been greedy. 'Thanks very much. Sorry to have troubled you. See you.'

'See you,' she said, waiting for the next customer. Hubert and I walked out, Hubert billowing admiration; I could sense he wanted to unload some comments but refrained from doing anything so out of place or unprofessional.

Outside, he looked at me expectantly, waiting for me to give the lead, clearly thinking, now what do we do? I remembered there was a very good fish restaurant around the corner. I chose to head there. Hubert whispered edgily: 'Aren't we going to run a bit?'

'No,' I said. Hubert obviously hadn't twigged that I was: (a) too old, (b) too fat and (c) too lazy to run, and that if I was going to be caught by the police I wanted to be collared in a dignified posture and state.

The police were slow. We were already scanning the entrées and sipping an aperitif when the first police car sped by, easy to observe from our table by the window.

The waiter didn't get on well with Hubert. Hubert seemed to me to be a stranger to first-class fish restaurants, and the waiter formed the same opinion. He had no doubt Hubert should be conducted to an open field and napalmed.

'Let me tell you about the specialities of the day,' the waiter urged.

'No, I don't want to hear about the specialities,' said Hubert. 'I want the bouillabaisse. We aren't tourists, you know.' He concluded by curling up his lip in the manner one associates with very aggressive dogs about to bite someone.

We were asked to move table when another party arrived. Hubert was brought the wrong dish and had to ask five times for his beer. For us, criminals in a criminally expensive restaurant, the service was nevertheless rubbish, despite the place being half-empty, my caving in and taking the speciality of the day as a peace offering and our drinking a small fortune. This is another heart-squashing element of life: no matter how good or expensive a restaurant, sooner or later you're going to be the recipient of offhandedness. The waiter rounded it off by pouring some buff-coloured sauce all over Hubert. I thought Hubert was going to hit him, but instead he insisted on leaving a tip as large as the bill.

'That'll teach him,' he said.

'I don't follow.'

'He thinks I'm a prick, and there's nothing as grating as a prick with money, not even a smack in the mouth.'

In among the cash, I found the piece of scrap that *she* had put in. In large writing so exciting that each character was worth a thousand pictures, was the name Jocelyne and a telephone number. I showed it to Hubert. He had noticed that look too.

'Phew!' he said, shaking his undetachable hand as if it were on fire. 'Now there's a woman . . . a woman who's hard to shock.'

On the way out, Hubert lifted someone's cap from the coat-rack and passed it to me. 'We mustn't push our luck,' he said as I muffled my baldness.

The police were making up for their earlier absence by a lot of presence, standing around, looking serious, talking into radios and acting as if they had important things to consider and do. We strolled through them, only stopping when Hubert asked one motorized copper leaning on his bike what had happened.

'Bank robbery.'

'Did you catch them? Or have you got a good description?' asked Hubert in his public-spirited voice.

'They won't get far,' was the response.

'Why did you do that?' I asked once we were out of earshot.

'Just checking.'

Back in our room, Hubert kicked the cushion into the wall.

'All I want to know is, are you a genius?' he exclaimed. 'Or is this what philosophy can do for you? In one morning you knock over a bank, invent the getaway lunch and you're in danger of being siphoned away by a woman who could drain the Atlantic with a straw. I've never seen anything like it.'

GRANTA

ITALO CALVINO
THE BLACK SHEEP

T here was once a country where everyone was a thief.
At night each inhabitant went out armed with a crowbar
and a lantern, and broke into a neighbour's house. On returning
at dawn, loaded down with booty, he would find that his own
house had been burgled as well.

And so everyone lived in harmony, and no one was badly
off—one person robbed another, and that one robbed the next, and
so it went on until you reached the last person, who was robbing
the first. In this country, business was synonymous with fraud,
whether you were buying or selling. The government was a criminal
organization set up to steal from the people, while the people spent
all their time cheating the government. So life went on its
untroubled course, and the inhabitants were neither rich nor poor.

And then one day—nobody knows how—an honest man
appeared. At night, instead of going out with his bag and lantern to
steal, he stayed at home, smoking and reading novels. And when
thieves turned up they saw the light on in his house and so went
away again.

This state of affairs didn't last. The honest man was told that
it was all very well for him to live a life of ease, but he had no
right to prevent others from working. For every night he spent at
home, there was a family who went without food.

The honest man could offer no defence. And so he too started
staying out every night until dawn, but he couldn't bring himself to
steal. He was honest, and that was that. He would go as far as the
bridge and watch the water flow under it. Then he would go home
to find that his house had been burgled.

In less than a week, the honest man found himself with no
money and no food in a house which had been stripped of
everything. But he had only himself to blame. The problem was his
honesty: it had thrown the whole system out of kilter. He let himself
be robbed without robbing anyone in his turn, so there was always
someone who got home at dawn to find his house intact—the house
the honest man should have cleaned out the night before. Soon, of
course, the ones whose houses had not been burgled found that
they were richer than the others, and so they didn't want to steal
any more, whereas those who came to burgle the honest man's
house went away empty-handed, and so became poor.

Meanwhile, those who had become rich got into the habit of joining the honest man on the bridge and watching the water flow under it. This only added to the confusion, since it led to more people becoming rich and a lot of others becoming poor.

Now the rich people saw that if they spent their nights standing on the bridge they'd soon become poor. And they thought, 'Why not pay some of the poor people to go and steal for us?' Contracts were drawn up, salaries and percentages were agreed (with a lot of double-dealing on both sides: the people were still thieves). But the end result was that the rich became richer and the poor became poorer.

Some of the rich people were so rich that they no longer needed to steal or to pay others to steal for them. But if they stopped stealing they would soon become poor: the poor people would see to that. So they paid the poorest of the poor to protect their property from the other poor people. Thus a police force was set up, and prisons were established.

So it was that, only a few years after the arrival of the honest man, nobody talked about stealing or being robbed any more, but only about how rich or poor they were. They were still a bunch of thieves, though.

There was only ever that one honest man, and he soon died of starvation.

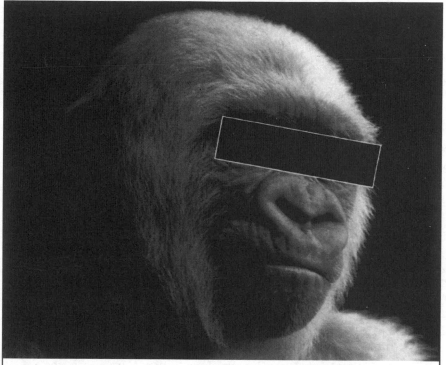

SEAN FRENCH

The Imaginary Monkey

An outrageous tale of an overweight, unwanted
underperformer and his remarkable transformation.

'Funny, perceptive and smart about English habits, neuroses and the rituals
involved in courtship and physical intimacy.' - *Literary Review*

'A cool, poised, comical book ... French is a writer of rare gifts.' - *Daily Telegraph*

'Sean French writes in a piercingly confident style: never opaque,
gassy or soggy; a joy to read.' - *Independent*

March 1994 Paperback £5.99

Notes on Contributors

James Ellroy was born in Los Angeles in 1948. His *LA Quartet* novels—*The Black Dahlia, The Big Nowhere, LA Confidential* and *White Jazz*—have won numerous awards. Dick Contino will also be the hero of Ellroy's next novel. **Hugh Collins** was released from prison last summer, on 5 July, and was married the following month. His sculptures and drawings were exhibited at the 369 Gallery in Edinburgh. His sculpture, 'Christ, the Sinner,' was commissioned by the St Columbus Church in Glasgow but rejected owing to its explicit depiction of Christ's genitalia. It is on permanent exhibition at the Demarco Gallery. A collection of Collin's work, *Evolution of the Special Unit*, was published in 1983. **Henry John Reid** is being held at Her Majesty's pleasure at a special prison hospital. He is currently writing a book about his life. **Hugh Barnes** worked as a reporter on the *Glasgow Herald* from 1986 to 1989. His first novel, *Special Effects*, will be published by Faber & Faber in April. **Andrew Savulich** is a photographer for the *New York Daily News*. His photographs have been collected by the Metropolitan Museum of Art and exhibited at the Opsis gallery in New York. **Tim Willocks** is a doctor specializing in the treatment of addictions. 'The Penitentiary' is taken from his novel, *Green River Rising*, that will be published by Jonathan Cape in June. **Allan Gurganus** is the author of *Oldest Living Confederate Widow Tells All* and *White People*. He is completing *The Practical Heart*, a collection of five novellas. He lives in North Carolina. **Peregrine Hodson** is the author of *Under a Sickle Moon* and *A Circle Round the Sun*. He is writing a book about the opium trade. 'Dizzy' is a chapter from **Paul Auster**'s new novel, *Mr Vertigo*, which will be published later this year by Faber & Faber in Britain and Viking in the United States. His last novel, *Leviathan*, was awarded the *Prix Medicis Etranger*. **Tibor Fischer** appeared in *Granta* 43, 'Best of Young British Novelists'. His first novel, *Under the Frog*, was short-listed for the Booker Prize. *The Thought Gang*, his second novel, will be published by Polygon later this year. **Italo Calvino** died in 1985. There are plans for four further books from the manuscripts of his unpublished writing.